DOMINICAN REPUBLIC

4th edition
Benoit Prieur
Pascale Couture

ULYSSES
TRAVEL PUBLICATIONS
Travel better... enjoy more

Editorial *Series Director:* Claude Morneau; *Editor:* Daniel Desjardins.

Research and Composition *Authors:* Benoit Prieur, Pascale Couture; *Contributors:* Marc Rigole.

Production *Design:* Patrick Farei (Atoll Direction); *Editing:* Jennifer McMorran; *Translation:* Jennifer McMorran, Tracy Kendrick, Danielle Gauthier, Sarah Kresh; *Cartography:* André Duchesne, Steve Rioux (Assistant); *Layout:* Sarah Kresh.

Illustrations *Cover Photo:* Grant V. Faint (Image Bank); *Interior Photos:* Tibor Bognar, Michel Gagné, D. Staquet, Herb Zulpier; *Chapter Headings:* Jennifer McMorran; *Drawings:* Lorette Pierson, Marie-Anik Viatour.

Special Thanks to: Mayeline de Lara (Dominican Republic Tourist Office, Montreal); Bolívar Troncoso, Ramón Cedano and Luis Martinez (Tourism Secretariat on the Dominican Republic); Barbara Polanco and Constance Haward (Signature Vacations); Jean-Maurice and Isabel Lemaire.

Thanks to SODEC (Québec government) and the Canadian Heritage Minister for their assistance.

Distributors

AUSTRALIA:
Little Hills Press
11/37-43 Alexander St.
Crows Nest NSW 2065
☎ (612) 437-6995
Fax: (612) 438-5762

BELGIUM AND LUXEMBOURG:
Vander
Vrijwilligerlaan 321
B-1150 Brussel
☎ (02) 762 98 04
Fax: (02) 762 06 62

CANADA:
Ulysses Books & Maps
4176 Saint-Denis
Montréal, Québec
H2W 2M5
☎ 1-800-748-9171 or
(514) 843-9882, ext.2232
Fax: 514-843-9448
www.ulysse.ca

GERMANY AND AUSTRIA:
Brettschneider
Fernreisebedarf
Feldfirchner Strasse 2
D-85551 Heimstetten
München
☎ 89-99 02 03 30
Fax: 89-99 02 03 31

GREAT BRITAIN AND IRELAND:
World Leisure Marketing
9 Downing Road
West Meadows, Derby
UK DE21 6HA
☎ 1 332 34 33 32
Fax: 1 332 34 04 64

ITALY:
Centro Cartografico del Riccio
Via di Soffiano 164/A
50143 Firenze
☎ (055) 71 33 33
Fax: (055) 71 63 50

NETHERLANDS:
Nilsson & Lamm
Pampuslaan 212-214
1380 AD Weesp (NL)
☎ 0294-465044
Fax: 0294-415054

SCANDINAVIA:
Scanvik
Esplanaden 8B
1263 Copenhagen K
DK
☎ (45) 33.12.77.66
Fax: (45) 33.91.28.82

SPAIN:
Altaïr
Balmes 69
E-08007 Barcelona
☎ 454 29 66
Fax: 451 25 59

SWITZERLAND:
OLF
P.O. Box 1061
CH-1701 Fribourg
☎ (026) 467.51.11
Fax: (026) 467.54.66

U.S.A.:
The Globe Pequot Press
6 Business Park Road
P.O. Box 833
Old Saybrook, CT 06475
☎ 1-800-243-0495
Fax: 1-800-820-2329

Other countries, contact Ulysses Books & Maps (Montréal), Fax: (514) 843-9448

Canadian Cataloguing in Publication Data
Prieur, Benoit 1965-
      Dominican Republic
      4th edition   (Ulysses travel guides)
      Translation of République dominicaine
      Includes index.
      ISBN 2-89464-064-1
1. Domincan Republic - Guidebooks. I. Couture, Pascale, 1966-   II. Title   III. Series.
F1934.5.C6813 1997   917.29304'54   C97-940915-2
© September 1997, Ulysses Travel Publications. All rights reserved
ISBN 2-89464-064-1
Printed in Canada

"May your highness believe that these lands are so greatly good and fertile, and especially those of this island of Hispaniola, that there is no one who can tell it; and no one could believe it he had not seen it."

Logbook of Christopher Columbus

TABLE OF CONTENTS

LIST OF MAPS

Help make Ulysses Travel Guides even better!

The information contained in this guide was correct at press time. However, mistakes can slip in, omissions are always possible, places can disappear, etc. The authors and publisher hereby disclaim any liability for loss or damage resulting from omissions or errors.

We value your comments, corrections and suggestions, as they allow us to keep each guide up to date. The best contributions will be rewarded with a free book from Ulysses Travel Publications. All you have to do is write us at the following address and indicate which title you would be interested in receiving (see the list at the end of guide).

Ulysses Travel Publications
4176 Rue Saint-Denis
Montréal, Québec
Canada H2W 2M5
www.ulysse.ca
E-mail: guiduly@ulysse.ca

TABLE OF SYMBOLS

🌴	Ulysses favourite
☎	Telephone number
⇄	Fax number
≡	Air conditioning
⊗	Ceiling fan
≈	Pool
ℜ	Restaurant
⊛	Whirlpool
ℝ	Refrigerator
ℂ	Kitchenette
△	Sauna
#	Screen
☉	Exercise room
tv	Colour television
pb	Private bathroom
sb	Shared bathroom
ps	Private shower
hw	Hot water
fb	Full-board
½b	Half-board (lodging + 2 meals)
bkfst	Breakfast

ATTRACTION CLASSIFICATION

★	Interesting
★★	Worth a visit
★★★	Not to be missed

HOTEL CLASSIFICATION

The prices in the guide are for one room, double occupancy, in the high season.

RESTAURANT CLASSIFICATION

$	$10 US or less
$$	$10 US to $20 US
$$$	$20 US or more

The prices in the guide are for a meal for one person, excluding taxes, drinks and tip.

All prices in dollars in this guide are in American dollars.

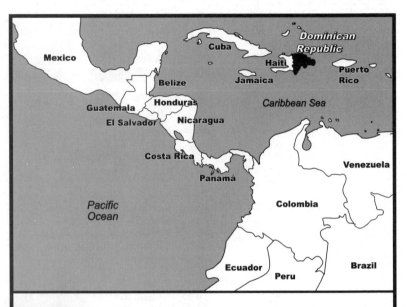

Where is the Dominican Republic ?

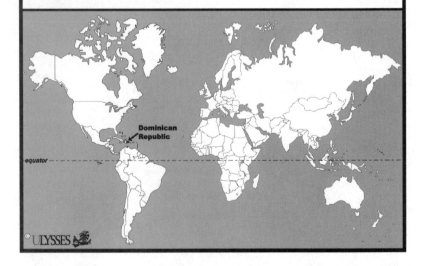

PORTRAIT

The Dominican Republic shares with Haiti the island of Hispaniola, the second largest island in the Caribbean after Cuba. Once the adopted land of the Tainos (Arawaks) and the Caribs, this island was "discovered" by Christopher Columbus and became home to the first European colony in the New World in 1492.

Known above all for the splendour of its white-sand beaches, the Dominican Republic is a country of tremendous diversity. The geography is a fascinating kaleidoscope, from the tropical rainforest to the desert-like expanses of the Southwest, from farming fields as far as the eye can see to the highest summit of the Caribbean, Pico Duarte, from the endless fields of sugar cane to verdant banana groves. The variety and spectacular beauty of its countryside is certainly one of its greatest riches.

But it is not the only one, for people also visit the Dominican Republic for the many remnants of its colonial past, of which the old area of Santo Domingo is one of the most shining examples, for its friendly hospitality and for the dynamic Caribbean culture and people.

GEOGRAPHY

With an area of 48,442 square kilometres, the Dominican Republic occupies the eastern two thirds of the island of Hispaniola. Traversing the country, it is hard not to seduced by the astonishing diversity of the countryside.

Mountains

Five mountainous massifs rise from the Dominican territory. The most impressive is the Cordillera Centrale at the heart of which stands Pico Duarte, which with an altitude of 3,175 metres is the highest summit in the Caribbean. Southwest of and extending from this range are two small mountain chains, called "Neiba" and Baoruco". To the north, the whole Atlantic coast is isolated from the rest of the country by the Cordillera Septentrionale, which runs from Monte Cristi to San Francisco de Macoris. Finally, traversing the Samaná peninsula in the eastern part of the island, is the Cordillera de Samaná.

The Plains

In between these mountain ranges stretch vast plains ideal for agriculture and grazing. In effect, 40% of Dominican land serves as grazing ground for animals, while one third is dedicated to agriculture. Fields stretch as far as the eye can see, especially sugar-cane fields, which have shaped the Dominican economy and countryside for centuries. The largest of these plains is the Cibao valley, in the centre of the country. This fertile land, where corn, rice, beans and tobacco are grown, is the country's most important agricultural region.

Tropical Rainforest

The heavy precipitation and constant humidity and temperature (never under 20°C) at the foot of the Cordillera Centrale have engendered the growth of a tropical rain forest. Three levels of vegetation can be distinguished in this verdant world. The first level, called the underbrush, consists of woody plants (young unmatured trees and shrubs that can survive in the shade) and her-

baceous plants. All of these plants thrive on the little light that manages to penetrate the canopy above them. The second level consists of epiphytes (plants that do not touch the earth, but rather grow on other plants), such as mosses, lichens, creepers and bromeliads. These plants have adapted to dark and dank surroundings while making optimum use of the space available. Finally, the last level, the canopy, consists of the tallest trees in the forest, whose leaves absorb almost all of the solar energy. This forest is also populated by an incredible variety of animals, mostly birds and insects.

The Beaches

Most of the Dominican Republic's coastline is lined with beach, in many cases of pristine sand. The prettiest beaches are located along the northern coast and are washed by the Atlantic Ocean, as well as in the Punta Cana region in the eastern extremity of the island. A very particular vegetation grows along these beaches, made up essentially of creepers, sea-grape trees and coconut palms.

Mangrove Swamp

This strange forest grows in the mud and salt water and consists essentially of a few varieties of mangrove, recognizable by their large aerated roots which plunge into the submerged earth. Farther inland, the river mangrove grows in less salty waters. Shrubs and plants also grow in these swamps. Amidst this impenetrable tangle of roots and vegetation live various species of birds, crustaceans and above all insects. The Gri-Gri lagoon in Río San

Juan is an excellent spot to view this world.

The Ocean Floor

The shallow, perpetually warm (about 20°C) waters just off the island provide a perfect environment for the growth of coral. Formed by a colony of minuscule organisms called coelenterate polyps growing on a polypary (calcareous skeleton), coral takes many different forms. The abundant plankton around these formations attracts a wide variety of marine wildlife. Fish of all sizes also gravitate around the coral. These include tuna, kingfish and on rare occasions sharks, plus more colourful fish like parrot-fish, boxfish, mullet and angel-fish. The coral is also home to numerous other animals, like sponges and sea urchins.

Fauna

Very few mammals, apart from rodents (rats and mice) and cattle, inhabit Hispaniola. The island separated very early from the American continent, and therefore has few of the indigenous species that evolved later on the mainland. In fact, most of the mammals here were introduced during the colonial era. Wild pigs were among the species imported during the colonization of the island, and can still be seen in certain parts of the country.

The **mongoose** was introduced onto the island by colonists in an effort to eliminate the snakes and rats that lived in the fields and attacked workers. However, this little animal, which resembles a weasel, doesn't only hunt snakes (in fact, none of the island's snakes are really dangerous); it also goes after reptiles and ground-nesting birds, actually threatening the survival of some species. Mongooses can be spotted near fields, if you keep your eyes peeled.

Mongoose

Among the few species that inhabited the island before the arrival of colonists, the **agouti** is a small rodent from the shrew family, which is about the size of a hare. Their numbers are few, and they are only spotted rarely.

Reptiles are more common. You are sure to see some little lizards sunning themselves here and there. Another, much larger reptile, the **iguana**, can be observed in the desert-like expanses of the southwest. This animal, which feeds on plants and insects, can grow to up to one metre long. Don't be afraid, though; the iguana is harmless. **Turtles** inhabit various areas, especially the islands of Siete Hermanos, north of Monte Cristi. Finally, **American crocodiles**, found only in Lago Enriquillo, are the largest animals on the island.

A few marine mammals populate the coastal waters, including the **manatee**, a huge, gentle animal that resembles a large seal. Unfortunately, their numbers have diminished greatly in recent years, and they are spotted rarely.

Another marine mammal, the **humpback whale**, which can grow to up to

16 metres, can be spotted near the coast of Bahía de Samaná. Arriving from the North Atlantic where they find an abundance of food during the summer, these whales head south to the warm waters of the Caribbean to repro duce and give birth (the gestation period lasts 12 months). Between January and March, whale-watching expeditions from Samaná allow visitors to become better acquainted with this fascinating mammal.

Birds

Winged wildlife abounds all over the island, making a bird-watcher out of just about anyone who looks around. To help you identify these animals, we have included a description of the most common species below. With a bit of patience and a good pair of binoculars, you are sure to spot a few.

The **brown pelican** has greyish brown plumage and is identifiable by its long neck, enormous bill and long grey beak. It is usually seen alone or in small groups, flying in single file. These birds, which can grow to up to 140 centimetres, are commonly found near beaches.

Brown pelican

The wingspan of the jet-black **magnificent frigate bird** can reach up to 2.5 metres. The colour of the throat is the distinguishing mark between the sexes; the male's is red, the female's white. These birds can often be spotted gliding effortlessly over the waves in search of food.

Magnificent frigate-bird

Herons are often found wading about near ponds and mangrove swamps. Among the different types found in the Dominican Republic is the **great heron**, which can grow to up to 132 centimetres tall. It is identifiable by the large black feather extending from its white head and down its neck. Its body is covered with grey and white plumage. The **cattle egret** is another bird in the same family commonly seen on the island, usually in the fields amongst the cattle. This bird is about 60 centimetres tall, with white plumage and an orange tuft of feathers on its head. It arrived in the Caribbean during the 1950s; before that it was found only in Africa. It has adapted well and is found in large numbers throughout the Antilles.

Cattle egret

Finally, you might hear the distinctive call of the small **green heron**, which stands about 45 centimetres tall and has greenish-grey feathers on its back and wings.

Green heron

The **pink flamingo**, another wader, is found along the shores of Lago Enriquillo. It feeds by turning its head upside down and dragging its beak through the mud while its tongue creates suction to trap organisms and small crustaceans.

Small green and red parrots called **coticas** can be seen in the gardens of several hotels. These domesticated birds are very popular with Dominicans, as they make friendly companions and can even learn to say a few words. The *cotica*, also known in Creole as the *verde cotorra*, is unfortunately being hunted into extinction.

Coticas

The minuscule **hummingbird**, with its dark blue and green iridescent plumage, rarely grows more than 12 centimetres long, and some types weigh no more than 2 grams. It feeds on insects and nectar, and can be seen humming about near flowering bushes and trees.

Hummingbird

The male **carib grackle** is completely black, while the female is paler. It is identifiable by its distinct yellow eyes. Its elongated claws allow it to run through fields in search of insects.

There are several types of turtledoves on the island, all about the size of a pigeon. The most widespread is the **zenaida dove**, with a brown back and a pinkish-beige breast, neck and head. It also has a blue spot on either side of its head. The **common turtledove** has greyish-brown plumage, with a black and white speckled neck.

Bananaquit

The **bananaquit**, also known as a yellow-breasted sunbird, is a small bird, about 10 centimetres tall, found throughout the Lesser Antilles. It is easily identifiable by its dark grey or black upperparts and its yellow throat and breast. It feeds on nectar and juice from various fruits including bananas and papaya. This greedy little bird often sets down on a patio table for a bit of sugar.

HISTORY

Well before the arrival of Christopher Columbus and the first Spanish conquistadors, large native populations inhabited the fertile island of Hispaniola. Like all native Americans, their ancestors were nomads from northern Asia who crossed the Bering Strait near the end of the ice age, and eventually inhabited almost all the American continent through successive waves of migration.

Because of its geographic isolation, the Caribbean archipelago was coveted much later on. It is believed that the first people to venture here had previously inhabited southern Mexico and Central America. Very little is known of them, since very early in the Christian era they were joined and then conquered or assimilated by the Tainos (Arawaks) and the Caribs. These two groups came from the banks of the Río Orinoco, in what is now Venezuela, and the Amazon forest. They gradually inhabited all the islands in the Caribbean archipelago and developed prosperous, structured societies.

The island of Hispaniola, except the eastern extremity, which was populated with Caribs, became the adopted homeland of the Tainos. At the time of Columbus' arrival most of the territory was divided into five distinct kingdoms (Marien, Magua, Jaragua, Maguana and Higüey). Each kingdom was governed by a grand chief, the *cacique*, and included several villages. The rest of the population was divided into three social strata: a group of nobles were in charge of all secular and spiritual ceremonies, while the common people worked the land with the help of slaves. The Tainos depended largely on agriculture for their survival, developing sophisticated irrigation and drainage techniques.

Columbus' first human contacts on the island of Hispaniola were with the Tainos, "Indians" that he judged to be fairly peaceable.

Scholars still do not agree on how large the native population of Hispaniola was at the time of the first Spanish explorations. Current estimations put the numbers at around 2 to 3 million individuals. Whatever the numbers, less than fifty years later, in 1535, only a few dozen native families remained on the island. A great many natives died because their immune systems were unable to combat the illnesses brought over by the Europeans. Many also perished in the colonial wars waged by Columbus and his successors. The survivors were then wiped out when the conquistadors imposed forced labour on them.

Christopher Columbus

On August 3, 1492, the Genoese navigator Christopher Columbus set sail from the Spanish port of Palos, on an expedition financed by the Catholic kings of Castille and Aragon. Setting out to find a new route to Asia, he sailed westward across the Atlantic Ocean, heading a flotilla of three caravels: the *Santa Maria*, the *Pinta* and the *Niña*.

More than two months later, the expedition landed on an island in the Bahamian archipelago then known by its Taino name, Guanahani. That day, October 12, 1492 marked the official "discovery" of America; Columbus and his men believed they were just off the shores of Southeast Asia.

For several weeks, Columbus explored Guanahani and the neighbouring islands, encountering the natives for the first time. He then headed towards Cuba. After following its shores, the three caravels headed towards another island, known by some natives as Tohio. On the morning of December 6, 1492, this island was "discovered" by Columbus and christened Isla Española (or Hispaniola). Columbus was charmed by the beauty of this large island and wrote about it enthusiastically in his

---

Taino Heritage

Barely two decades after Christopher Columbus "discovered" America, Hispaniola's Taino civilization had all but vanished. However, a number of Taino words have made their way into the English language. Notable examples are **canoe**, from the word *canoa*, designating a dugout canoe; **hammock** (the Tainos were the first to weave them); the names of various fruits and vegetable, including **tobacco**, **maize** and **guava**; **barbecue**, from *barbacoa*, the grill the Tainos used for cooking; and **manatee** from the word *manati*.

---

logbook. He sailed slowly along the northern coast, from west to east, making contact with natives and finding them peaceful and welcoming.

The island seemed to Columbus an ideal place to establish the first Spanish colony on the American continent, especially after gold deposits were discovered in some of the rivers.

It was actually the foundering of the *Santa Maria* that precipitated the settling of this first colony. A fort was built with material salvaged from the wreck. Completed on Christmas Day, 1492, it was christened Fuerte de la Navidad (Nativity Fort). A few weeks later, Columbus left 39 soldiers on the island under the command of Diego de Arana and returned to Spain, where news of his discoveries was received favourably by the Spanish monarchs.

This first Spanish colony on the American continent was soon wiped out. The details of what transpired after Colum

---

The Logbook of Christopher Columbus (December 16, 1492)

"May Your Highness believe that these lands are so greatly good and fertile, and especially those of this island of Hispaniola, that there is no one who can tell it; and no one could believe it he had not seen it. And may you believe that this island and all the others are as much yours as Castille; for nothing is lacking except settlement and ordering the Indians to do whatever Your Highness may wish. Because I with the people that I bring with me, who are not many, go about in all these islands without danger; for I have already seen three of these sailors go ashore where there was a crowd of these Indians, and all would flee without the Spaniards wanting to do harm. They do not have arms and they are all naked, and of no skills in arms, and so very cowardly that a thousand would not stand against three. And so they are fit to be ordered about and made to work, plant, and do everything else that may be needed, and build towns and be taught our customs, and to go about clothed."

---

bus' departure are not known; perhaps the Spanish sailors left on Hispaniola wore out their welcome. One thing is certain: conflict erupted between the two groups, and the natives easily won out.

When Columbus returned ten months later with 1,500 men, he found no trace of the fort or the 39 soldiers. The explorer then launched the first retaliatory expeditions, which continued for many years and lead to the death of thousands of natives. Columbus later imposed forced labour on the island's inhabitants, and many were even sent to Spain to be sold as slaves. It was thus Christopher Columbus himself who initiated a process that led to the complete extinction of Hispaniola's native population in the decades to come.

The goal of Christopher Columbus' second voyage to America was to found a real Spanish city on Hispaniola. Columbus and his 1,500 men, with supplies, seeds and farm animals, chose a spot not far from the present city of Puerto Plata and founded La Isabela, the first Spanish city in the Americas, in 1493. The city remained the centre of the colony for some time, until it was abandoned due to famines and epidemics.

Gradually, several forts were built closer to the centre of the country to oversee the exploitation of the island's gold deposits. Then, in 1496, Columbus' younger brother Bartoloméo, founded Santo Domingo, which became the young colony's nerve centre.

In 1500, Christopher Columbus was relieved of his duties as Viceroy of the Indies after Francisco de Bodadilla, appointed by Queen Isabela of Spain to investigate colonial management, accused him of poorly administering the colony, needlessly killing natives and encouraging the slave trade.

Gold and Sugar

During the first quarter century of Spanish colonization, gold mining fuelled Hispaniola's economy. Despite the *encomiendas* system, designed to protect natives from abuse, the island's inhabitants were used as slaves in the gold mines. Living conditions were deplorable, and natives died in such great numbers that the conquistadors eventually had to import slaves from other islands and from Central America.

By 1515, the gold deposits were becoming exhausted and the Spanish began to abandon Hispaniola in favour of other islands and regions in the Americas. Those who remained after the massive exodus of the Spanish population took up farming and stock breeding. On his second voyage to America, Columbus had provided the island with herds of cattle, which quickly grew in number, and crops such as sugar cane, which took well to the local climate. Sugar cane thus became Hispaniola's leading export and the driving force of its economy.

The sugar industry required a huge workforce, which the island simply did not possess. The Spanish therefore came to depend largely on African slaves, so much so that by the middle of the 16th century, the African population on the island had grown to more than 30,000 individuals.

The sugar boom did not last long, however. During the final decades of the 16th century, the European demand for Dominican sugar cane products began to decline, due in large part to increased exports from Brazil. As a result, the island experienced a second exodus of Spanish colonists.

Sugar cane and cattle nevertheless remained the staples of the economy, but Hispaniola was relegated to a position of marginal importance in the Spanish empire.

Pirates and Buccaneers

As the Spanish crown lost interest in the island and paid lower and lower prices for Dominican exports, the inhabitants of Hispaniola turned to smugglers to dispose of their merchandise. This angered the Spanish authorities, who decided to regain control of Hispaniola by forcing the Spanish colonists to move to the eastern part of the island, around Santo Domingo, and abandon the rest of the island. This harsh measure was enforced by the Spanish army in 1603 and 1604.

The western part of the island was thus completely deserted until several years later, when French buccaneers were drawn to the area. Many settled here permanently and tended the wild cattle that had been left behind. A very profitable business was set up between buccaneers, who slaughtered the animals for leather, and pirates, who transported the leather to Europe.

Although they tried several times, the Spanish authorities never succeeded in putting a stop to the trade. Taking advantage of the buccaneers' presence, France gradually took over this part of the island, which became an official French possession in 1697, with the signing of the Ryswick Treaty.

The eastern part of the island, still under Spanish control, experienced many decades of great economic hardship before finally attaining a certain level of prosperity towards the middle of the 18th century.

The division of Hispaniola between France and Spain led to the birth of the two countries that now share the island: the Dominican Republic and the Republic of Haiti.

Toward Independence

The French Revolution of 1789 had important repercussions even for Hispaniola. In 1791, inspired by the winds of change and the disintegration of France's control, a slave uprising led by Toussaint L'Ouverture broke out in the French colony in the western part of the island. From the start, the Spanish settlers of Santo Domingo supported the insurgency. However, things changed drastically in 1794, when France abolished slavery in the colony. All of a sudden, Toussaint L'Ouverture's men did an about-face and joined forces with the French to overthrow the Spanish colony on the eastern part of the island. Completely overwhelmed, the Spanish surrendered Santo Domingo to France (1795), which ruled over the whole of Hispaniola for a few years.

In the years that followed, France, under the rule of Napoleon Bonaparte, decided to combat the rising autonomy of Toussaint L'Ouverture's government. A military expedition was sent to Hispaniola in 1802, and L'Ouverture was taken prisoner and brought to France. However, the western part of the island continued to strive for independence from France. In fact, it only became stronger, this time under the leadership of Jean Jacques Desalines. The French forces were soon driven out by the rebels, and on January 1, 1804, the Republic of Haiti was declared.

The French maintained control of the eastern side of the island, but not for long; in 1809, Spanish colonists recaptured Santo Domingo for Spain with the help of British troops at war with Napoleon's France. However, Spanish authorities showed very little interest in the development of this far-off colony, leaving Santo Domingo's settlers little choice but to proclaim their independence in 1821. This independence also proved short-lived, for the Haitian army invaded Santo Domingo the following year. Then, for a period of more than 20 years, until 1844, the Haitians controlled the entire island of Hispaniola.

Haitian domination began to weaken near the end of the 1830s, when an underground Dominican organization began launching attacks on the Haitian army. This organization, known as *La Trinitaria*, was lead by three men: Juan Pablo Duarte, Ramón Mella and Francisco del Rosario Sanchez. After a few years of fighting, the Haitian army finally retreated, and the eastern half of the island declared itself officially independent. On February 27, 1844, this new nation adopted the name "Dominican Republic".

Years of Uncertainty (1844-1916)

Following the war of independence, *La Trinitaria* rebels faced opposition from several armed groups within their own country, who wished to take control for themselves. The members of *La Trinitaria* were quickly defeated at this game, and in September 1844 were completely ousted from power.

Thus began the battle for control, pitting the followers of General Pedro Santana against those of General Buenaventura Baez. For nearly a quarter century, the two military leaders wrestled for power through bloody civil wars. In 1861, General Santana even relinquished control of the Dominican Republic to Spain for a few years.

The Dominicans' string of misfortunes continued when General Ulysses Heureaux became president of the Republic in 1882. He headed a violent dictatorial regime, remaining in power until he was assassinated in 1899. During this time, his poor handling of internal affairs led the country into a series of economic crises.

Upon his death, a succession of governments took power for short periods, creating a period of instability and political chaos that exacerbated the country's economic problems.

It was this situation that precipitated the first of many incursions by the United States into the Dominican political arena. Worried that a European power might take advantage of the economic instability to gain a new foothold in the country, the United States, the new imperialist power that saw Latin America and the Caribbean as its private stomping ground, assumed control of the country's borders and economic affairs.

The American Occupation (1916-1924)

Attempts by the United States to increase their economic control in the Dominican Republic lead to an impasse in November of 1915, when Dominican authorities made it clear that they had no intention of giving in to American pressure. The U.S. reply was prompt: in May of 1916, the United States government ordered the invasion of the Dominican Republic; U.S. marines quickly took control of Santo Domingo and other major cities. Washington then ordered the dismantling of the Domini-

can army and the disarmament of the general population.

Under the eight-year American occupation, the Dominican economy was largely remodelled to suit the needs of the United States. For example, as the First World War had made the Americans fear a sugar shortage, the Dominican Republic increased its production of sugar, while the production of other goods needed locally was put aside. The United States also used this period to eliminate import barriers for American products in the Dominican Republic. The resulting American penetration into the Dominican market forced many small local enterprises out of business. The occupation did have some positive results, however, including an expansion of road and railway networks and an improvement of the educational system.

The American occupation of Dominican territory ended in 1924. In return, the Americans left a semblance of political legitimacy and a powerful National Guard.

The Trujillo Dictatorship

In 1924, Horacio Vasquez won the first free election held in the Dominican Republic. However, this period of democratic rule was short, as General Rafael Leonidas Trujillo, leader of the National Guard, took over the country by military force in 1930 and became the mastermind of one of the darkest periods in Dominican history.

During his "reign", Trujillo, backed by the National Guard and a solid network of spies, imposed an absolute dictatorship with a heinous combination of violence, intimidation, torture, political assassinations and deportations. Under Trujillo, elections were vulgar shams, held only to cover up the excesses of a regime that was nothing less than one of the most terrible dictatorships in the history of the continent.

Trujillo ran things as if they were his personal business. He exercised almost complete control over the development of the Dominican economy by maintaining, either directly or indirectly, a controlling interest in most of the country's industries. Rarely in history has a ruler been as extreme a megalomaniac as Trujillo. Portraits and statues honouring the Generalissimo, who declared himself the nation's "Benefactor", were put up everywhere in the country. In 1936, he even went so far as to change the name of the capital, Santo Domingo, to Ciudad-Trujillo (Trujillo City).

Relations between the Dominican Republic and Haiti were poor during Trujillo's reign. The dictator's rejection of Haiti and its "black" culture were central to Dominican nationalism. Trujillo actually believed that Dominicans had a "civilizing" mission on the island. Relations between the two countries deteriorated even further when, in 1937, under orders from Trujillo, the National Guard massacred between 10,000 and 20,000 Haitians living in the Dominican Republic.

In contrast to the situation between the Dominican Republic and Haiti, Trujillo established excellent relations with the U.S. by offering extremely favourable conditions to American investors and by taking a stand against communism. By the end of the 1950s, maintaining ties with Trujillo became burdensome for the U.S. In Washington, the fear was that the extreme brutality of Trujillo's regime only served to fire up communist revolutionaries in other parts of the continent. Trujillo finally succeeded in completely alienating the Americans in 1960, following the aborted attempt to assassinate Venezuelan president Romulo Bétancourt. From that point on, Trujillo's days were numbered.

This terrible dictatorship, which lasted more than 30 years, ended abruptly on May 30, 1961, when Trujillo was assassinated. At the time of his death, Trujillo was considered one of the 10 richest men in the world, with about 600,000 hectares of productive farmland to his name and a personal fortune valued at $500 million US. The three-decade-long Trujillo regime is estimated to have cost the lives of some 100,000 Dominicans.

The Second American Invasion

After Trujillo's death, the vice-president of the country, Joaquín Balaguer, took over. He soon had to relinquish control to a state council, which organized a presidential election on December 20, 1962. The people elected Juan Bosch of the Dominican Revolutionary Party (PRD). His term did not last long, however; believing that Bosch was determined to re-establish civil liberties, the army ousted him in a coup in September, 1963.

After two years of disastrous economic policies, the increasingly dissatisfied Dominican working classes rose up and, with the help of a dissident army faction, re-established constitutional order on April 24, 1965. Under the pretext that the uprising had been infiltrated by communists, the nervous American government reacted by sending in the marines to assist the Domini

A BRIEF SUMMARY OF DOMINICAN HISTORY

Near the end of the ice age, nomads from northern Asia cross the Bering Strait and in successive waves of migration inhabit most of the American continent. Later, some migrate to the islands in the Caribbean.

1492:   On his first voyage to the Americas, Christopher Columbus visits several islands, among them Hispaniola, where 39 soldiers stay behind while he returns to Spain.

1496:   Bartholoméo Columbus, Christopher's brother, founds the city of Santo Domingo.

1535:   Less than half a century after the arrival of the conquistadors, the native population on the island has been practically wiped out.

1603-1604:   To combat trading between colonists and pirates, Spain forces the colonists to abandon the western regions of the island and resettle in the vicinity of Santo Domingo.

1697:   France acquires the western part of the island under the Ryswick Treaty.

1795:   French troops take possession of Santo Domingo and occupy it for more than a decade.

1809:   Santo Domingo becomes a Spanish colony once again.

1822:   The new Republic of Haiti takes over Santo Domingo and occupies it until 1844.

1844:   After many years of guerilla fighting, the colonists of Santo Domingo oust the Haitian army. The newly independent nation adopts the name Dominican Republic.

1861:   After a long period of political instability, the Dominican Republic reverts to being a Spanish colony until 1865.

1916:   Already extensively involved in Dominican internal affairs, the United States invades the Dominican Republic, occupying it until 1924.

1930:   General Trujillo seizes power by military force and imposes an excessively repressive dictatorship. He remains head of state for more than 30 years, until he is assassinated in May 1961.

1965:	The United States sends in troops to prevent Juan Bosch, the legally elected president, from regaining the power he lost earlier at the hands of the military.
1966:	Joaquín Balaguer becomes president of the country, and stays in power until 1978. During his 12 years in office, Balaguer often relies on repression as a political tool.
1978:	Antonio Guzman, of the Dominican Revolutionary Party (PRD), is elected president. He is replaced in 1982 by Salvador Jorge Blanco, another member of the PRD.
1986:	Frustrated by the corruption in Blanco's government, the people re-elect Joaquín Balaguer. The former autocrat is once again re-elected by a very small majority in 1990.
1994:	Balaguer is elected once more, amid accusations by the opposition that he has fixed the election results. Under American pressure, Balaguer's term is cut to two years.
1996:	Leonel Fernández is brought to power. Dominicans invest much hope in this new government.

can military in putting down the "revolution". Fighting began, causing heavy casualties, and soon the rebels were forced to give in.

A provisional government led by Hector Garcia Godoy was established. Then in a rigged election, one of Trujillo's former comrades-in-arms, Joaquín Balaguer, was elected president in June 1966.

The Contemporary Period

Balaguer led the country for 12 years, winning rigged elections in 1970 and 1974, for which the opposition refused even to put up candidates. During this entire period, Balaguer ruled as an authoritarian, using violence and intimidation to maintain power.

Things took a new turn during the 1978 election, when the Dominican Revolutionary Party (PRD) supported Antonio Guzman in a bid for the presidency. Dominicans were ready for change, yet Balaguer had no intention of relinquishing his control. On election day, when poll results were leaning in favour of Guzman, Balaguer tried to put an end to the vote counting. He almost succeeded, but was forced to give in to outside pressure, mainly from the United States, and admit defeat.

Antonio Guzman remained in power until 1982, but his presidency ended on a tragic note, when he committed suicide upon learning that some of his closest allies had embezzled public funds. After an interim period of a few months, Salvador Jorge Blanco, the new head of the PRD, was elected president and remained so until 1986.

During the presidencies of Guzman and Blanco, many civil liberties were reinstated, which contributed greatly to the popularity of the two men. Unfortunately, with the collapse of sugar markets and the rise in oil prices, the Dominican Republic endured severe economic hardships during this period, leading to deep dissatisfaction among the population. The axe fell on the PRD, when its president, who was also the president of the country, Salvador Jorge Blanco, was personally found guilty of corruption.

In 1986, a disillusioned Dominican electorate facing an unprecedented political void opted to support the former dictator, octogenarian Joaquín Balaguer, in a national election. Balaguer was re-elected in 1990, defeating a disorganized and divided opposition. Once again, in 1994, he remained in power — not without difficulty, however, and despite accusations that he had fixed the election results in his favour. In a bid to silence critics who questioned the election results and under pressure from the Americans, Balaguer agreed to cut his term to two years and hold another election in 1996. During these last terms, Balaguer governed with a much softer hand than he had previously.

The 1996 election should have belonged to José Francisco Pena Gómez, of the Dominican Revolutionary Party (PRD). Everything indicated he would win, but it was not to be. On the second ballot, a coalition was formed between the Social-Christian Reform Party and the Dominican Liberation Party allowing the latter's candidate, Leonel Fernández, to narrowly defeat Pena Gómez. The results of the election were nevertheless greeted with enthusiasm by the Dominican people, as Fernández offers a real alternative to the Balaguer regime. Quite young (he is in his early-forties) and educated in the United States, Leonel Fernández intends to modernize the country by combatting corruption and investing in health and education.

POLITICS, THE ECONOMY AND SOCIETY

The 500 years that have passed since Columbus' first voyage to America in 1492 have seen an independent Dominican nation emerge. Like most populations in Latin America, Dominicans continue to struggle for real political, economic and social freedom. They must continuously deal with numerous uncertainties that linger over the future of their country. Whatever choices are made in the years to come, the country must first learn to invest in its extraordinarily young population.

Politics

Like the U.S. system, on which it is based, the Dominican legislative system is made up of two chambers, the Senate and the Chamber of Deputies. The Senate has 30 representatives, one for each province in the country and one for the national district; the Chamber of Deputies has 120 members. The president of the country has considerable power; he is elected by universal suffrage to a four-year term.

Though there are about 20 political parties, only three play a significant role in the political power play of the country. Up until 1996, the Social-Christian Reform Party (PRSC) (previously called the Reform Party or PR) dominated political life. As leader of the

PR and then the PRSC, Joaquín Balaguer was elected president in 1966, 1970 and 1974, then in 1986, 1990 and 1994. The PRSC is the result of the coming-together of the Reform party and the Social-Christian Revolutionary Party.

Founded in Havana (Cuba) by Juan Bosch, in 1939, the Dominican Revolutionary Party (PRD) is presently lead by José Francisco Pena Gómez (due to serious illness, Pena Gómez will undoubtedly step down soon). In 1973, in-party fighting forced Juan Bosch and his supporters to leave the PRD to found the Dominican Liberation Party. It was as head of the PRD that Juan Bosch was elected president in 1962 before being overthrown by a coup d'état the following year. The PRD was re-elected in 1978 and 1982 with Antonio Guzmán as their leader and then Salvador Jorge Blanco. The most recent election, held in 1996, was won by Leonel Fernández of the Dominican Liberation Party.

In the last few years, Dominican politics have been marked mainly by the growing impatience of the country's working classes, exasperated by the widespread corruption that has reached even the highest levels of government, and by a forced economic austerity plan that has greatly reduced consumer buying power.

Only a few months after his election, Leonel Fernández had to deal with general strikes, which broke out in certain regions of the country. These social ills, which shake things up politically from time to time in the Dominican Republic, are the result of a profound malaise that is particular to many Latin American societies and is linked to the constant growth of the immense gap separating the rich and the poor. Presently, in the Dominican Republic, while large segments of the society often cannot afford basic foodstuffs and live in humble shacks without running water or electricity, a small minority enjoys fabulous riches and material wealth. This marginalization of a large part of the population is a major stumbling block on the road to true democratization.

As well, until very recently the government of the Dominican Republic stood accused by the international community of participating in the exploitation of Haitian *braceros* (sugar cane cutters). Often surrounded by armed guards, thousands of Haitians had long worked in the fields for a pittance, barely making enough to survive. The Dominican government promised many times to rectify the problem; then, in June 1991, it deported all the illegal workers back to Haiti.

Many Haitians have nevertheless remained in the country, usually working at menial, low-paying jobs in the construction or agricultural sectors. Working conditions remain unbearable on sugar plantations, and, generally, the situation of Haitians living in the Dominican Republic is still a problem. The country's new president, Leonel Fernández, seems to show much more goodwill than his predecessor. A meeting with his Haitian counterpart at the end of 1996 lead to an agreement concerning the wages paid to cane-cutters.

The Economy

The Dominican economy has become somewhat more modern and diverse in recent decades, but farming and raising livestock are still central activities. More than 40% of the country's total surface area serves as pasture for cattle, and approximately one third is used for growing food for human consumption. Contrary to the situation in many Caribbean countries, most of the dietary staples consumed on the island are produced locally.

Sugar cane, which was introduced to the island by Columbus, is still the largest crop in the country. Its cultivation requires a large work force, and refined cane sugar is the country's primary agricultural export.

Among the other commodities exported by the Dominican Republic, the most important are tobacco, cocoa, coffee, rice and various tropical fruits. Dairy production and the breeding of cattle, pigs and poultry serve mainly to satisfy local demand.

The Dominican Republic is rich in mineral resources, though many are still largely untapped. The only large-scale mining operations focus on silver, gold, nickel and iron. In recent years, nickel has come to occupy an important place on the foreign markets. In terms of value, it is presently the most important export. The Dominican Republic also produces large quantities of salt, which is extracted primarily from deposits along the shores of Lago Enriquillo. In addition, hydroelectric facilities produce about 20% of the country's energy requirements. As with most Caribbean countries, the Dominican Republic is still largely dependent on foreign imports for energy.

Despite recent efforts to diversify industrial production, sugar cane refinement is still the biggest Dominican industry. Sugar cane is used mainly to produce raw sugar, and secondarily for rum and molasses.

Labour-intensive light industries, such as the production of textiles, shoes, clothing and food products, have grown steadily in the last few decades. The Dominican Republic's heavy industries are mostly in the plastic, metallurgy and oil refining sectors.

The Dominican government continues to favour the development of industrial zones near several large cities for the use of foreign businesses. As a consequence, many companies, mostly American, Canadian and Asian ones, now assemble their products in the Dominican Republic, thus taking advantage of a cheap labour force.

Tourism is also one of the mainstays of the economy; it is now the major source of foreign currency in the country. Though largely dominated by companies not owned by Dominican interests, tourism directly employs close to 200,000; realizing the economic importance of tourism with respect to the development of the country, the new government has sensibly increased its support for this sector.

Tourism began to develop in the 1980s, and since then the Dominican Republic has marketed itself as an inexpensive sun destination. Thanks to local production of most of the necessary foodstuffs, many hotel complexes are able to offer "all-inclusive" packages (room, meals and drinks) at very competitive rates compared to what is offered in other islands in the region.

Finally, the country's continued dependence on sugar markets constitutes a recurring problem for the structure of the national economy. The economic crisis that has plagued the Dominican Republic for over ten years is tied to a reduction in American sugar imports and the resulting sharp drop in the price of sugar. The Dominican Republic also has a considerable foreign debt, which seems out of control, further hindering the country's economic development. The employment situation is just as dismal, with more than a quarter of the potential workforce left idle.

Dominicans

Covering two thirds of the island of Hispaniola, which it shares with Haiti, the Dominican Republic has a population of 7,900,000, according to the most recent census. A majority of Dominicans live in either Santo Domingo or the Cibao valley. The population density in the country has reached 150 inhabitants per square kilometre, and the birth rate is among the highest in the Caribbean. Presently, 48% of Dominicans are under 14 years old. The poor economic conditions in recent years have pushed the number of Dominicans emigrating to Puerto Rico to as many as 500 per week.

Although it is difficult to present a precise picture of the Dominican Republic's racial composition, there are three main population groups in the country: mulattos make up about 75% of the population, while whites and blacks represent 15% and 10%, respectively. A marked economic disparity exists between whites and blacks, generally favouring whites.

The origins of the Dominican population are diverse, but most have Spanish or African backgrounds. A smaller percentage, typically working at lower-paying jobs, are of Haitian descent.

Generally speaking, citizens of Haitian origin are poorly accepted; the conflicts that have marked relations between the two countries are not soon forgotten. In addition, the country's large urban centres often have small Asian communities, while a number of the residents of Sosúa are descendants of Eastern European Jews who escaped Nazi Germany in the 1930s. There are no descendants of the indigenous peoples that once inhabited the island of Hispaniola; this group was completely wiped out at the beginning of colonization.

More than 95% of Dominicans consider themselves Catholic, while a small number of people, most of whom live in mountainous areas, practise voodoo.

The official language of the Dominican Republic, and the mother tongue of 95% of the population, is Spanish. Along the Haitian border a few people speak Creole. Throughout the country, even in tourist areas, visitors will be addressed in Spanish, though many people speak English and French as well.

CULTURE, TRADITIONS AND LIFESTYLE

The Dominican Republic was a Spanish colony for many years during which time it absorbed thousands of African immigrants. The artistic activity on the island has been shaped by these two cultures. During the early years of colonization, the arts flourished, especially in the 16th century. It was not until the 19th century, when the country gained independence and a certain stability, that artistic expression began to develop. From the end of the 19th century to the present, the arts have thrived continually. Unfortunately, censorship has often thrived as well.

Literature

The first writer to document the charms of Hispaniola was none other than Christopher Columbus; his log books provide the first descriptions of the region. Very early in the country's colonial history, Dominican writers emerged with a style of their own. The Santo Tomas de Aquino University, founded in 1538, was central to the development of this literature. The earliest Dominican works consist essentially of essays, journals and chronicles written by the first explorers and missionaries, and aim mainly to describe the territory and spread knowledge of its existence. Among the first texts of note are the *Historia Natural y General de Indias* by Gonzalo Fernandez de Oviedo, *Doctrina Cristina* by Brother Pedro de Cordoba, and *Historia de las Indias* by Brother Bartoloméo de las Casas.

The French invasion and the difficulties with Spain in the 17th and 18th centuries slowed the literary development of the country. Dominican literature did not enjoy a resurgence until the 19th century. Several influential writers emerged during that period, most notably Felix Maria del Monte, known for his patriotic poetry. The texts of Salomé Ureña, advocating an improvement in conditions for women on the island, are also significant. *Enriquillo*, a historical text written by Manuel de Jesus Galvan in the late 19th and early 20th centuries, also ranks among the most important works of the time.

The period immediately following the country's independence (1880), though marred by the American invasion (1916), saw the development of a literature that emphasized an awareness of social realities, as well as more patriotic writings. It was in this context that Federico Bermúdez wrote *Los Humildes*, denouncing the suffering of the Dominican people. Federico Garcia Godoy recounts the advent of independence in three powerful short stories: *Rufinito*, *Alma Dominicana*, and *Guanuma*. Though fairly conservative in his choice of subjects, Gaston Fernando Deligne is a master of the Spanish language and one of the country's most important poets. Another writer by the name of Domingo Moreno Jimines headed a group that sang the praises of the good and simple values of peasant life.

Later, during the dictatorship of President Trujillo, literary activity slowed down. In a climate of brutal repression, Dominican authors had much less freedom of expression. Writers such as Manuel Rueda and Lupo Fernandez Rueda used symbols and metaphors to protest covertly certain aspects of the political regime. Others were forced into exile. It was in such a context, while in Cuba, that Pedro Mir wrote his beautiful poem *"Hay un país en el Mundo"*.

During the 1940s, a greater openness toward foreign literary movements led to the emergence of the "surprise" poetry movement. Among the so-called "independent" poets, Tomas Hernandez Franco became known for his modern works, which protested the existing regime. Works with wider appeal were also created during this period. Antonio Fernandez Spencer published collections of poetry that gained international recognition. One of the most important authors of the 20th century, Juan

Bosch, did most of his writing during the Trujillo dictatorship. His engaging, beautifully written essays describe the daily life of Dominican peasants. After the fall of the Trujillo regime, Bosch led the Dominican Republic for a few months, and remained an important political figure for many years. However, during the 30 years of dictatorship, many authors opted for silence or exile, publishing their texts only after Trujillo's death in 1961. Despite these difficult years, Dominican literary movements remained dynamic and innovative.

Literary expression has since been granted more and more freedom and several authors, often influenced by foreign literary trends, stand out for the quality of their work. The most important are Ivan Garcia Guerra, Miguel Alfonseca, Jeannette Miller, Alexis Gómez and Soledad Alvárez.

Painting

The Dominican Republic has been and is home to numerous very talented painters who have gained renown in Dominican and international artistic circles. Usually richly coloured and joyful, paintings are truly a representation of the artistic intensity of this island. Among the distinguished artists of the country are Guillo Pérez, Elsa Núñez, Fernando Ureña Rib, Candido Bibo and Manuel Severino. Two other grand painters, Giorgi Morel and Jaime Colsón stand out and are among the country's masters.

Music and Dance

Music and dance occupy a very important place in the cultural landscape of the Dominican Republic. Much more than an occasional pastime, music accompanies every part of a Dominican day, whether its on a crowded bus, in the most modest of market stalls, at work, at home or, late into the night, in the nightclubs of Santo Domingo and of smaller towns.

Among the popular musical trends, the favourite of Dominicans is first and foremost the *merengue*, that rousing, furiously rhythmic music that originated on the island. The popularity of the merengue cuts across all social levels of the country. Originally the *merengue* was identified with the rural classes. It was in the Dominican countryside that this accordion, tambourine, saxophone and drum music, with its *son* rhythm, was created.

The *merengue* became omnipresent throughout the country in the 1930s, under the regime of General Trujillo, who was a true fan on this music. The talented artist Francisco Uloa made a name for himself during this period. At the end of the 1950s, the major groups had their turn at fame, most notably Johnny Ventura. Since then, while conserving its original rhythms, the *merengue* has been modernized, leaving more space for the saxophone and replacing the accordion with an electric guitar, the piano with a synthesizer. *Merengue* has also been influenced by various other styles, such as salsa, rock, zook and reggae.

For a while now, the fun appeal of the *merengue* has reached beyond the Dominican Republic. Some of the country's greatest talents have become international stars, as well known the world over as they are throughout the Caribbean and in other Spanish-speaking countries. In the 1980s, the group 4:40 and its leader Juan Luís Guerra were a huge success on the international scene.

Though Dominicans adore *merengue*, their national music, they are also very fond of other types of music. Spanish and Latin-American singers are omnipresent and very popular with locals. North American "top-40" music, as well as Afro-American and Caribbean movements, such as reggae, are very popular throughout the country. Lastly, classical music has a following too; Santo Domingo even has its own excellent symphony orchestra.

Baseball

Baseball is at least as popular in the Dominican Republic as it is in the United States, where it originated. Young Dominicans practise this sport more than any other; there are baseball fields in every neighbourhood in the capital and every village of the country. And with equipment requirements limited to a glove, a ball and a bat, it is very economical to play, a definite plus in a country where money is an issue for the majority of the population.

Baseball is the national sport of Dominicans, and is also a very popular pastime. The exploits of the big Dominican stars of professional baseball are followed passionately and reported upon at length in the local media.

Professional baseball has existed in the Dominican Republic for more than 100 years. The professional league currently numbers five teams, two in Santo Domingo and the others in San Pedro de Macoris, Santiago de los Caballeros and La Romana. Each team plays about 60 matches between the months of October and February, and the season ends with a championship series between the best teams in the Caribbean. Discussions currently underway grant Puerto Plata its very own professional team. The old stadium at the entrance to the city (near the Brugal rum distillery) would be completely renovated, and the Puerto Plata team should prove very popular with the tourists.

The reputation of Dominican baseball grew in the fifties following the successes of the first Dominicans to play in the majors. In 1956, Ozzie Virgil became the first player to make a name for himself in the United States. But it was thanks to the remarkable talent of right-handed pitcher Juan Marichal, signed by the San Francisco Giants and of the Alou brothers (Felipe, Mateo and Jesús) that the quality of Dominican players became known.

Since Virgil, Marichal and the Alou brothers, more than 200 young Dominicans have stepped up to the plate in the major leagues. Some of the more noteworthy players include Rico Carty, Manny Mota, César Cedeno, Pedro Guerrero, Frank Taveras, Pepe Fria, Alfredo Griffín, Rafael Landestoy, Joaquín Andujar, Tony Pena, George Bell, Damaso García, Pasqual Pérez, Mario Soto, Raul Mondesi, Julio Franco, Moises Alou, Mel Rojas and Carlos Pérez. After the United States, it is the Dominican Republic that has produced the most players to the major leagues. The city of San Pedro Macoris actually claims to have produced more players per capita than any other city in the world.

Felipe Alou: a star player and manager *par excellence* !

Born in 1935 in Haina, Felipe Alou has had a remarkable career in major-league baseball, a career that started in 1958 with the San Francisco Giants. Over the course of his 2,082 matches Felipe batted an average of .286, and hit 206 home runs. In 1966, *Sporting News* magazine named him first-base-man of the year in the National League. When his career as a player ended in 1979 he joined the Montreal Expos organization and was named manager in 1992 (Felipe Alou thus became the first "Latino" to occupy this position in the major leagues). His successes contributed to his being named manager of the year in the National League in 1994. Felipe Alou is very popular with Montreal fans, as well as with fans back in the Dominican Republic, for whom he is a pioneer for having a major-league career not only for a few seasons, but for several decades. Several members of his family have also had success as baseball players; his brothers Mateo and Jesús played in the major leagues, as does his son Moises.

Cockfighting

Introduced by the Spanish, cockfights are held all over the Dominican Republic. Men gather around the "pits" (packed-dirt arenas) to watch and cheer on a battle between two cocks. Before hand, there is a ceremony, during which the cocks are weighed and fitted with spurs, and their owners are introduced. Then, once the judges have decided that the birds qualify, the fight begins. Victory goes to the cock left breathing at the end.

PRACTICAL INFORMATION

Whether alone or with a group, it is easy to travel anywhere in the Dominican Republic. In order to make the most of your stay, it is important to be well prepared. This chapter is intended to help you plan your trip; it also provides information on local customs.

ENTRANCE FORMALITIES

Make sure you bring all the necessary papers to enter and exit the country. Though requirements are not very strict, you will need certain documents to travel in the Dominican Republic. You should therefore keep your important papers safe at all times.

Passport

To enter the Dominican Republic, citizens of Canada, the United States and the European Union are advised to bring their passport, making sure it is valid for the length of their stay. It is also possible to enter the country with an official birth certificate or a citizenship card. Be reminded though, that in case of problems with the authorities, the most official proof of your identity is your passport.

It is a good idea to keep a photocopy of the key pages of your passport, and to write down your passport number and its expiry date. This way, in case the document is lost or stolen, it will be much easier to replace (do the same with your birth certificate or citizenship card). If this should occur, contact your country's consulate or embassy to have a new one issued.

Tourist Card

To enter the country, all visitors are required to have a tourist card (*tarjeta del tourista*) which is valid for 60 days. In most cases the card is issued by the travel agent at the airport, or on the airplane. The price of your airline ticket or package will usually include the cost of the card, $10 US. Keep it in a safe place during your stay, as it must be returned to authorities upon departure.

Visas

A visa is not required for visitors from Canada, the United States, Great Britain or Germany. Citizens of other countries must contact the closest embassy or consulate of the Dominican Republic to obtain a visa.

Departure Tax

Each person leaving the Dominican Republic must pay a departure tax of $10 US. The tax is collected at the airport when you check in for your return flight. Remember to keep this amount in cash, as credit cards are not accepted.

Customs

Visitors may enter the country with up to one litre of alcohol, 200 cigarettes and up to $100 US worth of goods (not counting personal belongings). Bringing in illegal drugs and firearms is of course prohibited.

EMBASSIES AND CONSULATES

Foreign Embassies and Consulates in the Dominican Republic

Embassies and consulates can be an invaluable source of help to visitors who find themselves in trouble. For example, consulates can provide names of doctors or lawyers in the case of death or serious injury. However, only urgent cases are handled. It should also be noted that the cost of these services is not absorbed by the consulates.

Belgium Agencias Navieras Báez, 504 av. Abraham Lincoln, Santo Domingo, ☎ (809) 562-1661, ≈ (809) 562-3383.

Canada 30 Avenida Máximo Gomez, Santo Domingo, ☎ (809) 685-1136, ≈ (809) 682-2691.

United States At the corner of Calle Cesar Nicolas Pension and Calle Leopold Navarro, Santo Domingo, ☎ (809) 541-2171.

Germany 37 Calle Lic. Juan Tomás Mejía y Cotes, Santo Domingo, ☎ (809) 565-8811, ☎ (809) 565-8812 or Apartado Postal 1235, Santo Domingo.

Great Britain Saint George School, 552 Av. Abraham Lincoln, Santo Domingo, ☎ (809) 562-5015 or Apartado Postal 30341, Santo Domingo, Av. Romulo Betancourt, # 1302 apt. 202, Santo Domingo, ☎ (809) 532-4216.

Switzerland 26, av. José Gabria García, Santo Domingo, ☎ (809) 685-0126.

Dominican Embassies and Consulates Abroad

In Belgium 160-A av. Louise, 1050 Bruxelles, ☎ 648-0840, ≈ 640-9561.

In Canada 1650 de Maisonneuve West, Suite 302, Montreal, Quebec, ☎ (514) 933-9008 or 1-800-563-1611.

In the United States 1715 22nd St. N.W., Washington, D.C., 20008, U.S.A., ☎ (202) 332-6280.

1501 Broadway, 4th floor, New York, N.Y., 10036, U.S.A., ☎ (212) 768-2480.

1038 Brickell Ave., Miami, FLA., 33131, U.S.A., ☎ (305) 358-3221.

870 Market St., suite 915, San Francisco, Calif., 94102, U.S.A., ☎ (415) 783-7530.

In Germany Burgstrasse # 87, 5300 Bonn, 2nd floor, Germany, ☎ 00228-36-4956.

In Switzerland 16 rue Genus, Genève, ☎ 738-0018

TOURIST INFORMATION

Tourist Offices

These offices exist to help travellers plan their trips to the Dominican Republic. Their personnel can answer questions and provide you with brochures.

In Canada 2980 Crescent, Montreal, Quebec, H3G 2V8, ☎ (514) 499-1918, ≈ (514) 499-1393.

74 Front St. E., Unit 53 Market square, Toronto, Ontario, M5E 1B8, ☎(416) 361-2126 or 1-888-494-5050, ≈ (416) 361-2130.

In Italy lazza Castello 25, 20121 Milano, Italia, ☎ (392) 805-7781, ≈ (392) 865-861.

In Great Britain 1 Hay Hill, Berkely Square, London W1X 7LF, England, ☎ (171) 495-4322, ≈ (171) 491-8689.

In the United States 1501 Broadway, 4th floor, New York, N.Y., 10036, ☎(212) 768-2480 or 1-888-374-6361, ≈ (212) 575-5448.

2355 Salzedo St., Suite 307, Coral Gables, Miami, Fla., 33134, ☎ (305) 444-4592, ≈ (305) 444-4845.

561 West Diversey Bldg, Suite 214, Chicago, IL 60614-1643, ☎(773) 529-1336 or 1-888-303-1336, ≈ (773) 529-1338.

Tour Guides

You will likely be approached in tourist areas by Dominicans speaking broken English or French, offering their services as tour guides. Some of them are quite capable and trustworthy, but many have little valuable information to share. Be careful. If you want to hire a guide, ask for proof of his or her qualifications. These guides not only do not work for free, but often charge a substantial fee. Before starting off on a guided tour, establish precisely what services you will be getting and at what price, pay only when the tour is over.

ENTERING THE COUNTRY

Several airline companies offer packages including airfare on a charter flight, accommodation and dining. The advantage of these "all-inclusive" deals is that you have nothing to worry about once you arrive in the Dominican Republic. These packages generally place visitors in tourist villages like Playa Dorada, Sosua, Punta Cana or Juan Dolio. Check with your travel agent to find out what packages are available.

It is also easy to head off with just an airline ticket and to find accommodation in one of the numerous hotels all over the island once you arrive. The advantage of this type of travel is that you will see much more of the island and can choose where to stay each day. Except during peak travel times (Christmas vacation and the week leading up to Easter week), you should not have any trouble finding accommodation without reservations, either in out-of-the-way Dominican villages (if you don't require the utmost in comfort) or in the popular resorts.

Most flights from Canada are aboard charter flights, so check with a travel agent. At press time, American Airlines and Air France were among the major carriers offering flights to Santo Domingo.

By Plane

There are five international airports in the Dominican Republic; they are located in Santo Domingo (Las Américas),

Puerto Plata, Punta Cana, La Romana (Cajuiles) and Barahona. Only the airports in Santo Domingo and Puerto Plata receive flights regularly. The other three receive mainly small planes and charter flights.

The Airports

The Las Américas airport in Santo Domingo and the airport in Puerto Plata are sizeable, full-service airports with a good selection of boutiques. Not surprisingly, however, the shopping is more expensive here than it is in the cities.

At both airports, there are taxis and public buses that can take travellers to the surrounding cities. Though taxi rates are always posted (and are non-negotiable), to avoid any problems it is best to use the services of drivers who are members of the AILA association. When it comes to rates for buses, always ask the fare to the town where your hotel is located before getting on.

All of the car rental companies have small counters at the airports, so you can rent a car as soon as you arrive. They are all right beside each other, making it easy to compare prices.

Las Américas Airport
Located 20 km east of Santo Domingo
☎ 549-0651

Puerto Plata International Airport
Located 18 km east of Puerto Plata
☎ 586-0219

Punta Cana Airport
☎ 686-8790

By Car

To Haiti

To drive to Haiti, take the highway that leads to the town of Jimaní, in the Dominican Republic. Anyone wishing to visit Haiti must have a valid passport. Depending on your country of origin, you may or may not need a visa (Canadian residents, for example, do not). Visas can be obtained through the Haitian consulate in your country or in Santo Domingo:

33 Avenida Juan Sanchez Ramirez
Santa Domingo
☎ 686-6094

Excursions to Haiti are also offered, in the major resort towns (Sosua and Cabarete).

GETTING AROUND

Distances can be long in the Dominican Republic, especially since the roads, though generally in good condition, often go through small villages where drivers must slow down. Furthermore, very few roads have passing lanes, and the condition of some smaller roads is so pitiable that it is difficult to drive faster than 40 kph. It is therefore important to plan your itinerary carefully.

By Car

Renting a car in the Dominican Republic is easy, as most of the large companies have offices in the country. It will cost an average of $50 US a day (unlimited mileage) for a compact car, not including insurance and taxes. The minimum age for renting a car is 25. Choose a vehicle that is in good condition, preferably a new one. A few local companies offer low prices, but their cars are often in poor condition, and they don't offer much assistance in case of breakdown. Therefore, before heading off on a long journey, choose your car carefully.

It is strongly recommended that you take out sufficient automobile insurance to cover all costs in case of an accident. A $700 US deductible is fairly standard. Before signing any rental contract, make sure the methods of payment are clearly indicated. Finally, remember that your credit card must cover both the rental fees and the deductible in case of an accident. While some credit cards insure you automatically, you should check if the coverage is complete.

A valid driver's license from your country is accepted in the Dominican Republic.

Driving and the Highway Code

In general, the main roads and highways in the Dominican Republic are in good condition, but the odd pothole does crop up here and there. Furthermore, even though there are no shoulders, traffic still moves pretty fast.

Driving on the secondary roads is a whole other story. They are often gravel-covered, narrow and littered with potholes of all different sizes. As well, animals tend to wander across the roads (dogs and chickens in particular), forcing drivers to brake unexpectdly. Drivers must be

Table of Distances (km/mi)

Barahona	Higüey	La Romana	Monte Cristi	Puerto Plata	Samaná	San Francisco	Santiago	Santo Domingo
Barahona								
367/228	Higüey							
330/205	37/23	La Romana						
356/223	458/285	413/257	Monte Cristi					
373/232	402/250	342/213	137/85	Puerto Plata				
400/249	448/278	340/211	320/199	222/138	Samaná			
294/183	304/189	275/171	177/110	121/75	144/89	San Francisco		
312/194	341/212	305/190	117/73	61/38	204/127	269/167	Santiago	
200/124	166/103	131/81	292/181	235/146	243/151	75/47	166/103	Santo Domingo

particularly careful when passing through villages where there are many pedestrians. Cautious driving is imperative at all times.

Speed bumps have been placed on some village roads to slow down traffic, but unfortunately they are poorly marked. They are usually located on the way into villages and near military barracks.

Road signs, such as speed limit indications, stop signs or no-entry signs, are few and far between. The rules of the road are still to be respected, however. Slow down at intersections and do not go over the speed limit of 80 kph. Dominicans drive very fast, often with little regard for these rules, meaning travellers must be particularly vigilant. Many locals do not check their blind spot, and cars equipped with turn signals are rare. Motorcyclists are numerous and quite reckless. Finally, the most hair-raising experiences are almost always associated with passing. There are no passing lanes, except the lane for oncoming traffic... Some drivers weave in and out of traffic, passing at every chance, no matter how slim.

Although significant improvements have been made in recent years, road signs are still insufficient in many places. If you get lost, therefore, the only way of finding your way might be to ask local villagers, who are usually more than happy to help out.

Heavy traffic is rare on roads in the Dominican Republic, except in Santo Domingo, where driving can get tricky, especially at peak hours.

Due to the lack of signs and street lights on Dominican roads, driving at night is strongly discouraged. If your car breaks down you will be stranded. If you do have to drive at night, keep in mind that you are at greater risk of being robbed, so do not pick up hitchhikers or stop at the side of the road, and keep your doors locked.

The speed limit is 80 kph on the highways, 60 kph near cities and 40 kph within city limits.

Accidents

In the event of a road accident, the police will be called to the scene to assess the situation. If there are injuries or damages, witnesses will be asked to testify in court; the information they provide is central to the outcome of the case. Occasionally, the principal witnesses to an accident will be held in jail until the authorities can interview them. The wait can take up to 48 hours. This rarely happens, but should you find yourself in such a situation, stay calm and be patient.

Animals that roam freely along the roads near small villages can be hard to avoid, even for the most careful drivers (chickens seem to be particularly attracted to moving cars). If you do hit one, the local inhabitants might react aggressively, so it is best to drive to the nearest police station and deal with the situation through official channels.

Car Watchers

Throughout the Dominican Republic, youths will offer to wash or keep an eye on your car — for a small fee, of course. Sometimes they will even perform these services without asking, and still expect to get paid. Windshield washers are common at traffic lights. Usually a simple refusal is enough, though sometimes they'll wash it anyway. You have every right to refuse to pay; just make sure your windows are up, or you may get a bucket of water in your lap. When it comes to car watchers, it is often best to pay a small sum (to avoid some mysterious scratches appearing on the car). Expect to pay between 10 and 15 pesos for an evening of car surveillance and about 15 pesos for a car wash. Of course, you'll have to pay up front.

The Police

Police officers are posted all along Dominican highways. In addition to stopping drivers who break traffic laws, they are authorized to pull over any car they wish and ask to see the identification papers of the driver. The police have been told not to harass tourists, but occasionally some still ask for a few pesos. If you are sure you have not broken any laws, there is no reason to pay anything. Don't be alarmed if the police pull you over to check your papers. In general, they are approachable and ready to help if you have problems on the road.

Gasoline (Petrol)

There are gas stations all over the country; gas is reasonably priced, generally on a par with North American prices. Most stations are open until 10pm, and many stay open 24 hours. More and more stations now accept credit cards.

By Motorcycle or Scooter

In most resort areas it is possible to rent a motorcycle for $30 to $40 US a day. You will need to leave a deposit, such as your passport (or another valid piece of identification) or sometimes even your plane ticket. Drive carefully; even though motorcycles are common in the Dominican Republic, car drivers are not always cautious around them. Always determine the price and payment conditions before leaving with your rental.

By Taxi

Taxi services are offered in every resort area and moderate-sized city. The cars are often very old, but they will get you where you want to go. The rates are fairly high, and are usually posted at the taxi stand. They vary little from one city to another. Make sure to agree on the fare with the driver before starting out, and do not pay until you arrive at your destination.

By Motorcyle-taxi

Motorcyclists offer rides to pedestrians in most cities, providing a quick and inexpensive way to cover short distances. You will have to sacrifice some comfort and security, so avoid long distances and highways. Set a price before getting on; a few kilometres should cost about 10 pesos.

By Collective Taxi

In a collective taxi, the cost of the trip is shared between all the passengers, even if their destinations vary. These taxis operate within cities or travel between them. The vehicles are often in terrible shape (especially in Santo Domingo), but are still more comfortable than the bus. They are identifiable by their license plate reading *público*.

By Public Bus (*Guagua*)

Public buses, called *guagua*s by the Dominicans, (pronounced "oua-oua") travel along every type of road in the Dominican Republic and are an efficient way of getting around the island. To catch one, simply go to the local bus station (often near the central park) or wait by the side of a main road and flag one down. These buses stop frequently, and are often jam-packed and very uncomfortable. On the positive side, this is the cheapest way to get around the island. The table below will give you an idea of the prices.

By Coach

Coach service is offered by two bus companies, Metro Bus and Caribe

Rates for *guaguas*			
Santo Domingo	-	La Romana	18 pesos
Santo Domingo	-	Barahona	30 pesos
Santo Domingo	-	Santiago	25 pesos
Santo Domingo	-	Puerto Plata	50 pesos
Santiago	-	Constanza	20 pesos
Santiago	-	Puerto Plata	20 pesos
Puerto Plata	-	Samaná	60 pesos
Puerto Plata	-	Monte Cristi	60 pesos

Tours. While the vehicles in question are fairly old, they are air conditioned and reasonably comfortable. Coaches make fewer stops than *guaguas* and thus cover longer distances quite quickly. The fares are higher than those for *guaguas*, but you'll save a lot of time for long distances.

Hitchhiking

It is fairly easy to get around the country by hitchhiking. Dominicans are friendly and like chatting with visitors. However, a reasonable amount of caution is advised, especially for women travelling alone.

INSURANCE

Health Insurance

Health insurance is the most important type of insurance for travellers and should be purchased before your departure. A comprehensive health insurance policy that provides a level of coverage sufficient to pay for hospitalization, nursing care and doctor's fees is recommended. Keep in mind that health care costs are rising quickly everywhere. The policy should also have a repatriation clause in case the required care is not available in the Dominican Republic. As patients are sometimes asked to pay for medical services up front, find out what provisions your policy makes in this case. Always carry your health insurance policy with you when travelling to avoid problems if you are in an accident, and get receipts for any expenses incurred.

Theft Insurance

Most residential insurance policies in North America protect some of your goods from theft, even if the theft occurs in a foreign country. To make a claim, you must fill out a police report. Usually the coverage for a theft abroad is 10% of your total coverage. If you plan to travel with valuable objects, check your policy or with an insurance agency to see if additional baggage insurance is necessary. European visitors should take out baggage insurance.

Cancellation Insurance

This type of insurance is usually offered by your travel agent when you purchase your air ticket or tour package. It covers any non-refundable payments to travel suppliers such as airlines, and must be purchased at the same time as initial payment is made for air tickets or tour packages. This insurance allows you to be reimbursed for the ticket or package deal if your trip must be cancelled due to serious illness or death. This type of insurance can be useful, but weigh the likelihood of your using it against the price.

Life Insurance

By purchasing your tickets with certain credit cards you will get life insurance. Several airline companies offer a life insurance plan included in the price of the airplane ticket. However, many travellers already have another form of life insurance and do not need extra insurance.

HEALTH

The Dominican Republic is a wonderful country to explore; however, travellers should be aware of and protect themselves from a number of health risks associated with the region, such as malaria, typhoid, diphtheria, tetanus, polio and hepatitis A. Cases of these diseases are rare but there is a risk. **Travellers are therefore advised to consult a doctor (or travellers' clinic) for advice on what precautions to take.** Remember that it is much easier to prevent these illnesses than it is to cure them and that a vaccination is not a substitute for cautious travel.

Illnesses

Please note that this section is intended to provide general information only.

Malaria

Malaria (paludism) is caused by a parasite in the blood called *Plasmodium sp.* This parasite is transmitted by anopheles mosquitoes, which bite from nightfall until dawn. The parasite is present year round in the Dominican Republic, below 400 metres of altitude, in the rural and urban zones of the whole country, especially along the Haitan border. The risk is minimal and antimalaria drugs are not necessary for short stays in resort areas. It is nevertheless a good idea to take measures to prevent mosquito bites (see the section on mosquitoes, p 44).

The symptoms of malaria include high fever, chills, extreme fatigue and headaches as well as stomach and muscle aches. There are several forms of malaria, including one serious type caused by *P. falciparum*. The disease can take hold while you are still on holiday or up to 12 weeks following your return; in some cases the symptoms can appear months later.

Hepatitis A

This disease is generally transmitted by ingesting food or water that has been contaminated by faecal matter. The symptoms include fever, yellowing of the skin, loss of appetite and fatigue, and can appear between 15 and 50 days after infection. An effective vaccination by injection is available. Besides the recommended vaccine, good hygiene is important. Always wash your hands before every meal, and ensure that the food and preparation area are clean.

Hepatits B

Hepatitis B, like hepatitis A, affects the liver, but is transmitted through direct contact of body fluids. The symptoms are flu-like, and similar to those of hepatitis A. A vaccination exists but must be administered over an extended period of time, so be sure to check with your doctor several weeks in advance.

Dengue

Also called "breakbone fever", Dengue is transmitted by mosquitoes. In its most benign form it can cause flu-like symptoms such as headaches, chills and sweating, aching muscles and nausea. In its haemorrhagic form, the most serious and rarest form, it can be fatal. There is no vaccine for the virus, so take the usual precautions to avoid mosquito bites.

Typhoid

This illness is caused by ingesting food that has come in contact (direct or indirect) with an infected person's stool. Common symptoms include high fever, loss of appetite, headaches, constipation and occasionally diarrhea, as well as the appearance of red spots on the skin. These symptoms will appear one to three weeks after infection. Which vaccination you get (it exists in two forms, oral and by injection) will depend on your trip. Once again, it is always a good idea to visit a travellers' clinic a few weeks before your departure.

Diphtheria and Tetanus

These two illnesses, against which most people are vaccinated during their childhood, can have serious consequences. Thus, before leaving, check that your vaccinations are valid; you may need a booster shot. Diphtheria is a bacterial infection that is transmitted by nose and throat secretions or by skin lesions on an infected person. Symptoms include sore throat, high fever, general aches and pains and occasionally skin infections. Tetanus is caused by a bacteria that enters your body through an open wound that comes in contact with contaminated dust or rusty metal.

Other Health Tips

Cases of illnesses like hepatitis B, AIDS and certain venereal diseases have been reported; it is therefore a good idea to be careful.

Near the villages of Hato Mayor, Higüey, Nisibon and El Seibo, fresh water is often contaminated by an organism that causes schistosomiasis. This infection, which is caused by a parasite entering the body and attacking the liver and nervous system, is difficult to treat. It is therefore best to avoid swimming in fresh water.

Remember that consuming too much alcohol, particularly during prolonged exposure to the sun, can cause severe dehydration and lead to health problems.

Due to a lack of financial resources, Dominican medical facilities may not be as up-to-date as those in your own country. Therefore, if you need medical services, expect them to be different from what you are used to. The clinics outside large urban centres might seem modest to you. In general, however, clinics are better equipped than hospitals, so head to a clinic first. In tourist areas, there are always doctors who can speak English. Before a blood transfusion, be sure (when possible) that quality control tests have been carried out on the blood.

Insufficiently treated water, which can contain disease-causing bacteria, is the cause of most of the health problems travellers are likely to encounter, such as stomach upset, diarrhea or fever. Throughout the country, it is a good idea to drink bottled water (when buying bottled water, make sure the bottle is properly sealed), or to purify your own with iodine or a water purifier. Most major hotels treat their water, but always ask first. Ice cubes should be avoided, as they may be made of contaminated water. In addition, fresh fruits and vegetables that have been washed but not peeled can also pose a health risk. Make sure that the vegetables you eat are well-cooked and peel your own fruit. Do not eat lettuce, unless it has been hydroponically grown (some vegetarian restaurants serve this type of lettuce; ask). Remember: cook it, peel it or forget it.

If you do get diarrhea, soothe your stomach by avoiding solids; instead, drink carbonated beverages, bottled water, or weak tea (avoid milk) until you recover. As dehydration can be dangerous, drinking sufficient quantities of liquid is crucial. Pharmacies sell various preparations for the treatment of diarrhea, with different effects. Pepto Bismol and Imodium will stop the diarrhea, which slows the loss of fluids, but they should be avoided if you have a fever as they will prevent the necessary elimination of bacteria. Oral rehydration products, such as Gastrolyte, will replace the minerals and electrolytes which your body has lost as a result of the diarrhea. In a pinch, you can make your own rehydration solution by mixing one litre of pure water with one teaspoon of sugar and two or three teaspoons of salt. After, eat easily digested foods like rice to give your stomach time to adjust. If symptoms become more serious (high fever, persistent diarrhea), see a doctor as antibiotics may be necessary.

Food and climate can also cause problems. Pay attention to food's freshness, and the cleanliness of the preparation area. Good hygiene (wash your hands often) will help avoid undesirable situations.

It is best not to walk around bare-foot as parasites and insects can cause a variety of problems, the least of which is athlete's foot.

Mosquitoes

A nuisance common to many countries, mosquitoes are no strangers to the Dominican Republic. They are particularly numerous during the rainy season. Protect yourself with a good insect repellent. Repellents with DEET are the most effective. The concentration of DEET varies from one product to the next; the higher the concentration, the longer the protection. In rare cases, the use of repellents with high concentrations (35% or more) of DEET has been associated with convulsions in young children; it is therefore important to apply these products sparingly, on exposed surfaces, and to wash it off once back inside. A concentration of 35% DEET will protect for four to six hours, while 95% will last from 10 to 12 hours. New formulas with DEET in lesser concentrations, but which last just as long, are available.

To further reduce the possibility of getting bitten, do not wear perfume or bright colours. Sundown is an especially active time for insects. When walking in wooded areas, cover your legs and ankles well. Insect coils can help provide a better night's sleep. Before bed, apply insect repellent to your skin and to the headboard and baseboard of your bed. If possible, get an air-conditioned room, or bring a mosquito net.

Lastly, since it is impossible to completely avoid contact with mosquitoes, bring along a cream to soothe the bites you will invariably get.

The Sun

Its benefits are many, but so are its harms. Always wear sunscreen (SPF 15 for adults and SPF 30 for children) and apply it 20 to 30 minutes before exposure. Many creams on the market do not offer adequate protection; ask a pharmacist. Too much sun can cause sunstroke (dizziness, vomiting, fever, etc.). Be careful, especially the first few days, as it takes time to get used to the sun. Take sun in small doses and protect yourself with a hat and sunglasses.

First Aid Kit

A small first-aid kit can prove very useful. Bring along sufficient amounts of any medications you take regularly as well as a valid prescription in case you lose your supply; it can be difficult to find certain medications in small towns in the Dominican Republic. Other medications such as anti-malaria pills and Imodium (or an equivalent), can also be hard to find. Finally, don't forget self-adhesive bandages, disinfectant cream or ointment, analgesics (pain-killers), antihistamines (for allergies), an extra pair of sunglasses or contact lenses, contact lens solution, and medicine for upset stomach. Though these items are all available in the Dominican Republic, they might be difficult to find in remote villages.

CLIMATE

There are two seasons in the Dominican Republic: the cool season (from November to April) and the rainy season (from May to October). The cool season is the most pleasant, as the heat is less stifling, the rain less frequent and the humidity lower. Temperatures hover around 29°C during the day and dip to about 19°C at night. During the rainy season, the showers are heavy, but short, so it is still possible to travel. Rain is most frequent from May to mid-June. In the rainy season, the average temperature is 31°C during the day and 22°C at night. The number of hours of daylight remains fairly constant throughout the year. Hurricanes, though rare, occur during the rainy season.

PACKING

The type of clothing required does not vary much from season to season. In general, loose-fitting, comfortable cotton or linen clothes are best. When exploring urban areas, wear closed shoes that cover the entire foot rather than sandals, as they will protect against cuts that could become infected. Bring a sweater or long-sleeved shirt for cool evenings, and rubber sandals (thongs or flip-flops) to wear at the beach and in the shower. During the rainy season, an umbrella is useful for staying dry during brief tropical showers. To visit certain attractions you must wear a skirt that covers the knees or long pants. For evenings out, you might need more formal clothes, as a number of places have dress codes. Finally, if you expect to go hiking in the mountains, bring along some good hiking boots and a sweater.

SAFETY AND SECURITY

Although the Dominican Republic is not a dangerous country, it has its share of thieves, particularly in the resort towns and in Santo Domingo. Keep in mind that to the majority of people in the country, some of your possessions (things like cameras, leather suitcases, video cameras, and jewellery) represent a great deal of money, especially when you consider that the minimum monthly salary is 1,600 pesos ($115 US). A degree of caution can help avoid problems. For example, do not wear too much jewellery, keep your electronic equipment in a nondescript shoulder bag slung across your chest, and avoid revealing the contents of your wallet when paying for something. Be doubly careful at night, and stay away from dark streets, especially if there are strangers lurking about. Finally, some neighbourhoods of Santo Domingo — around the Puente Duarte and behind Calle Mella, for example — should be avoided, particularly at night. To be safe, don't wander into an area you know nothing about.

A money belt can be used to conceal cash, traveller's cheques and your passport. If your bags should happen to be stolen, you will at least have the money and documents necessary to get by. Remember that the less attention you draw to yourself, the less chance you have of being robbed.

If you bring valuables to the beach, you are strongly recommended to keep a constant eye on them. It is best to keep your valuables in the small safes available at most hotels.

MONEY AND BANKING

Currency

The country's currency is the peso. Bills are available in 100, 50, 20, 10, and 5 peso denominations; coins come in 50, 25 and 5 centavo pieces (100 centavos = 1 peso).

Banks

Banks are open Monday to Friday, from 8:30am to 3pm. They can be found in all large and medium-sized cities. Most can exchange US dollars, while fewer deal in other foreign currencies. In certain small villages and on holidays, it is impossible to change money. It is best to carry some cash with you at all times.

Cash advances from your credit card are easy to obtain. Most large banks offer this service. You can also withdraw money using your credit card from automatic teller machines, which are found mostly in Santo Domingo and in a few larger towns. However, it is difficult, sometimes impossible to use your bank card.

US Dollars

It is best to travel with cash or traveller's cheques in US dollars since they are easier to exchange and generally fetch a better rate.

Exchange Rates

$1 CAN	= 9.91 pesos	10 pesos	= $1.01 CAN
$1 US	= 13.67 pesos	10 pesos	= $0.73 US
1£	= 22.38 pesos	10 pesos	= £0.45
$1 Aust	= 10.15 pesos	10 pesos	= $0.99 Aust
$1 NZ	= 7.71 pesos	10 pesos	= $1.30 NZ
1 SF	= 9.02 pesos	10 pesos	= 1.11 SF
1 BF	= 0.36 pesos	10 pesos	= 28 BF
1 guilder	= 6.57 pesos	10 pesos	= 1.52 guilders
100 pesetas	= 8.76 pesos	10 pesos	= 114 pesetas
1000 lira	= 7.58 pesos	10 pesos	= 1319 lira

Exchanging Money

It is illegal to exchange money in the street. However, in some cities you may be approached by people offering to buy your dollars. It is safer to go to an official currency exchange bureau, especially since the rates are usually about the same.

Traveller's Cheques

It is always best to keep most of your money in traveller's cheques, which are accepted in some restaurants, hotels and shops (if they are in American dollars or pesos). They are also easy to cash in at banks and exchange offices. Always keep a copy of the serial numbers of your cheques in a separate place; that way, if the cheques are lost, the company can replace them quickly and easily. Do not rely solely on travellers' cheques, always carry some cash.

Credit Cards

Most credit cards, especially Visa and MasterCard, are accepted in a large number of businesses. However, many of the smaller places only take cash. Once again, remember that even if you have a credit card and traveller's cheques, you should always have some cash on hand.

When paying with your credit card, always check your receipt carefully to make sure that the abbreviation for the peso — "RDS" — appears, rather than the letters "US". If there is an error, make sure to have it corrected before signing.

Taxes and Service Charges

An 8% tax and a 10% service charge are automatically added to restaurant bills. For hotels the tax is 5%, and the service charge 6%.

TELECOMMUNICATIONS

Mail

There are post offices in every city, and some hotels offer mailing services and sell stamps. Regardless of where you mail your correspondence from, do not expect it to reach its destination quickly; the postal service in the Dominican Republic is not known for its efficiency. If you have something important to send, you are better off using a fax machine at a Codetel. Stamps are sold in post offices and in some shops.

Telephone and Fax

International telephone calls can be made from the larger hotels or from **Codetel** centres, which are found in all cities. Calling abroad from a Codetel is very easy. The simplest way is to dial direct, but collect calls can also be made. The length of a call is measured on a computer, and customers pay at a counter when leaving, eliminating the need for handfuls of change. Credit cards are accepted. Codetel centres also offer facsimile (fax) services.

The area code for the entire country is **809**. When calling the Dominican Republic from the United States or Canada, dial 1-809 and the number you wish to reach. The personnel at the Codetel centres can provide instructions (usually in Spanish, but occasionally in broken English) on how to dial long distance.

Using Foreign Operators

It is possible to use the operator in the country you are calling.

Canada Direct ☎ 1-800-333-0111
AT&T USA ☎ 1-800-872-2881
Sprint USA ☎ 1-800-751-7877 (from pay phone) or 1166 (wait for tone) 77 (from private phone)
MCI USA ☎ 1-800-999-9000

British Telecom Direct
☎ 1-800-751-2701

Toll-free 1-800 and 1-888 numbers included in this guide can only be reached from North America.

Direct Dialing

Direct dialed calls go through a Dominican operator and are charged accordingly.

To call North America, dial 1, the area code and the telephone number. For other countries dial 011 then the international country code (see below), the area code and the telephone number.

United Kingdom 44
Australia 61
New Zealand 64
Belgium 32
Italy 39
Germany 49
Netherlands 31
Switzerland 41

 ACCOMMODATIONS

When it comes to accommodations in the Dominican Republic, the choices are endless, especially in the tourist areas (Sosúa, Cabarete, Boca Chica) and in Santo Domingo. The rate varies enormously depending what type of establishment you choose, from the smallest hotel to the resort complex. Every room is subject to the 5% tax and the 6% service charge, however. It is customary to leave an extra 10 to 15 pesos per day for the room cleaning services; this can be left at the end of your stay. Most large hotels accept credit cards, while smaller hotels usually don't.

A few of our favourites...

For its old-fashioned charm
      Embajador (Santo Domingo)   p 82
      Palacio (Santo Domingo)   p 80

For its friendly atmosphere
      Méson de Isabela (Boca Chica)   p 102
      El 28 (Boca de Yuma)   p 106
      Waterfront (Sosúa)   p 179
      Caribe Surf (Cabarete)   p 181
      Bahía Blanca (Río San Juan)   p 181
      Tropic Banana (Las Terrenas)   p 199
      Araya (Las Terrenas)   p 199

For its superb view of the sea
      Marco Polo Club (Sosúa)   p 180
      Bahía Blanca (Río San Juan)   p 181
      Gran Bahía (Samaná)   p 201

For its peaceful setting
      La Catalina (Cabrera)   p 182
      Villa Serena (Las Galeras)   p 202

For children
      Club Med Punta Cana   p 117

For its beautiful setting
      Casa de Campo (La Romana)   p 105
      Bahía Principe (Río San Juan)   p 182
      Melia Bavaro (Punta Cana)   p 116
      La Hacienda (Playa Cofresi)   p 175
      Paradise Beach Club (Playa Dorada)   p 176

For its beautiful beach
      Club Med Punta Cana   p 117
      Punta Cana Beach Resort   p 117
      Melia Bavaro (Punta Cana)   p 116
      Iberostar (Punta Cana)   p 117
      Ríu (Punta Cana)   p 116
      Caribbean Village Playa Grande   p 182
      Playa Naco (Playa Dorada)   p 177
      Jack Tar (Playa Dorada)   p 176

Hotels

There are three categories of hotels. The low-budget places, near the downtown areas, offer only the basics in comfort. The rooms generally have a small bathroom and an overhead fan. Medium-budget hotels typically offer simple air-conditioned rooms that are reasonably comfortable. These can usually be found in resort towns and larger cities. Finally, there are the luxury hotels, found in resort towns and on large, secluded properties in Santo Domingo. They all try to surpass each other in comfort and luxury. Several hotels in this last category belong to international hotel chains like Occidental Hoteles, LTI, Caribbean Village, Jack Tar Village and Sheraton.

Except for budget hotels, most places have their own generator, as power cuts are frequent in the Dominican Republic. Security guards keep watch over medium- and high-priced hotels.

Some hotels offer all-inclusive packages, which usually include two or three meals a day, all locally produced drinks (such as rum and beer), taxes and the service charge. When a package deal is available, it will be indicated next to the room rate in the hotel listings.

Apart-hotels

Apart-hotels offer all the services of a hotel, but each room has an equipped kitchenette. This is the most economical option for longer stays in the Dominican Republic.

Cabañas

This type of accommodation is only slightly different than a hotel. *Cabañas* offer rooms in separate little buildings. They are usually inexpensive, and some are equipped with kitchenettes.

Bed and Breakfasts

Some people have adapted their homes to receive guests. However, the level of comfort varies greatly from one place to another. Generally, guests do not have a private bathroom.

Youth Hostels

There are no youth hostels in the Dominican Republic, but many of the country's small hotels offer very good rates.

Camping

There are no official campsites in the Dominican Republic, but some visitors occasionally camp out anyway.

 RESTAURANTS

There is something for every taste in the Dominican Republic, from little cafeterias serving local inexpensive dishes to gourmet restaurants offering refined fare. The choice is particularly varied in Santo Domingo and near the resort areas. Elsewhere, however, often the choice is limited to local specialties.

Spanish Menu Glossary

Abichuela	a bean dish
Abichuela con dulce	sweet red beans (Easter week only)
Agua	water
Ajo	garlic
Asopao	dish made with tomatoes, rice and seafood or fish
Arroz	rice
Batida	beverage made of fruit, ice and milk
Camarone	shrimp
Carne de res	beef
Carne	meat
Cerveza	beer
Chicháron	marinated and cooked meat or chicken
Chivo	goat
Chuleta	cutlet
Conejo	rabbit
Empanadas	small turnovers stuffed with meat or vegetables
Filete	steak
Granadilla	grenadine
Huevo	egg
Jalao	coconut and molasses
Jamón	ham
Jugo	juice
Lambi	shellfish
Langosta	crayfish
Leche	milk
Limón	lemon
Mangu	green bananas and meat
Mariscos	seafood
Masitas	floor, coconut and brown sugar
Mermelada	jam
Mofongo	ripe bananas with grilled sesame seeds
Mondongo	tripe
Naranja	orange
Pan	bread
Papas fritas	fried potatoes (French fries)
Postulad	wheat crust filled with seafood, meat or vegetable
Pescado	fish
Pica pollo	fried chicken
Piña	pineapple
Plátanos fritos	fried bananas
Pollo	chicken
Postre	dessert
Queso	cheese
Sancocho	meat boiled with vegetables
Sopa	soup
Tamarindo	tamarind
Tortilla	omelette
Tostada	toast
Vino	wine
Zanahoria	carrot

Service is usually friendly and attentive in both small and large restaurants. An 8% tax and 10% service charge are added to every bill.

Dominican Cuisine

Dominican cuisine is not too spicy, simple and nourishing and is prepared from local ingredients. Dishes are usually of meat, fish, chicken or seafood accompanied by rice, beans or plantain. By visiting a few local restaurants you'll certainly have the chance to enjoy some local specialties like *mondongo*, *asopao* or *sancocho*.

Drinks

There are a few local Dominican beers, these include Quisqueya, the new Soverana and El Presidente. All three are of export quality, though the most popular is El Presidente. Most hotels and restaurants also serve imported beers.

Wine is not very popular in the Dominican Republic, and not much local wine is produced. The imported wines served in restaurants are often quite expensive — particularly the French ones. Chilean wines are more affordable and often very good.

Rum, whether golden, white, dark or aged, whether served as an aperitif or digestif, is definitely the most sought after alcohol. Sold everywhere (it is sometimes easier to find than bottled water), rum has been close to the hearts of all Dominicans since sugar cane has been grown here, and grown well, we might add. Don't miss the chance to savour some Brugal Extra Viejo or Ron Bermúdez.

Tipping

Good service is generally rewarded with a tip. In addition to the 10% service charge automatically added to the bill, a 10% to 15% tip should be left depending on the quality of the service received.

 SHOPPING

Opening Hours

Most stores are open from 9am to 5pm. Stores rarely close at lunchtime, especially in resort areas.

Taxes

The Dominican government charges a tax on hotel rooms (see p 47) and another on restaurant bills (see above). The tax should be clearly indicated on the bill.

Mercados

You can buy all kinds of things in these little grocery stores, including food, beauty products, alcohol and cigarettes. In some smaller *mercados*, it is often easier to find bottles of rum than bottles of water.

Alcohol

Alcohol, most often rum and beer, is sold in all little grocery stores (*mercados*).

What to Bring Back

The boutiques in Santo Domingo and the resort areas are full of all sorts of merchandise like summer outfits and t-shirts. It can be difficult, however, to find good local crafts, an area, which is generally poorly developed. On the street and in the few craft shops in the tourist areas you might find something interesting amongst the wood sculptures, mahogany boxes, straw hats and naive (Haitian) art for sale. Jewellery made with amber (the price of which has increased since the release of the film *Jurassic Park*), *larimar* and shells are also sold throughout the country. Finally, rum is a must; it is both good and inexpensive.

Duty-Free Shops

There are duty-free shops in the airports and in Santo Domingo. Most of the products sold are foreign. All purchases must be paid for in American dollars.

HOLIDAYS

All banks and many businesses close on official holidays. Plan ahead by cashing traveller's cheques and doing last-minute souvenir shopping the day before. Things generally slow down during holidays.

January 1	New Year's Day
January 6	Epiphany
January 21	Nuestra Señora de la Altagracia Festival
January 26	Birthday of J.P. Duarte
Variable	Mardi gras
February 27	Independence Day
Variable	Good Friday
May 1	Labour Day
Variable	Corpus Christi
August 16	Restoration of the Republic Day
September 24	Nuestra Señora de las Mercedes Festival
December 25	Christmas Day

The Semana Santa

During the days leading up to Easter, called the *Semana Santa* or Holy Week, various festivities are organized by Catholics to celebrate this auspicious holiday. On Thursday, the pious visit churches throughout the country to pray. On Good Friday, the festivities reach their peak as countless processions take to the streets of the country's towns and villages. Many Dominicans take advantage of this holiday to travel within the country, and hotels are often full.

MISCELLANEOUS

Electricity

Like in North America, wall sockets take plugs with two flat pins and work on an alternating current of 110 volts (60 cycles). European visitors with electric appliances will therefore need both an adaptor and a converter. There are frequent power cuts in the Dominican Republic. The more expensive hotels compensate with generators.

Women Travellers

Women travelling alone should not encounter any problems. For the most part, people are friendly and not aggressive. Generally, men are respectful toward women, and harassment is uncommon, although Dominican males do have a tendency to flirt. Of course, a certain level of caution should be exercised; avoid making eye contact, ignore any advances or comments and do not walk around alone in poorly-lit areas at night.

Smokers

There are no restrictions with respect to smokers. Cigarettes are not expensive, and smoking is allowed in all public places.

Gay Life

The situation of gays and lesbians in the Dominican Republic is similar to that found in other Latin American countries. Gays still suffer from a certain form of repression, which stems from old family and chauvinistic values and politics. *Machismo*, the notion of male superiority, is alive and well and its influence of stereotypical behaviour based on gender contribute more than anything else to the oppression of homosexuals, while at the same time keeping women in traditional roles.

Prostitution

Veritable scourge of the Dominican Republic, prostitution became rampant in the 1980s following the arrival of masses of tourists. Whether its male or female prostitution, it exists in the every town that is the least bit touristy. In certain areas, notably Boca Chica and Sosúa, it became such a problem that merchants began to complain. Thus, toward the end of 1996, Dominican authorities, in an effort to restore order to Sosúa, had to intervene to put an end to prostitution by closing many bars.

Time Change

The Dominican Republic is one hour ahead of Eastern Standard Time, and four hours behind Greenwich Mean Time. In the winter it is one hour ahead of New York and Montreal and four hours behind London. There is no daylight savings time, therefore in the summer it is on the same time as New York and Montreal and five hours behind London.

Weights and Measures

Officially, the Dominican Republic uses the metric system. However, businesses often use the imperial system. The following conversion table may be helpful.

Weights
1 pound (lb) = 454 grams (g)
1 kilogram (kg) = 2.2 pounds (lbs)

Linear Measure
1 inch = 2.2 centimetres (cm)
1 foot (ft) = 30 centimetres (cm)
1 mile = 1.6 kilometres (km)
1 kilometres (km) = 0.63 miles
1 metre (m) = 39.37 inches

Land Measure
1 acre = 0.4 hectare
1 hectare = 2.471 acres

Volume Measure
1 U.S. gallon (gal) = 3.79 litres
1 U.S. gallon (gal) = 0.83 imperial gallon

Temperature
To convert °F into °C: subtract 32, divide by 9, multiply by 5
To convert °C into °F: multiply by 9, divide by 5, add 32

OUTDOORS

The Dominican Republic has a wide range of exceptionally beautiful natural attractions, including the highest summit in the Caribbean, Pico Duarte, at 3,175 metres. There are mountain ranges, blanketed with forests at times lush and other times sparse, and protected by national parks. The country also boasts idyllic beaches, stretches of golden sand that make it a veritable paradise for those who like to bask in the sun and enjoy the crystal-clear waters of the Caribbean Sea and the Atlantic Ocean. The coral reefs that have developed in the waters off these beaches attract a vibrant variety of plant and animal life that can be observed by scuba divers and snorkellers alike. Finally, visitors can seek out the fascinating wildlife that gravitates around the island, particularly in the winter, when humpback whales can be spotted in waters off Samaná. The resources in the Dominican Republic make it easy for outdoor enthusiasts to enjoy both a whole slew of activities and sports and the natural beauty of the setting.

This chapter contains tips and advice on various sports and activities to help you get the most out of them in a safe and environmentally conscious manner.

 ## SWIMMING

Along every coast of the Dominican Republic, there are beaches that are perfect for swimming or just lounging about. The currents can be strong, though, so be careful. You are better off staying close to shore when the waves get high. Furthermore, never swim alone if you don't know how strong the currents are.

Efforts have been stepped up to sensitize people about the importance of keeping the beaches clean, especially on the northern coast. Please respect these natural areas.

A completely deserted beach is a rarity in the Dominican Republic. The good beaches are usually overrun with visitors, and to satisfy their every need, vendors roam about selling juice, fruit, beach-wear and souvenirs of all sorts. Generally a *"no, gracias"* will suffice if you are not interested. Of course, if you look at the merchandise of one vendor, the others will assume you are a potential customer and will come along one by one to hawk their wares. Set a price first if you decide to buy.

Beach chairs and parasols can be rented at almost all beaches near resort towns; the cost is around 20 pesos per day per item.

Beaches are not private in the Dominican Republic. Hotels are nevertheless often built right on the ocean. Anyone is allowed to use the beach in front of a hotel, but not necessarily the facilities. These beaches have the advantage of being free of vendors, and are also better maintained.

SCUBA DIVING

Several diving centres offer visitors the opportunity to explore the underwater world. Reefs are numerous, and there are diving centres on both the northern (Sosúa, Playa Dorada, Cabarete) and southern coasts (Boca Chica).

Certified divers can explore the secrets of the Dominican coastline to their heart's content. Others can still experience breathing underwater, but must be accompanied by a qualified guide, who will supervise their descent (to a

depth of 5 m). There is little danger; however, be sure that the supervision is adequate. Before diving for the first time, it is very important to at least take an introductory course in order to learn basic safety skills: how to clear the water from your mask, how to equalize the pressure in your ears and sinuses, how to breathe underwater (don't hold your breath), to become comfortable with the change in pressure underwater, and to familiarize yourself with the equipment. Many hotels offer a resort course of about one hour before taking first-timers under water. Equipment can easily be rented from the different centres along the coasts.

Scuba diving makes it possible to discover fascinating sights like coral reefs, schools of multi-coloured fish and amazing underwater plants. Don't forget that this ecosystem is fragile and deserves special attention. All divers must respect a few basic **safety guidelines** in order to protect these natural sites: do not touch anything (especially not urchins, as their long spikes can cause injury); do not take pieces of coral (it is much prettier in the water than out, where it becomes discoloured); do not disturb any living creatures; do not hunt; do not feed the fish; be careful not to disturb anything with your flippers and, of course, do not litter. If you want a souvenir of your underwater experience, disposable underwater cameras are available.

SNORKELLING

It doesn't take much to snorkel: a mask, a snorkel and some flippers. Anyone can enjoy this activity, which is a great way to develop an appreciation

A Fragile Ecosystem

Coral reefs are formed by minuscule organisms called coelenterate polyps, which are very sensitive to water pollution. The high level of nitrates in polluted water accelerate the growth of seaweed, which in turn takes over the coral, stops it from growing and literally smothers it. Sea urchins (whose long spikes can cause severe injuries) live on the coral and play a major role in controlling the amount of seaweed that grows on the coral by eating what the fish cannot. An epidemic threatened the survival of many reefs in 1983, when the waters became so polluted that sea urchins were affected and seaweed flourished in the Caribbean waters. Scientific studies have since proved the importance of urchins to the ecological balance, and the species has thus been restored on certain reefs. However, these little urchins cannot solve the problem on their own. Pollution control is essential if the coral reefs, upon which 400,000 organisms depend, are to survive.

for the richness of the underwater world. Not far from several beaches, you can go snorkelling around coral reefs inhabited by various underwater species. Some companies organize snorkelling trips. Remember that the basic rules for protecting the underwater environment (see scuba diving section) must also be respected when snorkelling.

  ## SURFING AND WINDSURFING

Some beaches in the Dominican Republic, especially near Cabarete, are known for their great waves. Others, like those in Boca Chica bay, where the waters are usually calm, are better suited to novice sail-boarders. If you would like to try these sports, you can rent equipment on the beach (particularly at Cabarete, Boca Chica and Playa Grande). Some places offer courses as well.

If you have never tried these sports, a few safety pointers should be followed before hitting the waves: choose a beach where the surf is not too rough; keep well clear of swimmers; don't head too far out (don't hesitate to make a distress signal by waving your arms in the air if you need to) and wear shoes to avoid cutting your feet on the rocks.

 ## SAILING

Excursions aboard sailboats and yachts offer another enchanting way to freely explore the sea's sparkling waves. Some centres organize trips, while others rent sailboats to experienced sailors. You'll find a few addresses throughout the guide.

 ## JET-SKIING

These high-speed contraptions that fly across the water provide thrills for many travellers. Learning to drive them takes little time, but reasonable caution should be exercised in order to avoid accidents. If you are careening about, always give the right of way to slower, less-manoeuvrable boats (windsurfers, pedal-boats), and watch out for swimmers and divers. These are often hard to spot, so keep your eyes peeled and stay away from the shore.

 DEEP-SEA FISHING

Deep-sea fishing enthusiasts will be pleased to note that several places offer fishing excursions, particularly out of Boca Chica and Playa Dorada. Whether you are interested in big fish (like marlin, for example) or smaller ones will determine how far from the island you go. These trips usually last about 3 hours and are quite expensive. Equipment and advice are provided. Even if you come back empty-handed, this is still a great way to spend the day.

 NATIONAL PARKS

Much of the Dominican Republic's natural beauty is protected by the island's 12 national parks, which include an underwater park, five scientific reserves and one wildlife reserve. These parks, found in every corner of the country, each protect a distinct natural environment. More and more efforts are being made to allow visitors to discover these settings, but not all parks are easy accessible. Some, like Parque Los Haïtises, near Samaná, and Parque Armando Bermudes, around Pico Duarte, are starting to welcome more visitors, and companies are organizing excursions there. Still others, however, remain isolated from the resort areas, and have virtually no facilities or services to offer. These last parks are very hard to explore because they contain

few, if any, marked trails; visitors who head off the conquer these wild spaces should therefore be very careful. Theoretically, to enter a national park, you must have a permit issued by the National Parks Service *(Santo Domingo, ☎ 221-5340)*. Permits are also available on site, but often things are poorly organized, and it can be difficult to find the person in charge. The parks, however, are not well supervised.

 HIKING

Hiking and walking are undoubtedly the most accessible activities. However, parks with well-marked trails are hard to find, so anyone heading off to explore must be well prepared. A few trails near the resort towns are worth a quick visit; just be sure to bring along everything you might need during your outing.

There are a few things to keep in mind when hiking. Before heading off on any trail try to find out its length and level of difficulty. Remember that there are no maps available at the parks, and that if you should get lost, there are no rescue teams.

You will have to be well prepared and bring along anything you might need during your hike. The longer the hike, the better prepared you must be. First of all, bring a lot of water (you won't find any along the way) and sufficient food. Remember that the sun sets between 6pm and 7pm, and you can't do much hiking after, so plan to be back before dark. Ideally, you should start out early in the morning; that way you can avoid hiking when the sun is at its hottest, and get back before the day is done.

Sunstroke

Some trails include long sections in the open, with no shade. The risk of sunstroke, which threatens anyone hiking in the tropics, is thus even higher. Cramps, goose bumps, nausea and loss of balance are the first signs of sunstroke. If these symptoms arise, the affected person needs immediate shade, water and ventilation.

To avoid this problem, always wear a hat and a good sunscreen. By getting an early start, you'll have time to hike in cooler temperatures.

Clothing

Appropriate clothing is one of the best ways to avoid the little inconveniences of the outdoors. In light of that, remember to wear lightweight and light-coloured clothing; long pants to protect your legs from underbrush, thorny bushes and bug bites and thick-soled hiking boots that are lightweight but solid, with good traction. Bring water resistant clothing, as downpours are frequent, especially in the rainforest, and don't forget your bathing suit if you plan on cooling off in one of the many waterfalls in the mountains.

What to Bring

To be prepared in any eventuality, it is a good idea to bring along a few necessities, including a water bottle, a pocketknife, antiseptic, bandages (both adhesive and non-adhesive), scissors, aspirin, sunscreen, insect repellent, food and above all enough water for the trip.

 BICYCLING

The road system in the Dominican Republic is made up mostly of one-lane highways with no shoulders and secondary roads strewn with potholes. Not exactly a cyclist's dream. In addition, it gets very hot during the day, and the roads are not always shady. Caution is advised as people drive fast. This said, cycling can still be a very pleasant way to see the countryside outside the large cities. Bicycles can be rented in most of the larger cities for a few dollars. If you plan on travelling long distances, bring along a few tools, since bike repair shops are few and far between on the island.

 MOTORCYCLING

Motorcycles are the most common mode of transportation in the Dominican Republic, and can be rented in any tourist area for about $35 US per day. You may be asked to leave your passport or return plane ticket as a deposit. A motorcycle makes it easy to explore smaller roads, some of which lead to untouched beaches away from the touristy areas. Motorcycles are a convenient means of getting around, but once again, caution is strongly advised.

 HORSEBACK RIDING

A very popular activity among Dominicans, horseback riding is another interesting way to see the country. In some parts of the island, especially on the Eastern Point, the inhabitants use horses as their main form of transportation on the often narrow dirt roads of the region. Many of the large hotels, including Casa de Campo and Punta Cana organize excursions on horseback. Small riding stables can also be found in some cities, including Bayahibe and Río San Juan.

 GOLF

To meet the demands of golf enthusiasts, a number of golf courses have been developed around the country. Among the most renowned is the one at the Casa de Campo hotel complex; laid out along a stretch of the Caribbean coast, it is simply magnificent. There is also a lovely course at Playa Dorada and a brand new one at Boca Chica.

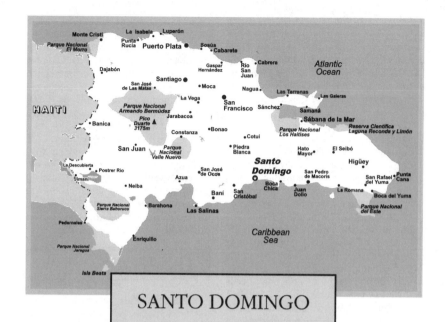

SANTO DOMINGO

The first city founded in the Americas, Santo Domingo has some 500 years of history under its belt. In 1496, after a fruitless effort to colonize the north shore of the island, Bartolomé, son of the great Genoese admiral Christopher Columbus, decided to build a city on the shores of the Caribbean Sea, at the mouth of the Río Ozama. Founded on the east bank of the river, this city was christened Nueva Isabel. A hurricane destroyed the first buildings, however, and in 1502, Nicolás de Ovando, the colonial governor at the time, decided to reconstruct the town on the west bank of the Ozama, a location he deemed more strategic.

The seat of the government of Spain's colonies in the New World, Santo Domingo thrived right from the start, as evidenced by the numerous buildings dating from that period. Spain began losing interest in Santo Domingo in

1515, when the island's gold mines were finally exhausted and fabulous riches were discovered elsewhere, most notably in Peru and Mexico, prompting the authorities to relocate the colonial government. Despite its decline in relation to the other Spanish colonies, Santo Domingo remained a nerve centre and continued to play a major role in the development of the Dominican Republic.

It was not long before Europe's other great powers started taking an interest in the New World colonies, and, envying the riches Spain had found there, tried to conquer them. Wars, invasions and destruction thus became the lot of the colonists. Santo Domingo was no exception, and many of its buildings were destroyed in an attack by English pirate Sir Francis Drake in 1586. An English offensive in 1655 and French domination from 1795 to 1809 disrupted life in the capital, whose inhabitants managed, often through bitter combat, to resist or drive back the invaders. Then, in the mid-19th century, Haitian troops invaded the country, taking control of it in 1822.

The 19th century brought a desire for independence, which changed the course of Dominican history. Juan Pablo Duarte, a fervent defender of these aspirations, succeeded in gaining the country's independence from Haiti in 1844. Santo Domingo was named capital of the Dominican Republic. The young republic was not safe from invaders, however, and was attacked repeatedly by Haitian troops, which the Dominicans succeeded, with considerable difficulty, in driving back. Less than 20 years later, in 1861, Spain annexed the country once again, putting an end to its independence and stripping Santo Domingo of its status as capital. This annexation only lasted a short time, however, and in 1865, the country was declared independent once and for all. Santo Domingo has been the capital ever since. Only its name has changed; during the Trujillo (1930-1961) dictatorship, the generalissimo renamed it Ciudad Trujillo (1936). Immediately following the president's death, the city became Santo Domingo again.

Trujillo's death also had harsh consequences for the capital, however, as it sparked major social unrest. The climate was so unstable that the Americans deemed it necessary to intervene to put some order back into the country's internal affairs. In 1965, American troops entered Santo Domingo and shelled parts of the old city, damaging a number of old buildings.

Today, with over 2,000,000 inhabitants, Santo Domingo is the largest and most populous city in the Dominican Republic. It is the country's financial, industrial and commercial centre. Its petrochemical, metallurgical, textile and plastic industries are thriving. It also has the busiest port in the country. Despite the frantic pace of life here, Santo Domingo is a pleasant city, especially in the colonial zone. Nicolás Ovando drew up the plans for the city in 1502. With the aim of reducing the existing traffic problems, he used a grid pattern for the streets. Elsewhere, however, the city has not always developed with such positive results.

 FINDING YOUR WAY AROUND

The road system in Santo Domingo is relatively modern. At rush hour, however, the streets swarm with an overwhelming number of *guaguas*, buses, motorcycles and cars heading in every direction at once, their drivers intent on weaving their way through traffic to get ahead. It is a truly "unforgettable" experience. Travelling by car between 8am and 9:30am and 4pm and 6pm is best avoided.

Although a road bypassing the downtown area is in the works, the project could take several years to complete. Until then, the main highway will continue to cut through the city, adding to the congestion of downtown traffic. It takes at least an hour to cross the city on the highway.

Las Américas International Airport

Las Américas Airport
Located 20 km east of Santo Domingo
☎ 549-0651.

One of the elegant residences bordering Parque Colón de Santo Domingo – T.B.

Santa María la Menor, the first cathedral in the Americas - Tibor Bognar

The fortress of Santo Domingo, standing guard over the city for the last 500 years - T.B.

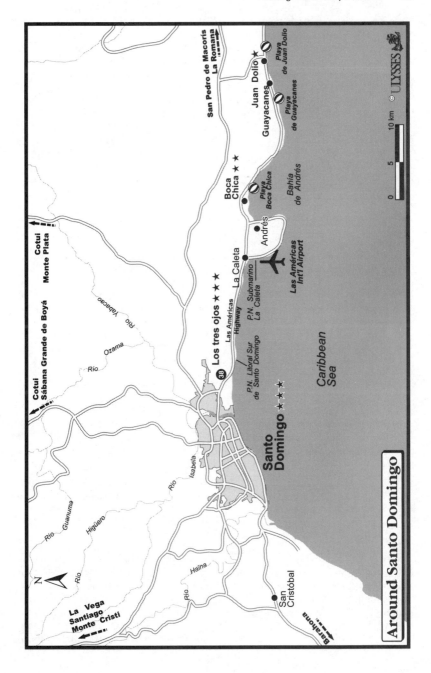

Around Santo Domingo

This airport, the largest in the country, has all the conveniences one would expect: ticket counters for major airlines, exchange offices, an assortment of boutiques and several restaurants.

Several major car rental agencies also have counters at the airport, including the following:

Avis ☎ 549-0468;
Budget ☎ 544-1244;
Hertz ☎ 549-0454;
Nelly Rent-A-Car ☎ 549-0505.

When arriving at the airport by car, you will likely be approached by employees offering to carry your bags to the check-in counters. A tip is expected in return. If you do not need help, make this clear right away.

It is easy to reach Santo Domingo and the surrounding cities from the airport. Taxis are available for the trip, but if you are on a tight budget, the public buses (*guaguas*) will get you to your destination. Comfort is not the first priority, but the trip will only cost you about ten pesos. If you decide to take a bus, make sure to agree on the price before leaving the airport. Drivers will sometimes take advantage of new arrivals, charging far more than the usual rate. It should not cost much more than ten pesos to get to Boca Chica or Santo Domingo from the airport.

Getting in and out of the City

If you are coming in by highway from the airport or from the eastern part of the country, you will cross the Río Ozama on the Puente Duarte. On the other side of this bridge, take a left on one of the main perpendicular roads, and you will soon be downtown.

To get out of Santo Domingo and head east, you can avoid a few headaches, not to mention many intersections and traffic lights, by taking the road that follows the river south of the Zona Colonial. At the end, turn left (follow the signs) to reach Puente Duarte.

The highway coming from San Cristóbal and the western part of the country becomes Avenida George Washington once it enters Santo Domingo; it then follows the shore all the way downtown.

If you are coming from Santiago or the northern part of the country, you will cross several main arteries, such as Winston Churchill, Abraham Lincoln and Máximo Gomez. Take one of these to the right, then turn left on Avenida Independencia or Avenida George Washington. The downtown area lies straight ahead.

Remember that there are toll booths at the western and eastern entrances to the city; the toll is two pesos.

In the City

The city's large arteries make it easy to get around. Running along the Caribbean Sea, Paseo Billini (which becomes Avenida George Washington) is a two-way street. Avenida Independencia, which is one-way, goes from west to east, while Avenida Bolivar, also one-way, runs in the other direction. The main streets running north-south are Avenidas Churchill, Lincoln, Tiradentes and Gomez. The Zona Colonial is bordered by the Río Ozama on one side and Parque Independencia on the other.

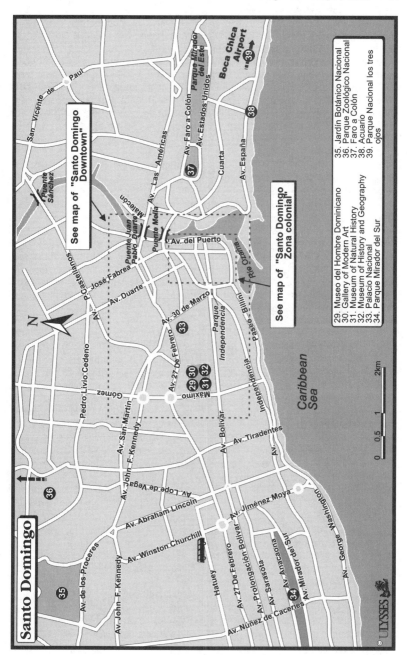

Santo Domingo

29. Museo del Hombre Dominicano
30. Gallery of Modern Art
31. Museum of Natural History
32. Museum of History and Geography
33. Palacio Nacional
34. Parque Mirador del Sur
35. Jardín Botánico Nacional
36. Parque Zoológico Nacional
37. Faro a Colón
38. Acuario
39. Parque Nacional los tres ojos

Caribbean Sea

© ULYSSES

See map of "Santo Domingo Downtown"

See map of "Santo Domingo Zona colonial"

Countless, inexpensive taxis, *guaguas*, and collective taxis crisscross the city. Always make sure you indicate your destination clearly. If you have any trouble finding your way around the city, do not hesitate to ask directions from a local. The following are a few tips for those getting around by car.

By Car

Once in the city, you'll find yourself in a maze of winding and one-way streets crowded with pedestrians. It can get quite confusing, especially because the road signs are sometimes inadequate. Decide where you're headed before you set out, keep your map in hand and don't hesitate to ask questions. This last solution may take a few tries, since many Dominicans don't know the street names, and their directions are often sketchy.

At intersections you will no doubt be harassed by crowds of vendors trying to sell you peanuts, fruit and just about anything else. They can be fairly insistent, but be patient and make your refusal clear if you are not interested. The "windshield washers" are the most troublesome; they see you coming, wash your windshield without asking and then expect a few pesos. Don't feel guilty about refusing (especially since you'll encounter this situation many times while crossing the city), but keep your windows rolled up or you may get a bucket of water in your lap!

Parking can also be a problem. Near Parque Colón and the Zona Colonial you will invariably be approached by some local offering to guard your car. To prevent having your car scratched, it is a good idea to accept and offer about 10 pesos in return. To avoid the

inconvenience completely, park a few streets away from Parque Colón.

If you are staying in one the hotels in the capital, you will probably be offered a car wash; once again, you are better off accepting (about 10 pesos). In any case, chances are you'll arrive to find the job already done!

Car Rental Agencies

The major car rental agencies have offices in Santo Domingo. The biggest companies downtown are: Avis ☎ 533-3530; Budget ☎ 567-0173; Ford Rent-A-Car ☎ 565-1818; Hertz ☎ 221-5333; and Toyota ☎ 566-7221. If you don't have to go downtown, pick up your rental at the airport, to avoid driving in the city.

Taxis

Taking a taxi is definitely the fastest and most convenient way to get around town. Rather than waiting to be flagged down, taxi drivers will often approach tourists to offer their services. Taxis can often be found near the major hotels and main tourist attractions as well. A ride within the limits of Santo Domingo rarely costs more than $5 US, but always negotiate the price beforehand. The vehicles are generally in good condition. This is definitely the quickest way to get around Santo Domingo.

Collective Taxis and Public Buses

Collective taxis can be identified by the word *Público* on their license plates. They are often in poor condition and jam-packed, but work well and cost very little to ride. For most destinations, you will be charged about 5 pesos. The drivers of collective taxis and buses tend to be honest, so it is not necessary to negotiate a price in advance. However, if you suspect you are being overcharged, ask other passengers how much they paid. To take a collective taxi or a bus, wait by the side of a main road and flag one down, since stops are often poorly marked. Buses and collective taxis heading east out of the city can be caught at the corner of Duarte and 27 de Febrero.

Motorcycles

Many Dominicans ride motorcycles, avoiding traffic jams by making their way between the backed-up cars. Some drivers take passengers for a few pesos; always negotiate the price first. This mode of transport can be unsafe in the busier parts of the city and is best reserved for the quieter neighbourhoods.

PRACTICAL INFORMATION

The following section includes the addresses of several organizations that might be of help to you during your stay in the Dominican capital. Because the offices of some of these organizations are not always easy to find, it is often simpler to ask locals for directions.

Tourist Information Office

This office is not as helpful as it could be in providing tourists with pertinent information. To begin with, its opening hours*(Mon to Fri 9am to 2pm)* are not particularly convenient. However, the staff will go to great lengths to assist you if they can. The tourist information office lies opposite the Palacio Nacional, on the second floor of a building at the corner of Avenidas 30 de Marzo and Mexico *(☎ 689-3657)*.

National Parks Service

If you are planning to visit any of the parks in the Dominican Republic, be aware that permits are required. Most outfitters furnish these permits, so in theory it is only those travellers planning to visit parks without the benefit of a tour operator who must obtain permits at the national parks office *(Independencia, behind the Sheraton hotel, ☎ 221-5340)*. Security at park entrances is generally relatively lax, and it is also possible to buy permits in villages on the outskirts of parks (if you succeed in finding the parks official!).

Post Office

The post office is located on Calle Isabela la Católica (in the Zona Colonial), at the corner of Calle Arzobispo Portes.

Codetel Centres

Santo Domingo has about 15 Codetel centres. In the Zona Colonial, the easiest one to find is at 20 Calle El Conde.

Safety

Despite its size, Santo Domingo is not a particularly dangerous city. While it is important to maintain a level of caution, you can walk about most parts of the city without worry. Tourists may run into trouble if they make a display of material goods (camera, jewellery) in certain poorer sections; other areas are to be avoided altogether, especially north of Calle Mella. Outside these areas, anyone walking about is generally treated well. Of course, if you decide to explore at night, avoid dark streets and be careful.

A number of children wander the streets of the city begging for small change from passersby; some have no family, while others just want to make some money. They offer their services, usually a shoe-shine, to tourists and locals alike for a few pesos. The younger ones usually just wait for a charitable soul to give them a few centavos or a bit of food. Though these children can be brusque, they are generally harmless.

 EXPLORING

Of its rich history, Santo Domingo has preserved fabulous treasures, concentrated in the Zona Colonial. Whether you visit Catedral Santa María la Menor, built in 1521, Las Casas Reales museum, Alcázar de Colón, or any other building in this sector of the city, you will not be able to help but be awestruck at these stone buildings that have dominated the city for centuries. While history has proffered these priceless gifts, the capital is also endowed with sites of natural beauty such as Los Tres Ojos park and of the typical Dominican neighbourhoods that are disorienting and fascinating at once. To help you become familiar with this vibrant capital, and allow you to appreciate its treasures, we first lead you to the Zona

Colonial. Then follow descriptions of every tourist attraction worth mentioning.

Santo Domingo's many attractions are scattered across the city. To make it easier to find them, they have been identified on the maps by a series of reference numbers. These numbers appear in parentheses immediately after the name of the attraction in the descriptive texts that follow.

The Zona Colonial ★★★

To visit the Zona Colonial is to climb streets that are imbued with memory and history, discovering buildings that may be as much as 500 years old, to marvel at the still palpable colonial past. For those interested in old stonework this is doubtless the most rewarding visit in the country. A stroll through these streets is even more pleasant than it is effortless, the buildings being set in a relatively limited perimeter and the traffic being much lighter than in nearby downtown.

Once called "Mayor place", **Parque Colón (1)** *(at the corner of Calle Arzobispo Meriño an Calle El Conde)*, at the centre of which stands a bronze stature of the Genoese sailor, is the departure point for the tour. Many guided tours leave from this park and buses full of tourists stop here in great numbers, which explains the hordes of vendors and self-proclaimed private-tour guides who make the park less pleasant than one would hope.

The magnificent **Catedral Santa María La Menor ★★★ (2)** *(facing Parque Colón)*, constructed during the 1540s on the order of Real Miguel de Pasamonte, dominates an entire side of

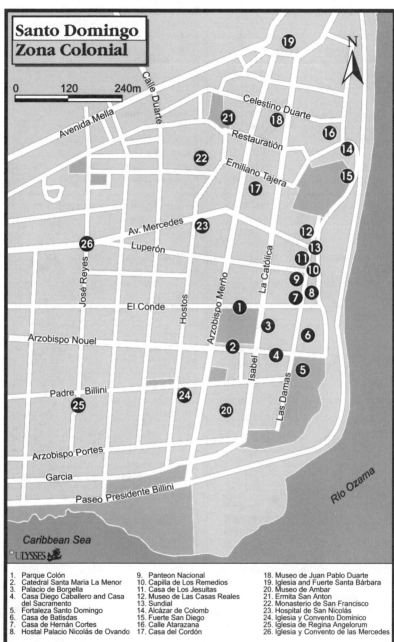

Santo Domingo
Zona Colonial

0   120   240m

1. Parque Colón
2. Catedral Santa Maria La Menor
3. Palacio de Borgella
4. Casa Diego Caballero and Casa del Sacramento
5. Fortaleza Santo Domingo
6. Casa de Batisdas
7. Casa de Hernán Cortes
8. Hostal Palacio Nicolás de Ovando
9. Panteon Nacional
10. Capilla de Los Remedios
11. Casa de Los Jesuitas
12. Museo de Las Casas Reales
13. Sundial
14. Alcázar de Colomb
15. Fuerte San Diego
16. Calle Atarazana
17. Casa del Cordón
18. Museo de Juan Pablo Duarte
19. Iglesia and Fuerte Santa Bárbara
20. Museo de Ambar
21. Ermita San Anton
22. Monasterio de San Francisco
23. Hospital de San Nicolás
24. Iglesia y Convento Dominico
25. Iglesia de Regina Angelorum
26. Iglesia y Convento de las Mercedes

the park. It is famous as the first cathedral constructed in the Americas and also constitutes the oldest building of the Plateresque-Gothic style (which allies the characteristics of Gothic and Spanish Renaissance architectural styles with baroque ornamentation). From the outside this squat building of grey stone can seem heavy but it conceals an extremely graceful interior. First there is its elegant door, and then once your eyes have adjusted to the dimly-lit interior, its graceful arches, its magnificent mahogany altar dating from 1684 and its 14 little chapels dispersed on either side of the cathedral. Until 1992 one of these chapel enclosed the tomb of Christopher Columbus, which is now located at the **Faro a Colón** (see p 79). After being allowed to deteriorate over many years, the cathedral has just been restored. Visits to the cathedral are free. Proper dress (no shorts or mini-skirts) is required.

The **Palacio de Borgella (3)** *(on Isabel la Católica, facing Parque Colón)*, dates from the 19th century, and was once the seat of executive power for the country. It now houses administrative offices.

*After visiting the area around **Parque Colón**, turn left on Calle Pellereno Algaz (the first little stone passage).*

The **Casa Diego Caballero** and the **Casa Sacramento (4)** *(Calle Pellereno Algaz)* both face a small cobblestone lane, the first pedestrian street in Santo Domingo. The latter was home to many important colonial figures, including archbishop Alonso de Fuenmayor, who ordered the construction of the city walls. The Casa Diego Caballero was built around 1523. Its façade is distinguished by two square towers, while its interior features galleries formed by solid stone arches.

Keep walking until you reach Calle Las Damas.

Calle Las Damas ★★★

Calle Las Damas is like nothing else in Santo Domingo. This splendid little street, where some of the oldest and most beautiful buildings in the old city stand in succession, will doubtless be indelibly inscribed in your memory and constitute one of the most remarkable moments of your trip.

Fortaleza Santo Domingo ★ (5) *(7 pesos; every day 9am to 4pm; Calle Las Damas)*, the oldest military building in the Americas, stands proudly at the edge of a cliff presiding over the Caribbean and Río Ozama at once, a location originally chosen for its strategic value in the protection of the colony. The walls surrounding this vast military complex shelter an attractive garden, at the centre of which stands a statue of Gonzales de Oviedo, which you'll notice upon entering. The munitions building is located to the right of the entrance. At the end of the garden, there is a square structure known as the **Torre del Homenaje**, whose construction began in 1505 by order of Nicolás de Ovando.

The **Casa de Bastidas (6)** *(Calle Las Damas)* was built at the beginning of the 16th century for **Don Rodrigo de Bastidas**, a comrade of Nicolás de Ovando's who arrived in Santo Domingo in 1502. The neoclassical portal was added in the 17th century. A charming inner garden enhances the beauty of the residence. Two small art galleries have been set up in the rooms adjoining the entrance.

The **Casa de Hernán Cortes (7)** *(Calle Las Damas)* was constructed in the early 16th century to accommodate representatives of public institutions. It has been restored and now houses the offices of the Maison de la France (French Tourist Board).

Now a hotel, the **Hostal Palacio Nicolás de Ovando (8)** *(Calle Las Damas)* was the residence of the governor of the Dominican Republic from 1502 to 1509. Nicolás de Ovando was an important figure in Santo Domingo's history, for he enhanced the development of the city by instituting various construction standards. The house is certainly among the most beautiful and elegant residences of its era. Built from high quality cut stones, it has a Gothic-style portal, a very rare feature in the architecture of the New World.

Formerly the Iglesia Companía de Jesús, the **Panteon Nacional ★ (9)** *(Calle Las Damas)* was built between 1714 and 1745. This imposing neoclassical church is made of large grey stones; a sculpted Dominican coat of arms adorns the façade. The interior consists of a single nave hung with magnificent wrought-iron chandeliers. In 1955, Trujillo ordered that the building be renovated and transformed into a pantheon in honour of the country's heroes. It is open to the public; you must, however, be appropriately dressed (no shorts or mini skirts).

In the 16th century, the **Capilla de Los Remedios (10)** *(Calle Las Damas)* was a private church belonging to a wealthy family, the Davilas. The pretty little red brick chapel has a campanile with three arches. The building was restored at the end of the 19th century after being abandoned and partially destroyed.

The **Casa de Los Jesuitas ★ (11)** *(Calle Las Damas)*, made of brick and stone, is one of the oldest buildings in the city. Constructed by order of Nicolás de Ovando, it was given to the Society of Jesus in 1701. The Jesuits used the building for a college, which became a university in 1747. In 1767, when the Jesuits were expelled from the Dominican Republic, the house was taken over by the Spanish Crown.

The **Museo de Las Casas Reales ★★ (12)** *(10 pesos; Tue to Sun 10am to 5pm; Calle Las Damas, at the corner of Calle Las Mercedes)* is located in two impressive palaces that originally housed the offices of royal institutions governing the territories, hence the name: museum of the "royal houses". The buildings were completed in the 1520s. Although they look fairly modest from the outside, their interior is richly decorated. Objects relating to the social, political, economic, religious and military history of the country are on display. Among other things, there is a magnificent collection of weapons from different countries. The museum makes for an interesting visit, though not all rooms contain treasures.

At the end of Calle Las Damas stands the **sundial (13)** *(at the corner of Calle Las Mercedes)* built in 1753. This spot offers a splendid view of the port and the Río Ozama. Four canons are lined up here.

The **Alcázar de Colón ★★★ (14)** *(20 pesos; Tue to Sun 9am to 5pm; Calle Las Damas at the far end of the park)* dates from 1509-1510 and was built for Christopher Columbus' son, Diego Columbus, and his family. Diego Colum

Alcázar de Colon

bus succeeded Nicolás de Ovando as Viceroy of the colony in 1509. The beautiful façade, graced with 10 stone arches looks out onto a large paved park where visitors will find a handful of benches and, in the centre, a statue of Nicolás de Ovando. The Alcázar was abandoned for many years until architect Javier Borroso undertook reconstruction work in the 1950s. It has since been opened to the public. Each room is decorated with beautiful period furniture, making this a visit not to be missed.

Near the Alcazár de Colón is the **gate** and a section of the **Fuerte San Diego (15)** *(Calle Las Damas)*, which served for many years as the main entrance to Santo Domingo. Part of the wall of the fortress that protected the city in the early colonial days can be seen here. Construction of these fortifications began in 1571.

At the edge of Parque Colón, follow the first little street on the right to reach **Calle Atarazana ★ (16)** where, in 1509, the first group of shops in the New World was built. Visitors will find a row of small white houses with brick foundations, whose architectural style is unique in the country. Besides their architectural significance, they form a harmonious ensemble, which still houses a few little shops to this day.

Double back to Calle Emilo Tejera and turn left on Isabel la Católica.

Calle Isabel la Católica

The architecture on Isabel la Católica is less harmonious than that on Calle Las Damas. There are, however, a few beautiful colonial buildings scattered among the much more recent additions.

The **Casa del Cordón (17)** *(Calle Isabel la Católica, at the corner of Calle Tejera)*, constructed in 1502, was one of the first stone residences in the New World. Upon arriving in 1509, Diego Colón lived here with his family before moving into the palace in 1510. The house is easy to spot, thanks to a large sculpted sash on the façade, the symbol of the Franciscan religious order.

The **Museo de Juan Pablo Duarte** ★ **(18)** *(10 pesos; Mon to Fri 9am to noon and 2pm to 5pm, Sat and Sun 9am to noon; on Calle Isabel la Católica, at the corner of Calle Celestino Duarte)* is located in the house where Juan Pablo Duarte was born on January 26th, 1813. This national hero became famous as the leader of *La Trinitaria*, a secret organization that sought to liberate the Dominican Republic from Haitian domination. As a result of his efforts, the country declared independence on February 27th, 1844. Ousted from power, Duarte took exile in Venezuela, where he stayed until 1864, when Spain annexed the Dominican Republic (1861-1865). He returned to the Dominican Republic to oppose the Spanish takeover, but in vain. Forced to leave the country again, he was never able to return and died in Carácas, Venezuela on July 15th, 1876. The museum highlights the important moments in his life, and displays many of his belongings. The building itself is unremarkable, but the exhibit is quite good.

The **Iglesia Santa Bárbara** and its connected **fort (19)** *(Calle Isabel la Católica, at the corner of Avenida Mella)* erected in 1562, form a unique construction featuring elements from various architectural styles, including Gothic and baroque. The façade is distinguished by two square towers of different sizes and three brick arches at the entrance.

After leaving the fort, take Calle Arzobispo Meriño to get to the Ermita San Anton.

Calle Arzobispo Meriño

The privately funded **Museo del Ámbar** ★ **(20)** *(452 Arzobispo Meriño)* aims to increase public knowledge of amber, the hardened sap of an extinct species of pine. It takes no more than 30 minutes to tour the museum, where you can learn about how amber was created and how insects and leaves could get trapped in it. A number of fine specimens are displayed. Visitors will also have a chance to see amber of all different colours—not just yellow, but red, green and blue as well. The exhibit is also intended to help consumers learn to distinguish between real and imitation amber, and some useful tips are provided.

The **Ermita San Anton (21)** *(Calle Hostos, at the corner of Calle Restauración)* is located just a few steps from the Monasterio San Francisco. Built of brick and stone, this single-nave hermitage was erected in 1586.

Built on a small hill in the heart of the old city, the **Monasterio de San Francisco** ★★ **(22)** *(4 pesos; everyday except Sun, 10am to 5pm; Calle Hostos, at the corner of Calle Tejera)* is impressive, though only ruins remain. The monastery was nearly completed during the 16th century, but in 1673, an earthquake completely destroyed it. Originally, it consisted of three distinct but connected buildings: the convent, the church and the chapel. The thick wall that surrounded the monastery still stands. Among the ruins, the little chapel is the easiest building to identify, as its brick vault remains.

After visiting the monastery, continue to Calle Hostos. A portion of the road is lined with pretty, colourful little houses.

Soon after Santo Domingo was rebuilt on the right bank of the Río Ozama, Nicolás de Ovando ordered the construction of the **Hospital de San Nicolás (23)** *(Calle Hostos, at the corner of Calle Mercedes; you will need to double back)* to provide care for the city's poor and needy. In ruins today, the building was shaped like a cross, a traditional Spanish design. It was surely the first hospital in the New World.

Parque Duarte (24) is a little island of tranquillity, the perfect place to relax. It is beautifully landscaped and well worth a stop.

Dominating an entire side of the park, the **Dominican monastery ★** *(Calle Hostos, at Calle Padre Billini)* is a magnificent stone structure that was built in several stages: the monastery itself dates from 1510, the church from 1517 (though the original building was destroyed by an earthquake in the 16th century) and the rosary chapel in 1649. The monastery also had the privilege of housing the first university in the Americas, Universidad Santo Tomás de Aquino. The building is still in good condition, but is scheduled for renovations and is thus closed to the public for the time being.

Calle José Reyes

To continue your tour of the Zona Colonial, take Calle Arzobispo Portes to Calle José Reyes, where you'll find another series of interesting buildings dating from the 16th century. These are somewhat out-of-the-way, however, so you'll have to walk a bit farther to reach them.

The plateresque-style **Iglesia de Regina Angelorum (25)** *(Calle José Reyes, at* the corner of Paseo Padre Billini) is one of the city's major 16th century constructions. The cut-stone exterior features a small campanile with three arches. The church, having been seriously damaged by seismic activity and hurricanes since the end of the 16th century, required a thorough restoration. Though the interior is very simple, with only one nave, its ornamentation is striking. Take the time to admire the magnificent wood retable behind the altar.

The **Iglesia y Convento de las Mercedes (26)** *(Calle José Reyes, at the corner of Calle Las Mercedes)* were built during the first half of the 16th century, in homage to the Virgin Mary. The cut-stone church has a massive tower. The richly-carved wooden retable is one of the most beautiful in the city. The convent, even more stark-looking than the church, was heavily damaged when Sir Francis Drake attacked the city. The cloister is the only extant structure of its kind from the era.

At the Edge of the Colonial Zone

Located at the end of Calle El Conde, the **Parque Independencia (27)** is surrounded by noisy, traffic-ridden streets, making it seem even more like an oasis of greenery and peace. A monument containing the tombs of three Dominican heroes who fought for the country's independence, Mella, Sanchez and Duarte, stands in the centre of the park.

Sundays on Calle Mella once brought out droves of Dominicans to sample unique dishes prepared according to African culinary traditions. The street has changed considerably and is no longer an African neighbourhood but a

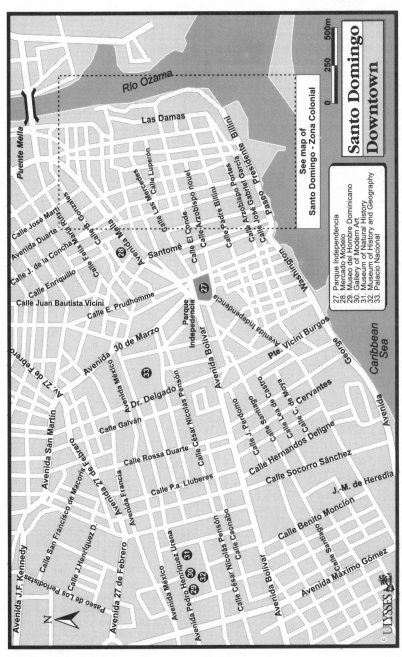

Santo Domingo Downtown

0   250   500m

See map of
Santo Domingo - Zona Colonial

27. Parque Independencia
28. Mercado Modelo
29. Museo del Hombre Dominicano
30. Gallery of Modern Art
31. Museum of Natural History
32. Museum of History and Geography
33. Palacio Nacional

Río Ozama

Las Damas

Puente Mella

Calle José Martí
Avenida Duarte
Calle J. de la Concha
Calle Enriquillo
Calle Juan Bautista Vicini
Calle E. Prudhomme
Calle Félix M. Ruíz
Calle G. González
Avenida Mella
Santomé
Calle Las Mercedes
Calle Luperón
Calle El Conde
Calle Arzobispo nouel
Calle Arzobispo Portes
Calle Gabriel García
Calle José Gabriel presidente
paseo presidente
Billini
Calle Padre Billini

Parque
Independencia
Avenida Independencia
Washington

Avenida 30 de Marzo
Avenida México
Dr. Delgado
Calle Galván
Calle Rossa Duarte
Calle P.a. Lluberes
Calle César Nicolás Pensón
Avenida Francia
Avenida San Martín
Av. 27 de Febrero
Avenida J.F. Kennedy
Paseo de Los Periodistas
Avenida San Francisco de Macorís Febrero
Calle J.Henríquez D.
Avenida 27 de Febrero
Avenida México
Avenida Pedro Henríquez Ureña
Calle César Nicolás Pensón
Calle Caonabo

Avenida Bolívar
Pte. Vicini Burgos
Calle J. Perdomo
Calle Santiago
Calle Lea de Castro
Calle C. de Moya
Calle C. Cervantes
George
Calle Hernandos Deligne
Calle Socorro Sánchez
J.-M. de Heredia
Calle Benito Monción
Avenida Bolívar
Calle Santiago
Avenida Máximo Gómez
Caribbean Sea
Avenida

27
28
33
29
30
31
32

N

© ULYSSES

large commercial artery with countless shops selling all kinds of products. The **Mercado Modelo ★ (28)** is also located here. Dominicans come to this enormous indoor market to sell foodstuffs, jewellery made of shells, *larimar* or amber, beachwear and crafts. This place is picturesque, but be careful (the aisles are narrow and sometimes dark) and always bargain before buying.

Plaza de la Cultura

The **Plaza de la Cultura** *(Calle Máximo Gomez, between Calles Cesar Nicola Penson and Pedro Henriquez Urena)*, or cultural centre, includes four museums and the Teatro Nacional. The museums can all be visited on the same day.

The **Museo del Hombre Dominicano ★★ (29)** *(10 pesos; Tue to Sun 10am to 5pm)* is certainly the most interesting museum in Santo Domingo, if not the whole Dominican Republic. A rich collection of Taino art is displayed on the main floor. This indigenous people had been living in the Dominican Republic for over a thousand years when Columbus arrived, and large numbers of them were wiped out during colonization. The entire ground floor of the museum is devoted to an exhibit of the art, religion and daily life of this society, which changed radically following the arrival of the Europeans. The few information panels in the museum are written only in Spanish.

The exhibits on the second floor retrace various events that have marked the colonization of the country. Many subjects are explored, and slavery is given special attention. The difficult living conditions faced by the thousands of Africans forced to come to the Dominican Republic are described. The last room houses a magnificent collection of carnival masks from different regions of the country (see p 150).

The **Gallery of Modern Art (30)** *(20 pesos; Tue to Sun 10am to 5pm)* houses a beautiful collection of modern art by Dominican and foreign artists and offers visitors a chance to familiarize themselves with local trends in modern art. While the extensive permanent collection merits a visit on its own, the museum presents interesting temporary exhibitions as well.

The mandate of the **Museum of Natural History (31)** *(10 pesos; Tue to Sun 10am to 5pm)* is to further the public's knowledge of various aspects of the country's natural history. Some rooms contain taxidermy exhibits, focusing on animals found in the Dominican Republic, including some beautiful birds. Unfortunately, some of these specimens have been around for a long time and look more like the remains of dried birds than the work of a taxidermist. Other rooms deal with more general themes, such as astronomy. The information provided is a little brief (as well as being only in Spanish), but covers a multitude of subjects relating to animal life, vegetation and minerals.

The **Museum of History and Geography (32)** *(10 pesos; Tue to Sun 10am to 5pm)* houses a collection of objects from everyday and military life in the Dominican Republic. It is divided into three rooms, each with exhibits covering a specific period: 1822 to 1861, 1861 to 1916 and 1916 to 1961. Although certain objects on display belonged to important figures in Dominican life, such as President Trujillo, this museum holds few objects of great interest and has limited appeal, unless you are a specialist or a real fan of these types of exhibits.

Other Attractions

The **Palacio Nacional ★ (33)** *(Calle Dr. Delgado)* was built in the 1940s to house President Trujillo's government offices. The long, imposing building is neoclassical in design and has an elegant dome, 34 metres high and 18 metres across. The building is still the seat of government. The main façade looks onto a quiet little street. An impressive staircase, flanked by two stone lions, leads to the main entrance. The building is surrounded by a pretty park, which is unfortunately closed to the public. To enter the palace, visitors must wear long pants or skirts that cover the knees.

Extending over several kilometres, the **Mirador del Sur (34)** park is a welcome green space perfect for a stroll far from the hustle and bustle of Santo Domingo.

The **Jardín Botánico ★★ (35)** *(everyday; Avenida de Los Proceres)* is the largest park in the city, and without a doubt the most pleasant. The multitude of tropical plants and trees on display are well laid out and provide a good introduction to the plant life of the island. Another attraction is the pretty Japanese garden. We recommend taking the little train *(10 pesos)* that crisscrosses the garden, carrying passengers through a lush forest one moment and flowering gardens the next. This is an ideal way for those in a hurry to visit the entire garden. These gardens provide a welcome break from the frantic pace of the city.

The **Parque Zoológico Nacional (36)** *(Paseo de Los Reyes Católicos)* is home to a good number of animal species, some of African origins (giraffes, lions, rhinoceros) and others from the Dominican Republic (pink flamingos). Special care has been taken to recreate the natural environments of these animals. A big section of the park has been laid out without any cages, thus allowing visitors to observe the animals roaming almost freely. There is also an aviary with a large variety of tropical birds. A little train *(5 pesos)* can take you on a tour of the park.

The idea of building a mausoleum for Columbus was first put forward during the final years of President Trujillo's reign. In keeping with the famous explorer's character, a huge lighthouse was built. The **Faro a Colón ★ (37)** *(10 pesos; on the east shore of the Río Ozama, in the Parque Mirador del Este)* took a number of years to build and was not completed in time for the 1992 celebrations marking the 500th anniversary of Columbus' arrival in the Americas. The project is said to have cost about $250 million! The aim was to build a monument worthy of the great Genoese navigator. Unfortunately, despite its impressive size, the cruciform, concrete, windowless building is not particularly charming. The marble tomb in the heart of the building seems very small. It is guarded around the clock by four military guards. The building also contains a number of exhibition halls.

The many tanks of the **Acuario Nacional ★ (38)** *(Boul Sans Souci)* contain specimens of the colourful fish species and crustaceans that inhabit the waters around the island. One small room contains various species indigenous to Venezuela. There is also an ingenious display tank with a tunnel-like walkway right through it, allowing visitors to observe the fish from all angles. All explanatory texts are in Spanish only.

The **Parque Nacional los Tres Ojos ★★★ (39)** *(every day 8am to 5pm; at the east side of Parque Mirador del Este, on Avenida de Faro a Colón)* is located on the outskirts of Santo Domingo, on the east bank of the Río Ozama. It has a few pleasant trails, but most visitors come for its enormous open-air grotto. Stone steps lead down into this cavern, which is home to a surprising abundance of tropical plantlife. A narrow path disappears into the vegetation, guiding visitors to the shores of the three extraordinary but beautiful subterranean lakes, or "eyes", for which the park was named. Stalactites and other natural formations can be seen here as well. Outside the grotto, a trail leads to a fourth lake, which resembles a volcano crater. This is a truly extraordinary spot.

To reach the park from downtown, cross the Puente Duarte and continue along the Las Américas highway. Keep an eye out for the single small sign that points the way to the park.

ACCOMMODATIONS

The Zona Colonial

Though there are few hotels here, it is possible to stay in the Zona Colonial — and what a pleasure to sleep in a centuries-old building at the heart of old Santo Domingo.

The **Hostal Nader** *($50 US; ⊗; at the corner of Duarte and Luperón, ☎ 687-6674, ↮ 687-7887)* is an adorable old house, which stands out for its beautiful stone façade. Upon entering you will find yourself in an interior courtyard surrounded by the balconies of the guest-rooms. The rooms themselves are all well kept and have a certain charm.

 Not far from the Hostal Nader, and still on this relatively calm part of Calle Duarte, is the **Palacio** *($60 US; ≡, ⊗; 106 Calle Duarte, P.O. Box 20541, ☎ 682-4730, ↮ 687-5535)*. This is another charming inn set up inside a beautiful old house, just a few steps from the alluring streets of the Zona Colonial. The wrought-iron light fixtures adorning its façade make it easy to spot. With its tasteful decor, this is an extremely pleasant place.

The former home of Nicolás de Ovando, the country's first governor (see p 73), the **Hostal Nicólas de Ovando** *($US 75; Calle Las Damas, ☎ 687-3101, ↮ 688-5170)* would be in a class of its own if it hadn't been neglected. Unfortunately, however, it would have to have a major overhaul to regain its former elegance. Still, this hotel will appeal to visitors who would like to stay on magnificent Calle Las Damas, have a penchant for old buildings and are ready to compromise a bit as far as comfort is concerned.

Avenida George Washington and Surroundings

Avenida George Washington follows the Caribbean offering exceptional views over the vast expanse of shimmering waves. It is therefore the perfect spot for a big hotel complex. Hotels ideal for those on a tighter budget can also be found close by.

The **Palmeras del Caribe** *($25 US; ⊗; 1 Cambronal, at the corner of Malecón, ☎ 689-3872)* offers small, sparsely furnished rooms. Though not incredibly comfortable, they are relatively well kept. The rooms run along either side of a long, open-air corridor, giving the place an unusual but nonetheless appealing look.

The **Hotel El Señorial** *($30 US; ⊗, ≡; 58 Pte. Vicini Burgos, ☎ 687-4359, ≈ 687-0600)* is an ordinary-looking white stucco building. It is located in front of a park near the sea, enabling visitors to enjoy some peace and quiet. The rooms are fairly large and attractively decorated.

Behind the green and white façade of the **Sea View** *($40 US; ≡, K; Avenida Cambronal, at the corner of George Washington, ☎ 688-3979)* are clean, comfortable apartments with well-equipped kitchenettes. Though the decor lacks style, rooms are functional.

The **Napolitano** *($50 US; ≡, ≈, ℜ; Avenida George Washington, ☎ 687-1131, ≈ 689-2714)* is a long building with a plain façade. It looks out on the sea, giving some rooms a beautiful view. The hotel is comfortable, though the decor is outdated.

The **Sheraton Santo Domingo** *($130 US; ≡, ≈, ℜ; 365 Avenida George Washington, P.O. Box 1493, ☎ 221-6666, ≈ 687-8150)* faces the sea, so most of the rooms have wonderful views. The high standard of comfort and wide range of services are in keeping with the well-known Sheraton hotel chain. The spacious rooms are decorated with functional modern furniture. Unfortunately, the lobby is not very elegant.

The **Ramada Renaissance Jaragua Resort** *($180 US ½b; ≡, ≈, ℜ; 367 Avenida George Washington, P.O. Box 769-2, ☎ 221-2222, ≈ 686-0528)* also faces the sea. A vast lobby adorned with flowers and elegant furnishings welcomes visitors. The rooms are tastefully decorated as well. Finally, the hotel has a lovely garden where visitors can escape the hurried pace of the city.

Formerly known as the Centenario V, the **Inter-Continental** *($US 170; ≡, ≈, ◯, ♠, ℜ; 218 Avenida George Washington, ☎ 221-0000, ≈ 221-2020)* is definitely one of the chicest hotels in town. Upon changing hands, the building was renovated and the lobby is now much more inviting. The rooms, as impeccable as ever, offer a superb view of the sea.

Elsewhere in Town

Looking for a place with adorable rooms? You'll love the **Maison Gautreaux** *($US 32; 8 Calle Felix Lluberes, at Avenida George Washington, ☎ and ≈ 687-4856)*, where everything has been designed to create an inviting atmosphere for travellers. The well-kept rooms are decorated with paintings by Dominican artists, and the staff is gracious. A small green house adorned with balconies, it also has the advantage of being located on a quiet street.

Avenida Independencia, where the **Duque de Wellington** *($US 35; ≡; 304 Avenida Independencia, ☎ and ≈ 682-4525)* is located, is anything but peaceful, especially at rush hour. Still, this spruce little hotel is a perfectly decent place to stay in the Dominican capital without spending a fortune. The rooms are small but decorated with pretty wooden furniture, and the beds, with their white sheets, create an atmosphere of well-being.

Located near the Plaza de la Cultura, the clean and pretty **Plaza Florida** *($40 US; ≡, K; 203 Avenida Bolivar, ☎ 541-3957, ≈ 540-5582)* offers rooms with well-equipped kitchenettes.

The decor at the 72-room **San Geronimo** *($45 US; ≡, ≈, ℜ, ♠; 1067 Avenida Independencia, P.O. Box 15, ☎ 533-8181)* hotel is outdated and a bit unattractive, orange and brown being the dominant colours. Hardly elegant, the rooms are nonetheless comfortable and well-kept. The hotel also has a casino.

The **Delta** *($65 US; ≡, ℜ, K; 53 Avenida Sarasota, P.O. Box 1818, ☎ 535-0800, ≈ 535-5635)* is a lovely pink building with a typically Caribbean air about it. It is ideally located in a peaceful part of the city. The rooms are decorated with distinctive modern furniture.

The five-story yellow building of the **Hispaniola** *($70 US; ≡, ≈, ℜ, ♠; Avenida Independencia, at the corner of Abraham Lincoln, ☎ 221-7111, ≈ 535-4050)* hotel is easy to spot on the western edge of the city. Though this hotel is not in the most convenient part of town, it offers large, comfortable rooms, a big pool and a casino.

A handsome hotel with all the modern comforts, the **Gran Hotel Lina** *($105 US; ≡, ≈, ♠, ℜ; Maximo Gomez, at Calle 27 de Febrero, ☎ 563-5000,*

≈ 686-5521) is located downtown. It is a modern building that rises several stories high, looking out over this bustling part of the capital. Some people are sure to consider it a plus, furthermore, that both a casino and a good restaurant (see p 85) can be found on the premises.

If you're looking for another good place to stay in Santo Domingo, you might consider the modern, comfortable **Hotel Naco** *($75; ≡, ≈, ♠, ℜ; 22 Tiradentes, ☎ 562-3100, ≈ 544-0957)*.

The chic hotel **Embajador** *($US 90; ≡, ≈, ℜ, ♠; Avenida Sarasota, ☎ 221-2131, ≈ 532-4494)* was built under the Trujillo dictatorship. The rooms are decorated in an outdated fashion but have a certain charm and meet all the modern standards of comfort. Guests also enjoy access to a vast and magnificent tropical garden, a rarity in the Dominican capital. This edenic spot, where you can enjoy a meal or take a dip in the pool, feels far from all the hubbub of the city. The huge, elegant lobby, where the hotel's casino and bar are located, attracts a well-groomed crowd every night. One last little thing: take a good look at the trees around the hotel; there are *coticas* (see p 14) living in them.

The grand and luxurious **Hotel Santo Domingo** *($120 US; ≡, ≈, ℜ; Avenida Independencia, at the corner of Avenida Abraham Lincoln, P.O. Box 2112, ☎ 221-1511, ≈ 535-1511)* is located in a peaceful neighbourhood slightly removed from the downtown area. The rooms are spacious and attractively decorated.

RESTAURANTS

The Zona Colonial

You are certain to find a good place for lunch among the restaurants that line the pedestrian street, El Conde. One of these is **Bariloche** *($)*, which is very popular with Dominicans at lunchtime. The cafeteria-style layout is quite simple; choose your meal at the counter, and sit down to eat it in the large nondescript room with the television. This place is ideal for a filling, inexpensive meal (*pollo*, *arroz* and *habichuela*).

Not far from Bariloche, is the **Petrus Cafetería** *($)*, another plain-looking restaurant where you can grab a quick bite (sandwiches, pizza or ice cream). For a good sandwich, try **Café Paco's** *($; facing Parque Colón)*, which has a nice little terrace.

The charming little cafés facing the Alcázar de Colón offer a delightful setting in which to enjoy a drink and a bite to eat. Besides the Wendy's, a somewhat unwelcome sight here, there is the **Museo del Jamón** *($)* which serves delicious deli meats.

For tasty *empanadas*, head to **De Nosotros** *($; Calle Hostos)*. Ready in minutes, they are delicious and well-garnished. Ask for a take-out order and have a picnic in Parque Duarte, just around the corner.

Calle Duarte has a few restaurants where you can go for a quick lunch. **Panadería Sum** *($)* is a good place for sandwiches and *empanadas*.

Henry's Bar & Grill *($; 7 Calle Isabel la católica)* is the perfect place to enjoy a simple meal (steaks, hamburgers) in the Zona Colonial to the sounds of live blues and rock. Pool players make up a portion of the regular clientele, as there are several tables here.

An elegant white stucco façade that seems untouched by time conceals the charming restaurant **Retazos** *($$; Padre Billini, ☎ 688-6141)*. The decor is hardly luxurious, but the dining room, laid out in a pleasant inner court, has a certain charm about it. It is in this relaxed atmosphere that guests select their meal from a vast choice of local and international specialties.

In the colonial zone, just steps away from the cathedral, you'll have no trouble finding the **Briciola Café** *($$; Calle Arzobispo Meriño)*, another good place to enjoy a delicious Italian meal in a quiet atmosphere in the old city.

Follow Calle Las Damas and you'll soon cross Calle El Conde. Here, at the heart of the prettiest part of the Zona Colonial, is **Don Camillo** *($$)*, which serves fine French and Dominican cuisine. With an outdoor terrace surrounded by beautiful buildings and a dining room offering shelter from the sun, this place boasts an incomparable atmosphere.

Housed in one of the many historic buildings on charming old Calle Atarazana, **Fonda Atarazana** *($$$; Calle Atarazana, ☎ 689-2900)* is a very well-situated restaurant. Upon entering the little house, you'll find yourself in beautifully decorated and utterly charming surroundings. What better setting to enjoy some local specialties?

Avenida George Washington

Opposite the fancy hotels that line Avenida Washington there are a number of food stalls and open-air bars. This lively, unpretentious area is popular with local inhabitants who come to enjoy an evening snack and the seaside.

It is hard to miss the green and red façade of the **Pizzeralli** *($; Avenida George Washington)*. This place is very popular with Dominican families, who arrive in large numbers and often become quite boisterous. The tasty pizza is served in large portions.

The proprietors of the **Vesuvio Pizzeria** *($; Avenida George Washington, ☎ 685-7608)* also own the chic Vesuvio restaurant. The atmosphere of the pizzeria is more relaxed, however. The menu features simple dishes, including, of course, a variety of pizzas.

La Parilla *($; 533 Avenida George Washington, ☎ 688-1511)* is a modest-looking restaurant that serves a good selection of deliciously prepared Creole dishes.

The **Triomphe Café** *($$; Avenida George Washington, next to the Ramada hotel)* is a pretty little seaside restaurant with an inexpensive and varied menu including succulent crepes. Comfortable cushioned benches lend themselves well to an intimate tête-à-tête meal.

To savour Chinese food in a unique atmosphere, head to the **Palacio de Jade** *($$-$$$; José Maria de Heredia, close to George Washington)*. The exterior, which vaguely resembles a medieval castle, may be a bit surprising, but the interior is beautifully decorated and the dishes are succulent.

The **Jardin de Bagatelle** *($$$; 39 Avenida George Washington, ☎ 682-1625)* faces the sea. While unassuming from the outside, this restaurant has a very attractive dining room. The menu lists traditional French dishes, each more delicious than the last.

Restaurante Vesuvio *($$$; 521 Avenida George Washington, ☎ 221-3333)* serves excellent Italian food, with seafood as the specialty. A friendly atmosphere adds to the charm of this elegant restaurant, among the best in town.

Elsewhere in Town

A few family restaurants can be found in the vicinity of Parque Mirador del Sur. The unique Mesón de la Cava restaurant is also in this area.

The **Comida del Pais** *($; Avenida Jiménez Moya)* is another typical Dominican cafeteria-style restaurant, where guests choose from a wide assortment of dishes to be enjoyed in a large adjoining dining room or as takeout. This inexpensive place is particularly busy on Sundays at lunchtime.

Right next door, **La Pizza** *($; Avenida Jiménez Moya)* serves, of course, great pizza. The restaurant has a pleasant terrace looking onto the street.

🦀 If you are craving linguini with crab or shrimp, or a delectable *tiramisú*, head straight to the Italian restaurant **Mangiaridi** *($$-$$$; 302 Avenida Independencia)*, which serves a fine selection of dishes, each more delicious than the last. To make things even better, you get to savour your meal comfortably seated in an air-conditioned dining room, attended by a courteous staff. Only the slightly kitschy paintings of Italy adorning the walls leave something to be desired.

Jai Alai *($$-$$$; 411 Avenida Independencia)*, located on noisy Avenida Independecia, offers visitors an excellent chance to familiarize themselves with the local cuisine or treat themselves to one of the delicious seafood dishes for which the place is reputed.

For years, the restaurant **Lina** *($$$; Maximo Gomez, at Calle 27 de Febrero,* ☎ *563-5000)*, in the hotel of the same name (see p 82) has been concocting Spanish dishes of a quality found nowhere else in Santo Domingo, winning over the palates of many fans of that cuisine. Each specialty served here, in particular the paella, is a delicious invitation to discover the culinary traditions of Spain.

If there is one place that seems far from the frenzied activity in Santo Domingo, it is the garden of the **Hotel Embajador** *(Avenida Sarasota)*, and it is in this peaceful spot that the hotel restaurant is located. The restaurant only takes up a small part of this vast stretch of land planted with trees and flowering bushes, enabling guests to enjoy an outstanding setting and serene atmosphere while eating. In addition to its location, the restaurant offers a varied menu and consistently good, honest food.

For a memorable meal, head to the **Mesón de la Cava** *($$$; Avenida Mirador del Sur,* ☎ *533-2818)*, set in

natural caves. Comfortably seated next to a stone wall, guests enjoy delicious meals in an extraordinary decor.

 ENTERTAINMENT

Cultural Activities

You can spend an evening taking in one of the plays presented at the renowned **Teatro Nacional**, where the best theatre companies in the country perform. Of course, the plays are all in Spanish.

In the last two weeks of July, when the *merengue* **festival** is in full swing, *merengue* fever reaches its peak in Santo Domingo. The Malecón is transformed into a huge, open-air stage, where some of the best bands in the country give free concerts. People from all over the country flock to the capital to party and kick up their heels to the rousing rhythms of this music, which is native to the Dominican Republic. *Merengue* music also sets the mood at many bars and discotheques during this period.

Casinos

The **Hotel Hispaniola** *(Avenida Independencia at the corner of Avenida Abraham Lincoln,* ☎ *535-9292)* has the biggest casino in the city, and it attracts a varied crowd. This huge and opulently decorated casino is worth checking out, and is a good place for beginning gamblers to try their luck.

The **Ramada Renaissance** *(367 Avenida George Washington,* ☎ *221-2222)* hotel has a large casino, where gamblers from the world over play to win.

The big casino at the **Sheraton Santo Domingo** *(365 Avenida George Washington,* ☎ *687-8150)* attracts a crowd of "serious" gamblers.

The casino at the **San Geronimo** *(1067 Avenida Independencia,* ☎ *533-8181)* hotel is smaller and less luxurious than the other three and caters to a largely Dominican clientele.

Bars and Discos

Discotheques are popular in Santo Domingo, and there are many to choose from. Avenida George Washington is a very lively street with a lot of bars, including the **Bella Blue**, a huge dance bar that attracts crowds of Dominicans.

The capital's most impressive disco would have to be the **Güácara Taina** *(Wed to Sun 8pm to 3am; 165 Parque Mirador del Sur)*, set in a series of caves. A stone staircase leads into the caves, where a real party atmosphere prevails. Several hotels organize trips to the bar for their guests. The place is also frequented by a gay clientele.

Fram Boyan *(Avenida George Washington, one street west of Cervante)* is another spot for drinks and dancing.

Those looking for a place to have a beer and gaze out at the endless sea should stop by **D'Frank** *(Malecón)*. Besides its great location, it offers a friendly, relaxed atmosphere.

A trip to Santo Domingo wouldn't be complete without a drink at **Bachata Rosa** *(9 Atarazana,* ☎ *688-0969)*, which books some of the best-known artists in the country.

On the other hand, if you've had your fill of *merengue* and would rather spend an evening in an entirely different kind of atmosphere, head to **Chez Drake** *(Arzobispo Meriño, at the corner of Portes)*, where you can sip a drink while grooving to jazz and blues tunes.

The tapas bar **Museo del Jamón**, right opposite the Alcazar de Colón, is a wonderful spot for a late afternoon drink and a view of the setting sun.

Among the bars in the big hotels, the following are worth mentioning:

The **Piano Café Concerto** *(Avenida Sasasota)*, in the Embajador hotel, is a popular spot come nightfall, when guests can sip their drinks to soft, relaxing music.

The **Euroclub** *(22 Tiradentes)*, in the Hotel Naco, is the perfect place to spend a fun evening shaking your thing to boisterous music.

Las Palmas *(Avenida Independencia, at the corner of Avenida Abraham Lincoln)*, at the Santo Domingo Hotel, is a good place to dance the *merengue*. The atmosphere is lively and the dance floor is often crowded. Thursdays and Fridays are the most popular nights.

The **Jubilee** at the Ramada Renaissance Jaragua Resort *(367 Avenida George Washington)* has been recently renovated and is now one of the hottest places in town to enjoy music from the Caribbean and elsewhere.

$ SHOPPING

The noisy, bustling downtown core extends from Calle 27 de Febrero to Calle Mella between Calle 30 de Marzo and Vincente Noble. This part of town is teeming with street vendors selling candies, fresh fruit and lottery tickets, and crowded with stores of every kind; if you look around a little, you can find almost anything!

There are several banks on Calle Mella where visitors can exchange their foreign currency for pesos (a branch of the Bank of Nova Scotia will change Canadian dollars). On the same street, the **Mercado Modelo** sells a variety of crafts, from wooden figurines and straw hats, to jewellery and t-shirts (see p 78).

A panoply of other shops right next to the Mercado Modelo also sell all kinds of Dominican products. If you didn't find what you were looking for at the Mercado Modelo, take a stroll along Calle Mella. One shop you'll find is the **Casa del Café**, a good place to stock up on Dominican coffee.

For a quieter shopping experience, stroll along **Calle El Conde**, a very pleasant pedestrian street with many small shops selling lovely local crafts and different types of clothing. Here are some of the more interesting ones:

A book and stationery store at the corner of Calle Hostos sells books on the Dominican Republic in Spanish and in other languages.

There are two sporting-goods stores, **Sporto** *(at the corner of Santome)* and **El Molino Deportivo** *(at the corner of Duarte)*, both with a good selection of snorkelling equipment and clothing (t-shirts, swimsuits, shoes).

For music, head to **Disco Mundo** *(at the corner of Santome)* or **Musicalia** *(at the corner of Santome)*.

Several small souvenir shops selling local crafts can be found on Calle Arzobispo Merino, next to the cathedral. The quality of these items varies greatly, so choose carefully.

If you take Calle Arzopispo Meriño next to the Santa María la Menor cathedral, you'll soon come to **Mi País**. Perfect for visitors in search of Dominican souvenirs, this store is packed with great gift items: locally made handicrafts, amber and larimar jewellery, cigars, dolls, statuettes, books, etc. There is something here for everyone!

Facing the cathedral, **Monte Cristi de Tabaco**, sells Dominican cigars and cigarillos.

On Atarazana, you'll find an unpretentious shop called **Ambar Tres**, which is another good place in town to buy amber.

On the ground floor of the **Museo del Ámbar** there is a large store, located in the last gallery of the museum. Jewellery, statuettes and scores of other amber items are available for purchase here. The pieces are of high quality and the salespersons are always right at hand, but not too insistent.

Art lovers can stop by the **Sala de Arte Rosamaría** *(Calle Ataranza)*, where a small number of paintings by Dominican artists are exhibited and sold.

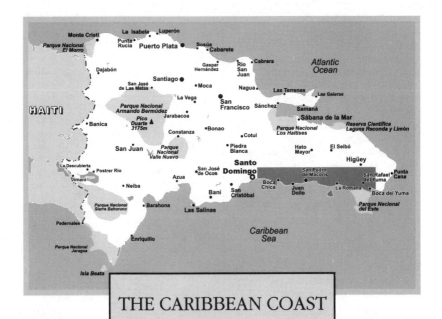

THE CARIBBEAN COAST

The miles of beautiful coastline in the southeastern region of the Dominican Republic are popular with visitors from around the world. Numerous hotel complexes have been built to accommodate all these visitors. Tourist complexes, like Juan Dolio and Casa de Campo, have sprung up in previously uninhabited areas, near beautiful sandy beaches. Luxurious modern complexes have also been built in the centre of typical Dominican villages, alongside modest Creole cottages. Although the juxtaposition is at times disquieting, these hotels have the advantage of being right in the thick of the island's daily hustle and bustle. The coastline features some outstanding attractions as well, including **Altos de Chavón**, a reconstruction of a 14th century Italian village. The southeast has also attracted rich Dominicans, who have built magnificent houses here to escape the hectic pace of Santo Domingo.

This whole coastline, from Boca Chica to Boca del Yuma, is lapped by the shimmering waters of the Caribbean Sea. The vegetation is sometimes lush, a patchwork of palm groves and fields of sugar cane, other times sparse, as in the region of Bayahibe. Just off the southern shores lie charming little islands like Catalina and Isla Saona, each a veritable paradise of sand and palm trees where horseback riding is enjoyed on daytime excursions.

FINDING YOUR WAY AROUND

It is easy to reach the coast by car or *guagua* (public bus) from the capital. This last mode of transport is the least expensive; for example, it costs 10 pesos to get to Boca Chica.

A single highway leads to the southeastern part of the island. It begins in Santo Domingo and follows the Caribbean coast to the town of La Romana. The importance of tourism to the area and the recent development boom ensure that the highway is well maintained. The section between Santo Domingo and the Las Américas airport even has a special installation of concrete columns (in bad shape these days), each representing a South American country. Tourist destinations are often off the highway, so visitors must keep an eye out for billboards advertising specific destinations. This is an interesting region and well worth a visit.

To reach the southwestern coast from Santo Domingo, take the highway over the Puente Duarte and continue straight along Avenida Las Américas.

Boca Chica

Boca Chica is about 30 kilometres from the capital. Avenida Las Américas follows the sea all the way to and through the town. To reach downtown Boca Chica from the highway, take Calle Juan Bautista Vicini or Avenida Las Caracoles and then turn on Calle Duarte.

The car rental agencies in Boca Chica tend to have older vehicles on hand. A better alternative is renting a car at the Las Américas airport. The following agencies have offices at the airport: **Avis**(☎ 5490468), **Hertz** (☎ 549-0454), **Budget** (☎ 5441244).

There are many *guaguas* between Santo Domingo and Boca Chica. They pick up passengers along Avenida Los Caracoles.

Juan Dolio

A few kilometres from Boca Chica, the village of Juan Dolio is actually nothing more than large resort complexes and a few restaurants. Although the village is off the highway and you won't see many signs for it, it is easy to find: watch for a shopping centre and two large hotels near the two beach entrances.

There is a *guagua* to Juan Dolio; just head out of town and wait for it to come along the highway.

The **Budget** (☎ 526-1907) car rental agency has an office in front of the casino.

San Pedro de Macorís

The highway passes through the village and traffic can be heavy at peak times. Be careful, because people drive very fast and there are many pedestrians.

The *guagua* station is next to the Iglesia San Pedro.

La Romana

The highway runs alongside the village. To reach the seashore or Casa de Campo, you must head south across town to join up with the road along the coast.

Casa de Campo lies on a vast property east of La Romana. As you leave La Romana by the road along the coast, you'll easily spot the signs for both the tourist complex and Altos de Chavón,

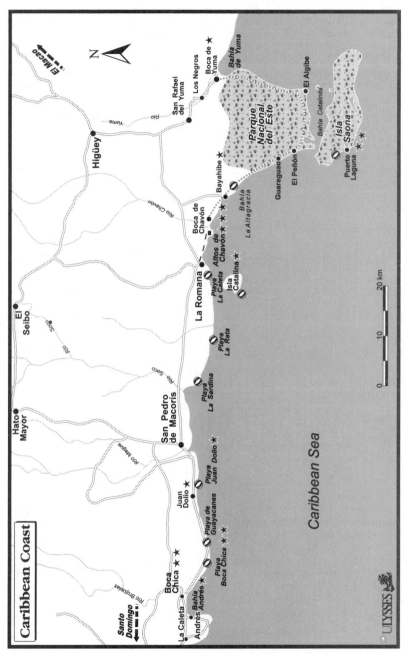

which is located on the grounds of Casa de Campo.

Bayahibe

The highway, a narrow strip of asphalt snaking through the shrubs and undergrowth, goes all the way to the village of Bayahibe. It might seem odd that a highway in such excellent condition serves such a small village; in fact, the road was built mainly for the Club Dominicus hotel complex, not far from the village.

Boca de Yuma

To get to Boca de Yuma from La Romana, continue on the main road. Don't take the little road leading to Bayahibe. After about 30 kilometres, you'll come to an intersection; the road heading left goes to Higüey (see p 112), the one to the right to Boca de Yuma, passing through the villages of San Rafael del Yuma and Los Negros along the way.

PRACTICAL INFORMATION

Boca Chica

In the downtown area of Boca Chica, essentially limited to the section of Calle Duarte between Juan Bautista Vicini and Caracoles, you will find a number of little shops and restaurants, some of which sell attractive local crafts. The **Banco Popular** will exchange American and Canadian money. The **post office** (at the corner of Juan Bautista Vicini) and the **Codetel** (at the corner of Caracoles) are located on the same street.

San Pedro de Macorís

The highway crosses through the heart of San Pedro de Macorís. The town is centred around a park located at Avenida Independencia and Calle Gran Cabral. This area contains many shops and restaurants. The **Codetel** is on Avenida Independencia.

La Romana

The main streets in downtown La Romana are Calle Santo Rosa and Avenida Libertad. Several banks can be found near the park along Calle Duarte. You can catch a *guagua* out of the city on this last street. The **Codetel** is on Avenida Padre Abreu, at the corner of Calle Santo Rosa.

EXPLORING

La Caleta

On the Autopista Las Américas, just before the road to the airport, you will come across Parque La Caleta. This green space along the highway consists essentially of a few trees, some benches and a beach often overrun with young Dominicans. Somewhat surprisingly, it is also home to the **Museo la Caleta**, a little house containing the remains of the Taino tombs discovered during construction of the airport. This museum makes for a short but interesting visit.

Boca Chica ★★

Boca Chica is a bustling town popular with both foreign and Dominican visitors. Its main street is lined with hotels, restaurants and boutiques ready to serve the needs of tourists. Indeed, the whole town is geared toward tourism, and suffers as a result from an aesthetic standpoint. However, the beach — a magnificent long stretch of white sand caressed by the turquoise waters of the Caribbean — is sufficiently breathtaking to make up for the jumbled architecture of the town, where little hotels are crowded in with big ones. The bay at Boca Chica is sheltered from rough seas by coral reefs making it great for swimming. In fact, this magnificent beach, located close to Santo Domingo, has been attracting residents of the capital for weekend visits for several decades.

Although Boca Chica is no paradise lost, and prostitution is unfortunately very evident, it is an enchanting spot for visitors in search of a beautiful beach where they can enjoy all sorts of exciting water sports. Many foreigners have opened small businesses here, and you may often find yourself in a hotel or restaurant run by Italians or Canadians.

Boca Chica is practically a suburb of Santo Domingo. Getting to the capital from Boca Chica to do some sightseeing is easy; the distance can be covered in about 30 minutes and the route is beautiful. Quieter than Santo Domingo, Boca Chica nevertheless offers all the same services and comforts. A popular option is to spend the day in Santo Domingo and sleep in Boca Chica.

Take a ten-minute walk along the beach in Boca Chica and you will find yourself in the neighbouring village of **Andrés**, where several attractive marinas organize deep-sea fishing and scuba diving expeditions. Be careful walking along here at night, since it is not lit.

Juan Dolio ★

Juan Dolio is located about 40 kilometres east of Santo Domingo. A small shopping centre and several hotels line the highway near the beach. The road to the beach is indicated by commercial signs (rather than regular road signs), so watch carefully. All the local hotels lie on either side of the only road that passes through Juan Dolio.

The resort town of Juan Dolio is located on a long beach, which is quite beautiful, but less spectacular than some in other parts of the country. The village, once just a few fisherman's huts, has only recently sprung up in response to the growing tourist boom. Today, Juan Dolio lives by tourism alone. Each hotel occupies a vast property and most have direct access to the beach. Unfortunately, the lots between these hotels are often empty save for a few shrubs growing here and there. If you stay in one of these hotels, you will enjoy superb tropical gardens and a safe environment. Nevertheless, be careful if you explore the area, as there have been reports of thieves. These hotel complexes offer a panoply of services. You may also notice the luxury apartment buildings of rich Dominicans. A few shops and restaurants have also opened for business. As a result of the still ongoing construction in Juan Dolio, the road is not in the

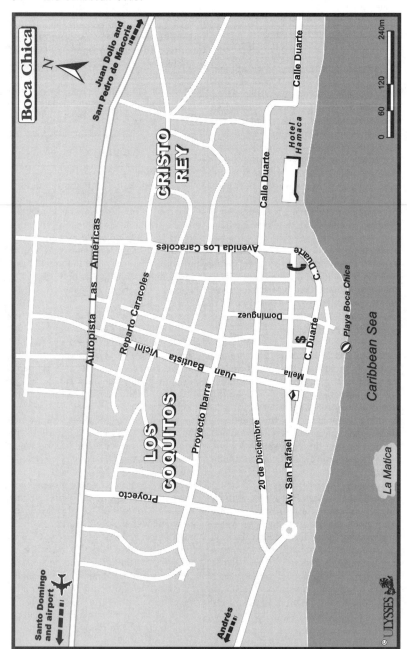

best condition. Nonetheless, this is an attractive spot.

San Pedro de Macorís

San Pedro de Macorís was founded near the end of the 19th century by Cubans fleeing the terrible war of independence that was ravaging their country. The immigrants, many of whom were wealthy, had extensive experience in sugar-cane farming. They began to cultivate the crop throughout the region, thus developing a sugar industry that boosted the local economy. The beginning of the 20th century was a particularly prosperous time in San Pedro de Macorís, and many beautiful buildings in the town date from that era. Among them is the lovely **Iglesia San Pedro** (San Pedro Church), built in the British Gothic style, as well as other buildings, such as the **Post Office** and the **Fire Station**. Today, this medium-sized, typically Dominican town is known among baseball fans as the birthplace of some of that sport's biggest stars. Supposedly, San Pedro de Macorís has contributed more players per capita to the American professional leagues than any other town. If you like baseball, you might be interested to know that the town's team is a member of the Dominican league, and that games are held here.

La Romana

When arriving from the northern part of the country (Seibo), enter La Romana on Calle Santa Rosa; from the west (Higüey, Bayahibe, San Pedro), turn onto Avenida Libertad from the Las Américas highway to reach downtown.

With a population of nearly 100,000, La Romana is the biggest urban centre in the southeastern part of the Dominican Republic. The economy of the city prospered for much of this century, fuelled by sugar production at the Puerto Rica Sugar Co. refinery. However, in the seventies, a drop in sugar prices brought a period of recession. To help the economy of the city and the region, the tourist industry was developed, since La Romana had the right resources — beautiful beaches on the Caribbean Sea — for promoters to undertake such a project. In order for the plan to be successful, hotels able to comfortably accommodate guests from all over the world had to be built. The first step was to renovate the Hotel La Romana, just outside the city. This was a success; the hotel became the gigantic **Casa de Campo** complex, which now welcomes thousands of wealthy visitors a year. It has become the biggest holiday resort in the southeastern Dominican Republic.

While tourism has become very important to La Romana, the city retains a typically Dominican downtown area characterized by rows of simple wooden houses. There is also a much more opulent neighbourhood by the sea, just outside the centre of the city, where affluent Dominicans have built luxurious houses.

The region is flat and is dotted with palm trees, sugar-cane fields and scrub growth. Excursions inland on the **Río Chavón** are a good way to see the countryside up close. The La Romana region also includes several surprises; for example, just off the coast lies **Isla Catalina** ★, with its cache of idyllic beaches (see p 100).

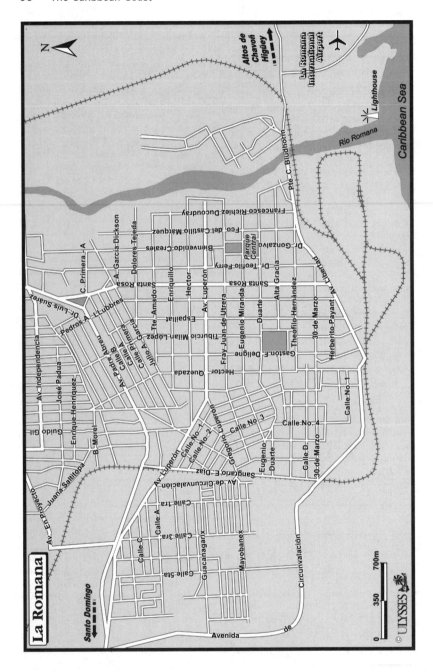

La Romana

N

Santo Domingo

Altos de
Chavón
Higüey

La Romana
International
Airport

Lighthouse

Caribbean Sea

Rio Romana

Pte. C. Bitudhorn

Francesco Richlez-Ducoudray

Fco. del Castillo-Márquez

Bienvenido-Creales

Dolores-Tejeda

A. García-Dickson

C. Primera-A

Pedros A.-LLubbres

Dr.-Luis-Suárez

Santa Rosa

Tte.-Amado

Enriquillo

Hector

Av.-Luperón

Santa Rosa

Alta Gracia

Dr.-Teófilo-Ferry

Parque
Central

Dr.-Gonzalvo

Av.-Liberación

Av.-Independencia

José Padua

Enrique-Henríquez

Guido Gil

B.-Morel

AV.-Padre Abreu

Calle-B

Calle-A

Calle-Primera

Julio-A.-García

Espaillat

Fray-Juan-de-Utrera

Tiburcio Milan-López

Eugenio Miranda

Duarte

Gastón-F.-Deligne

Theófilo-Hernández

Herberito-Payant

30-de-Marzo

Hector-Quezada

Calle-No.-1

Av.-En-Proyecto

Juana-Saltitopa

Av.-Luperón

Calle-No.-1

Calle-No.-2

Sangrario-E.-Díaz

Gregorio-Luperón

Calle No. 3

Calle No. 4

Eugenio
Duarte

Calle-D.

30-de-Marzo

Calle-No.-1

Av.-de-Circunvalación

Calle-1ra.

Calle-A

Calle-3ra.

Calle-C

Calle-3ra.

Guacanagarix

Mayobanex

Calle-5ta.

Circunvalación

de

Avenida

ULYSSES

0   350   700m

Altos de Chavón

Altos de Chavón ★★★ *(free admission; Avenida Libertad)*, located to the east of La Romana, is a surprisingly beautiful reconstruction of a late 14th century Italian village. It was built by ambitious entrepreneurs from Casa de Campo in order to add a major tourist attraction to the region. This replica is faithful in many ways to the original village, due to an incredible attention to detail. Built entirely of stone, Altos de Chavón includes a fountain, a small museum of pre-Hispanic art, period houses containing several shops and restaurants, a small church and an amphitheatre. Because of its size, the amphitheatre is the most impressive structure in the village; renowned artists occasionally play here. Built on a hill overlooking the sea, the village also has a terrace with a spectacular view of the region. To really get a feel for Altos de Chavón, also known as the "artist's village", take the time to explore its narrow streets, each more charming than the last.

Altos de Chavón is part of the Casa de Campo hotel complex. Small buses shuttle hotel guests between the hotel and the village. As you enter the village you will be met by people offering to act as your guide, for a fee of course. Keep in mind, however, that the narrow streets of the village are easy to explore on your own.

To build the section of road heading east, high cliffs had to be dug out. On the way to Bayahibe, motorists now pass through an impressive otherworldly canyon known as the Canyon Boca de Chavón.

Bayahibe ★

The road from La Romana to Bayahibe is in relatively good shape, considering that it leads to a simple small isolated village. It passes through a landscape of shrubs and undergrowth, with not a soul in sight for several kilometres before reaching Bayahibe.

Bayahibe is a charming little fishing village made up of modest wooden houses. Everything seems to depend on the sea here, and while there are more and more businesses dedicated to tourism, including a few hotels in the centre of the village, nothing has marred the authenticity of the setting. The main attraction is a superb fine-sand beach washed by the Caribbean Sea with colourful little boats dotting the horizon. This is a peaceful, attractive place far from big towns and major tourist developments.

A large-scale hotel complex, the Club Dominicus, has been built on a beach neighbouring Bayahibe. This huge, luxurious place, which already attracts a lot of visitors, never seems to stop growing, surrounding construction sites indicate that it is to be substantially enlarged.

Excursions to **Isla Saona** ★ (see p 99, 100) and **Isla Catalina** ★ (see p 100) are organized from Bayahibe. Both islands have magnificent white-sand beaches and palm trees. **Isla Saona** has only a small number of residents divided between two hamlets. Life on the island is as peaceful as can be when it is not overrun by visitors. These quiet periods are becoming rare as more and more people discover the charms of this lush island. The Parque Nacional Del Este, which also includes the southeastern point of the Dominican Republic was created to protect Isla Saona's exceptional flora and fauna, featuring a wide variety of birds.

Boca de Yuma ★

The village of Boca de Yuma sits atop steep cliffs that plunge into the Caribbean at the mouth of the Boca de Yuma river. The cliffs offer a fascinating view of the waves crashing against the rocks below. The area is rich in aquatic bird life, attracting interesting species such as the pelican. The town is perhaps best known for the **natural pools** the ocean has formed in the cliffs along the shore. There is a small half-moon shaped beach at the mouth of the river, but the most impressive stretch of sand is the one circled by cliffs. A hole in the rock wall allows the water to enter this spectacular pool.

 PARKS

Parque Nacional del Este protects the southeastern peninsula of the Dominican Republic. It encompasses most of the peninsula as well as Isla Saona, located at the southeastern extremity of the country.

The park is accessible from the coastal road that connects Bayahibe and Boca del Yuma. The entrances to the park are a few kilometres south of Bayahibe (near Guaraguao), and south of Boca de Yuma. Before heading off, be reminded that the road is not much more than a narrow, sandy trail, only accessible with an all-terrain vehicle. There are no villages or gas stations along the road so make sure you fill your tank beforehand. If your vehicle gets stuck, use a palm leaf to dig it out of the sand.

The park's coastline is dotted with magnificent wild beaches; the isolated beach at **Puerto Laguna**, for example, will make you feel like you are the only person on earth. Besides these oases of white sand, the peninsula and island feature a wealth of tropical plant and animal life. A subtropical forest covers a large portion of the territory and is home to a multitude of bird species.

The park is also a stop along the migration path of some birds. If you're lucky, you'll spot some manatees along the coast; these large aquatic mammals usually live at the mouths of rivers. Unfortunately, the manatee population has dropped considerably and the animal is quite rare.

Work is underway to improve access to the park (the peninsula region); it is unknown when the project will be completed.

Covering almost 100 square kilometres, **Isla Saona** ★★, is a haven of tranquillity. The only human inhabitants of this vast palm grove are a few families of fishermen; in the high season, however the island's beaches come under siege. To reach Isla Saona, you can take part in the excursion from Bayahibe *(1,500 pesos for 10 people)*. These are organized at restaurants along the beach, in particular the La Bahia restaurant.

Theoretically, visitors require a permit to enter a Dominican park *(Santo Domingo, ☎ 2215340)*, but surveillance is virtually nonexistent. The companies that organize excursions to Isla Saona usually arrange for permits.

 BEACHES

La Caleta

The craze for the minuscule beach at **La Caleta** is quite strange indeed. The sea rushes into a tiny bay formed by the coastal cliffs, and hordes of young people come here to go swimming. Space is so limited that they appear to be swimming on top of each other.

Boca Chica

The beach ★★ is magnificent: large coral reefs have developed offshore, forming a natural breakwater; as a result, the waters are always calm. Swimmers must venture out several metres before the shallow waters of Boca Chica bay drop off to any considerable depth, creating a natural swimming pool. The sea holds its share of treasures as well: scuba divers and snorkellers can observe the multitude of tropical fish that gravitate around the coral reefs.

In an effort to beautify the area, the countless wooden stalls that used to line the beach have been torn down. However, crowds of vendors now roam the beach hawking anything and everything, often very aggressively. If you aren't interested, avert your gaze from the merchandise and make your refusal clear. Despite this inconvenience, which is all too common in touristy areas, the beach is very pleasant, since much care is taken to maintain it; it is cleaned every day. Beach-goers can thus enjoy the best this natural site has to offer.

Following the shoreline towards Andrès, you'll come upon another portion of the **beach** ★, which is literally overrun on Sundays by crowds of Dominicans relaxing with friends and family. This is the peak time, and finding an empty spot is no picnic, not to mention trying to spread out a towel. This part of the beach is not bordered by the village, but that doesn't stop vendors from coming here. Though the beach is pleasant, it is not as nice as the one near the centre of town.

Juan Dolio

The long **beach** ★ is trimmed by a beautiful ribbon of sand, which is unfortunately not as fine as at Boca Chica, but is much less crowded. Palm trees offer welcome shade from the noonday sun and frame the beach nicely. Furthermore, there are none of those shabby wooden stalls displaying all sorts of merchandise, which all too often cheapen touristy beaches. Instead, there are a few inconspicuous water-sports centres.

La Romana

The very private grounds of the Casa de Campo include a magnificent beach, which is only accessible to guests of the complex. Just outside of town is another beach, the Caleton, which is pretty average.

Isla Saona

The island, protected as part of Parque Nacional del Este, is ringed by a magnificent strip of golden sand and the warm, shimmering waters of the Caribbean Sea. The **beach** ★★ is so lovely that many hotel complexes arrange daytrips to it, arousing concern about the area's ecological equilibrium. For this reason, certain precautions aimed at protecting this remarkable natural site should be taken.

Boca de Yuma

The village of Boca de Yuma lies on the west bank of the Río Yuma, at the top of some steep cliffs. It thus has no beach. However, on the other side of the river, a short distance from the village, there is a lovely sandy beach where you can relax or go for a swim. It is easy to get there, as the local fishermen will take you across the river for a few pesos. There are plans to build a small bridge to make the beach even more accessible. The spot is particularly impressive at the end of the day, when hundreds of cattle egrets take refuge for the night in the trees near the river.

Isla Catalina

Less popular than neighbouring Isla Saona, lush **Isla Catalina** ★ is no less enchanting. It boasts superb white-sand beaches, perfect for a relaxing swim and catching some rays. More and more people are making their way here, as the island is an interesting dive site. Boats bring visitors from Bayahibe *(1,300 pesos for 10 people)*.

Bayahibe

Among the prettiest **beaches** ★ in the region, this long, tree-studded crescent of soft sand lies alongside a tranquil town. Surprisingly, this magnificent spot is often ignored by many visitors. This beach is still wild and not as well maintained as some others but nonetheless has a charm all its own. The section of beach right next to the Club Dominicus is better maintained and busier.

By following the road along the water through the Parque Nacional Del Este (assuming your vehicle does not get stuck), you'll discover a series of unspoiled, isolated little beaches great for sunning or swimming. Be careful though: these beaches are very remote, and you will be far from help if problems arise.

 OUTDOOR ACTIVITIES

  Scuba Diving and Snorkelling

The coral reefs offshore in Bahía de Boca Chica make this an ideal spot to observe underwater life, and several diving excursions are available. The **Don Juan** *(☎ 523-4511)* rents snorkelling equipment for about $6 US per hour. Its diving centre, **Treasure Divers**, organizes excursions and diving courses. Beginners can try a day of lessons and a dive for $75 US.

The **Boca Chica Resort** *(☎ 223-0622)* offers a day-long *(10am to 5pm)* package deal that includes access to the pool, tennis courts, snorkelling equipment and a windsurfer for 300 pesos.

The beach at **Juan Dolio** is another good diving site with an abundance of underwater attractions. The diving centre at the entrance to Juan Dolio organizes excursions, and many of the larger hotels also have snorkelling and scuba diving equipment on hand. Those wishing to go scuba diving can head to the **Marena Beach Resort** (see p 104), which has a diving centre.

Bayahibe also has a diving centre, **Casa Daniel** *(☎ 2230622)*, which offers excursions for experienced and novice divers.

  Sailing and Windsurfing

The **Don Juan** hotel in Boca Chica rents windsurfers for $12 US an hour. The gentle waters in the bay off Boca Chica are perfect for novice windsurfers. Small sailboats are available from the same hotel.

The **Boca Chica Resort** *(☎ 223-0622)* also rents out windsurfers.

 Deep-sea Fishing

Several species of fish, including seabream, swordfish and sometimes barracuda, might be your catch of the day after partaking in one of the deep-sea fishing excursions offered by the **Hamaca** and **Don Juan** hotels. While prices vary depending on the length of the trip, you can expect to pay about $50 US per person.

 Jet-skiing

If you are in the mood to whiz across the waves, then head to the **Don Juan** hotel, where you can rent a jet ski. Expect to pay about 250 pesos for an unforgettable 20-minute ride.

 Cruises

Cruises to **Isla Saona** *(1,500 pesos for 10 people)* and **Isla Catalina** *(1,300 pesos for 10 people)* are organized by Madrugadora Tour *(☎ 556-5055)* and depart from Bayahibe.

Bicycling

The **Hotel Hamaca** in Boca Chica rents bicycles for $8 US a day. **Alpha 3000** also rents for $5 US.

 Motorcycling

To explore the area beyond the reaches of a bicycle, consider renting a motorcycle (but watch out for dangerous drivers). Motorcycles can be rented at the **Guest House No.14** *(Calle Juan Bautista Vicini)*, or at **Alpha 300** *(Calle Pimera, ☎ 5236059)*. Expect to pay $22 US a day for a scooter and $35 US a day for a motorcycle. Harley Davidsons are available for real enthusiasts.

Motorcycles can also be rented from **Alpha 3000** in Juan Dolio. Expect to pay about $35 US per day. In Bayahibe, in the centre of town, **Tom M.** rents motorcycles.

 Golf

A nine-hole golf course has been laid out 5 kilometres west of Boca Chica. Several hotels in Boca Chica offer package deals that include greens fees. If you want to play a round expect to pay 150 pesos per round and 140 pesos for clubs.

The golf course at the **Casa de Campo** hotel complex in La Romana is one of the most beautiful in the Caribbean. It lies stretched along the Caribbean coastline enabling golfers to enjoy some stunning views.

 Horseback Riding

The surroundings of Bayahibe can be explored on horseback. **Casa Daniel** *(☎ 223-0622)* provides well-cared-for horses for pleasant tours of the area.

 ACCOMMODATIONS

All sorts of accommodations, from modest hotels to the grand resort complexes, dot the southeastern coast. Since these places are always located near one of the many beautiful sandy beaches along this coast, visitors have only too many options to choose from.

Boca Chica

All of the hotels in Boca Chica have been built near the centre of town. Some lie on pretty streets in quiet neighbourhoods, while others are right by the water downtown. Boca Chica definitely has the largest choice of accommodations in the region, and it doesn't take long to find what you are looking for.

The **El Cheveron** *($20 US; ⊗, ℜ; Calle Duarte)* is a downtown hotel that can be a bit noisy, but has the advantage of being right on the beach. It has small, ordinary rooms.

Some inns make you want to go back to a village again and again. This is certainly the case with the **Meson Isabela** *($35 US, ⊗, ≈, K; Calle Duarte, behind the Hamaca Hotel, ☎ 523-4224)*. A Dominican and a native of Québec are your friendly hosts. This isn't the place for late night carousing; instead, guests enjoy a magnificent, peaceful garden, a pool rarely used by more than two swimmers at a time, and rooms in well-maintained buildings. The owners can also help familiarize you with the country. Finally, for those wishing to avoid the hustle and bustle of the town, there is private access to the beach. Golf packages and rooms with equipped kitchenettes are also available here.

The **Villa Sans-Soucy** *($40 US, bkfst and dinner incl.; ≡, ≈, ℜ; 48 Calle Juan Bautista Vicini, ☎ 1-800-463-0097 or 523-4461)* is set back from the street for added peace and quiet. The pleasant rooms open onto a inner courtyard with a pool. The premises are well tended.

La Belle *(40 $US; ≈; 9 Juan Bautista Vicini, ☎ 523-5959, ≈ 523-5077)* is located by the side of the highway on the way into the village, but offers a relatively peaceful atmosphere nonetheless. Though hardly a tropical paradise, the place is new and well maintained. Its small, clean rooms are equipped with balconies. Perfectly acceptable for the price.

For many people, the name "Neptuno" refers to one of the finest restaurants (see p 107) in Boca Chica. The restaurant now operates a small inn, **Neptuno's Guest House** *($US 45; ≈, K; 12 Duarte, ☎ 523-6534, ≈ 523-4251)*, located in the residential part of town, across from the Hamaca hotel. A former home enlarged to serve its present purpose, it has comfortable rooms, each of which is equipped with a kitchenette. The place is well kept and inviting, but unfortunately has no garden.

The green balcony of the **Terrazas del Caribe** *($45 US; ≈, ⊛, K; 7 Calle Sanchez, ☎ 523-4488, ≈ 523-4444)* is easy to spot behind the downtown area. The buildings stand next to an uninteresting empty lot, but the rooms, equipped with kitchenettes, are perfectly adequate.

Set back from the beach, the **Condo Carey** *($US 50; ≡, K; 8 Calle Francisco del Rosario Sánchez, ☎ 523-5436, ≈ 523-5435)* has large, relatively comfortable rooms, each with a private bath, a kitchenette and a dining nook.

The **Don Juan Beach Resort** *($US 140 all-inclusive; ≡, ≈, ℜ; Abraham Nunez, ☎ 523-4511, ≈ 523-6422)* consists of several buildings on a large piece of property right on the beach. The owners have made the most of the available space. The restaurant was recently expanded, and there are two gardens giving onto the beach, one of which looks a little neglected. The place is quite comfortable and offers easy access to the sea. Some rooms afford a view of the shimmering waves. Finally, there is a water sports centre right on the property, enabling guests to enjoy a variety of activities.

In order to be close to the sea, the **Hamaca** *($140 US all-inclusive, ≡, ≈, ℜ, ♣; Calle Duarte, ☎ 523-4611, ≈ 566-2354)* had to build right over the main road. The back of this large pink building, at first sight hardly inviting, is easily spotted from downtown, and you have to drive around it to get to the other side of Boca Chica. The lobby, restaurants and guest rooms, are all tastefully decorated. There is also a splendid beach nearby.

The large **Boca Chica Resort** *($150 all-inclusive; ≡, ≈, ℜ; 20 Calle Juan Bautista Vicini, ☎ 567-9238, ≈ 686-6741)* hotel complex stands on a vast piece of property, well protected from intruders. Although the hotel is a short distance from the sea, the range of services offered here is extensive and makes up for this inconvenience. The location, furthermore, ensures a relaxing, peaceful stay. Some of the rooms could be better kept up, and the staff, while ever-courteous, is not always friendly. Golf packages are available.

Juan Dolio

This tourist village consists essentially of large, luxurious hotel complexes. Most guests reserve ahead of time, and opt for an all-inclusive package. Budget travellers who choose their accommodation on a day to day basis won't find much here.

La Santa *($US 40; ≈, ≡, ℜ; ☎ 526-1011, ⇥ 526-1706)* is the only small inn in Juan Dolio. It is a charming, quiet place with pretty rooms and a lovely garden with flowering shrubs and plants. A good choice for those who prefer a pleasant inn to a large, often impersonal hotel complex.

A lovely complex looking out onto the sea, the **Punta Garza** *($US 125 all-inclusive; ≈, ≡, ℜ; ☎ 687-6887, ⇥ 526-3814)* has a few pretty villas, as well as several pink buildings adorned with balconies with white friezes. These take up the larger part of the garden, but the property has been carefully landscaped so that lovely flowering plants grow all over, lending the place a remarkably calm atmosphere. The pool and restaurant are located on the part of the property facing the sea, thus offering a magnificent view of the waves.

The **Marena Beach Resort** *($US 125 all-inclusive; ≈, ≡, ℜ; ☎ 581-9495, ⇥ 226-1690)* is divided into two sections. The first is a big white building containing the reception desk and the guestrooms; the other, across the street, by the sea, consists of several outbuildings scattered across a pleasant garden. The outbuildings definitely offer a more beautiful setting, but all the rooms are decorated with pretty wood furniture.

Those who prefer more intimate hotels are sure to like the **Colonial Tropical** *($US 75; ≈, ≡, ℜ; ☎ 526-1660, ⇥ 526-2538)*, which is not right next to the water but nevertheless offers a peaceful setting far from all the hustle and bustle. The rooms, brightened up with pretty tropical colours, are divided up among several Spanish-style buildings laid out around a pretty cobblestoned courtyard with a pool in it.

The **Embassy** *($40 US; ≡, ≈, ◉, ℜ; 98 Jose Contreras, ☎ 535-8389, ⇥ 526-1251)* is a hotel complex located on the highway between Boca Chica and Juan Dolio, well away from any villages. It consists of several buildings, each housing a few rooms, which are spread across a property stretching from the highway to the sea. At the far end, a lovely terrace with a pool overlooks the waves. The location would be very pleasant were it not for the highway bordering the beach.

The **Metro Marina** *($140 US; ≡, ≈, ℜ; Juan Dolio, ☎ 526-2811, ⇥ 526-1808)* stands right on the beach, and stretches along the sea. As a result, many of its rooms have a great view. On first impression, the building seems less attractive than the more recently built hotels nearby, but the rooms are pleasant, and the back of the hotel, opening onto the beach, is certainly the envy of the neighbours.

The gigantic **De Cameron** *($170 US all-inclusive;* ≡, ≈, ℜ, ☉; *Juan Dolio,* ☎ *526-2009)* hotel complex sits on a vast property in the centre of town. It is almost a world unto itself, complete with exercise rooms, a casino, and a selection of bars and restaurants to satisfy any and all its guests needs. Part of the garden is taken up by a huge swimming pool, where nonstop music creates a festive atmosphere for fun-seekers. The hotel is a member of the Caribbean Village chain.

The **Villa Jubey** *($200 US all-inclusive;* ≡, ≈, ℜ; ☎ *541-6989)* with its elegant tastefully decorated lobby and guestrooms, is set back a bit from the beach. A large swimming pool takes up almost all of the garden, which is nevertheless nicely appointed with waterfalls.

The **Renaissance Capella Resort** hotel complex *($200 US all-inclusive;* ≈, ≡, ℜ; ☎ *526-1080)* stretches over a vast and beautiful garden. In addition to this wonderful, verdant setting, the hotel offers a horde of amenities including a large swimming pool.

🏆 At the **Coral Caribe Resort** *(all-inclusive package;* ≡, ≈, ℜ; ☎ *526-2244,* ⊷ *526-3142)* is another hotel offering all-inclusive packages, where guests are treated like royalty from morning to night. Modern buildings, ideally located on the beach, house comfortable, nicely decorated rooms, and the hotel's garden, facing the beach, is exceptionally pleasant.

The **Costa Linda** *($240 US all-inclusive;* ≡, ≈, ℜ; ☎ *526-3909)* has long buildings running along the sea, but not quite on the beach. Although the main attraction is a lovely flowering garden where guests can stroll about, the carefully chosen decor adds to the charm of this hotel.

San Pedro de Macorís

San Pedro has no luxurious hotels. Though there are some simple inexpensive places, we suggest staying in Boca Chica, where you'll have a wider choice, or in Bayahibe, where the hotels have more charm.

La Romana

La Romana offers two very different types of accommodations: low-budget, low-comfort hotels and a gigantic hotel complex that is definitely the most luxurious on the island, Casa de Campo.

The **Tío Tom** *($35 US;* ≡, ≈, ℜ; *on the highway to San Pedro de Macorís, at the edge of La Romana,* ☎ *556-6211,* ⊷ *556-6201)* is located on the highway on the outskirts of town. The surroundings are not particularly interesting but the rooms are functional, if not the most comfortable. Next door is the **Adamaney Hotel**, offering a similar level of comfort. Besides these two, there are few budget hotels in the city.

🏆 The **Casa de Campo** *($230 US;* ≡, ≈, ℜ; *P.O. Box 140, La Romana,* ☎ *523-3333,* ⊷ *523-8548)* hotel complex, one of the most luxurious on the island, offers an incredible variety of services, including stables, tennis courts, equipment for various aquatic sports and a beautiful golf course. The property covers an area of 2,800 hectares, and minibuses shuttle from one end of the complex to the other. The rooms, available in little villas or in the main buildings, are comfortable and tastefully decorated. This is a real little paradise.

Bayahibe

This tiny hamlet hidden on the shores of the Caribbean has a few hotels to satisfy the needs of the still small numbers of visitors who come here.

The very basics (no electricity or hot water) in non-luxurious but nonetheless pleasant rooms are offered at the **Villa Bayahibe** *($15 US; ⊗)*, a green and white building in the centre of town.

The **Trip Town Bungalow** *($15 US; ⊗)*, located in the centre of town next to the Villa Bayahibe, offers similar rooms in modest pink and white cottages, which are more than adequate for those looking for budget accommodation. The rooms are well maintained, and the beach is just a few steps away.

The **Club Dominicus** *($200 US all-inclusive;* ≡, ≈, ℜ; ☎ *686-5658,* ⊶ *687-8583, 1-800-847-4502 for reservations)* is located on a beach next to Bayahibe. Although there is a lot of construction in progress, this is the only hotel thus far, so the setting remains quite peaceful and secluded. Beautiful stone buildings with palm-thatched roofs house the guestrooms. Besides the delightful peace and quiet, guests enjoy the proximity of a beautiful sand beach.

Boca de Yuma

Club El 28 *($US 18 or $US 35 fb;* ≈, ⊗; ☎ *476-8660)* is one of those small, family hotels that don't have luxurious facilities but offer warm hospitality, a peaceful setting and well-kept rooms, which are basic but perfectly acceptable for the price. Packages including three delicious meals at the hotel restaurant are available—an excellent option for those looking to spend a few days of peace and quiet without breaking their budget.

If you'd rather stay in a hotel that's not quite as hospitable but offers a more majestic setting, head to the **Hotel Saina** *($US 35;* ☎ *223-0681)*, which stands atop a cliff alongside the natural pool in Boca de Yuma, offering up this impressive natural site, as well as the Caribbean. The hotel has small, no-frills rooms in the main building and in several little houses right near by. The prettiest have balconies.

 RESTAURANTS

Boca Chica

Many food stalls downtown sell grilled and breaded fish. One of the best spots for chicken is the stall next to the Boca Chica Gift Shop. While **De Nosotros**, across from the central park, at the corner of Calles Juan Bautista Vicini and Duarte, sells delicious *empanadas*. As well, the restaurant at the corner of Calle Abraham Nuñez and Juan Bautista Vicini serves good breakfasts.

The menu at the **Villa Sans-Soucy** *($; Calle Juan Bautista Vicini)* lists simple but delicious Québec dishes like roast chicken and hot chicken sandwiches. There's nothing refined about these meals, but they are always good and the portions are generous. Courteous service.

El Cheveron *($; Calle Duarte)*. This little restaurant has a good location near the beach and an attractive terrace looking out onto the street. The menu features deliciously prepared Dominican specialities from a menu based mainly on fish and seafood. This is a good and inexpensive place to sample the local cuisine. The restaurant also serves pizza and pasta dishes.

For good Italian food, try the lively **Portofino** *($$; Calle Duarte)*, located by the water. The menu lists a wide variety of tasty pasta and meat dishes. Breakfast is also served.

Countless signs lead the way to **Willy's B.B.Q.** *($$)*, located behind the main street. The succulent ribs cooked over a wood fire alone are reason enough to go. The setting is pleasant as well, featuring a garden, filled with bird cages, where all sorts of birds flutter about. This is a very appealing spot.

The **Hamaca Hotel** *($$; Calle Duarte)* offers a complete buffet in its larger dining room overlooking the sea. The more intimate **Las Chorales** *($$$)* serves excellent Dominican and international dishes in a relaxing, cosy atmosphere.

At the very end of Calle Duarte, steps away from the Hamaca, you'll find an Italian restaurant called **Romagna Mia** *($$; Calle Duarte)*. The first thing that will catch your attention is the ice cream counter, but don't just think about indulging your sweet tooth, as

the restaurant offers a good daily selection of Italian specialties that are invariably delicious.

Neptuno *($$$; Calle Juan Bautista Vicini, at the corner of Calle 20 de Diciembre)* is without a doubt the best place in town for fish and seafood. Everything from traditional Dominican food to paella is prepared with great flair and served on a beautiful seaside terrace.

Juan Dolio

L'Écrevisse *($$-$$$)* occupies a pretty building facing onto the street, right next to the De Cameron hotel complex. This is one of the few good restaurants in town that is not located in a hotel. In addition to its attractive decor, it offers succulent dishes that are a pleasant change from the food served at the hotel buffets, which is often not hot enough.

La Romana

Calle Santa Rosa has several small restaurants serving simple, inexpensive fare such as sandwiches and hamburgers.

The **El Pici** *($)* pizzeria is located on Calle Duarte, along with the **El Polo** *($)* which serves *pica pollo*.

It's breakfast time and you're craving a thick, delicious sandwich made with French bread with a nice crispy crust. Or perhaps you're in the mood for a croissant... In any case, head to the café-cum-bakery **Trigo de Oro** *($; 8am to 12:30pm and 3pm to 8:30pm; Calle*

Trinitaria), where you can enjoy your meal on the terrace.

There are a number of pleasant, quaintly decorated restaurants at **Altos de Chavón**. Particularly noteworthy are the **Café del Sol** *($$)* pizzeria, the Italian restaurants **Piazzeta** *($)* and **Giacosa** *($$)*, and the **Sombrero** *($$)* a Mexican restaurant. Prices are a bit high, but the beautiful setting makes it all worthwhile.

Bayahibe

The **Bar Billard** *($)* doesn't look like much, but it is a good, friendly spot for a quick bite. The menu offers sandwiches and burgers.

Besides a great location right by the sea, **La Punta** *($$)* offers mouthwatering seafood dishes. The interior is simply decorated, but very pleasant.

Right by the water as well, **La Bahia** *($$)* is another place to remember for Dominican specialties, including great fish and seafood dishes.

Boca de Yuma

Club El 28 *($$$;* ☎ *476-8660)* is a wonderful surprise in this tiny Dominican village. Run by an Italian family that recently immigrated to the country, this restaurant is the place to go if you feel like tucking into delicious Italian specialties—something hard to come by in this area. You'll enjoy your meal beneath a big wooden roof, in a big dining room that opens onto the street. Unpretentious and as pleasant as can be.

 ENTERTAINMENT

Boca Chica

Sipping a drink while enjoying the last golden rays of sun is a pleasant way to end the day. The bar at the **Hamaca** hotel, located in a structure built over the waves, is definitely the most charming in town.

If you're willing to brave the hustle and bustle of a noisy street, then head for one of the many terraces along Calle Duarte, from late afternoon into the night.

The bigger hotels, such as the **Hamaca** and the **Don Juan**, have good discos.

Newly opened in Boca Chica, the **River Club** *(10 pesos; Calle Juan Bautista Vicini, facing the Belle hotel)* has become *the* place in town for an evening out. Set in a basement (so it is always cool), the interior of the is dance bar has been made to look like a grotto; drinks and dancing to anything from rock to *merengue* are the order of the night.

The **Hamaca** hotel now houses the only casino in town. You can try your luck at slot machines and various games such as roulette.

Juan Dolio

At present the **De Cameron** is the only hotel in town with a casino; give it a whirl! For dancing, try the Caligula, also in the **De Cameron**. Many little bars open in the afternoon and evening are spread along the beach.

SHOPPING

Boca Chica

In Boca Chica, Calle Duarte is the main drag and the best place to find souvenirs. The quality of the goods sold varies, however, so choose carefully.

La Romana

There are boutiques and small markets in downtown La Romana, along Calle Santa Rosa and Avenida Libertad.

Altos de Chavón

At Altos de Chavón, a few shops sell good local arts and crafts, but the prices are high. There is also a little bookstore, which sells books written in a number of different languages.

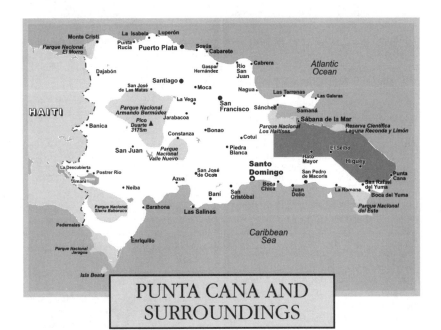

PUNTA CANA AND SURROUNDINGS

The Dominican Republic's eastern point is characterized by an almost unbroken succession of sugar cane fields and orange groves. Picturesque, pastel-coloured villages pop up here and there on the landscape. It is common to see people travelling by horse, a much more popular means of transport than the car in some villages. In fact, Higüey is the only sizeable urban centre in this sparsely populated region, where you can drive for tens of kilometres without encountering any towns. The eastern point thus offers curious travellers an intriguing look at the traditions and customs of the Dominican countryside. Most travellers, however, come to this region for another reason: its beaches are among the most beautiful in the country, if not the whole Caribbean.

In just over a decade, the once nearly uninhabited northeastern shore of the Dominican Republic, known as the Coconut Coast, has become a major holiday destination. Most developers have followed the same general plan, building grand luxury hotels on large properties, at the edge of breathtaking and completely isolated beaches. Relaxation, the beach and outdoor activities are what attract vacationers to Punta Cana and the surrounding area.

FINDING YOUR WAY AROUND

Punta Cana Airport

Punta Cana's small airport is the point of arrival for most guests who have reserved ahead for a room in one of the region's resort complexes. The airport is located near most of the big hotels (just a few kilometres north of Club Med). The waiting room has a small restaurant that serves light meals, and accepts both American dollars and pesos.

A network of excellent roads connects all the hotels complexes. Getting from Santo Domingo to Punta Cana is easily accomplished on the road that passes through Romana, San Rafael de Yuma and Higüey. Other roads in the region are in poorer condition. The section along the coast north of Higüey is particularly bad.

Sabana de la Mar

The road from Hato Mayor had not yet been paved. This situation should change very soon, if it has not already. Sabana de la Mar can also be reached by boat from Santa Barbara de Samaná, on the other side of the Bahía de Samaná. The **Codetel** is located at 47 Calle Diego de Lira.

Higüey

The road from Romana provides quick access to Higüey. Higüey's **Codetel** is on Avenida Bertilio.

The Coconut Coast

To reach Punta Cana, the main tourist area of the region, drive along the full length of the basilica in Higüey, then turn right. Continue along the main road to reach the Club Med or the Punta Cana Beach Resort (about 40 km from Higüey). To reach the other large hotel complexes, turn left at Kilometre 27. As public buses (*guaguas*) in this area is not very efficient, visitors who want to explore the countryside are better off renting a car or motorcycle,

or taking taxis. Taxis wait outside some of the major hotels, and can take you just about anywhere (fares are always posted).

EXPLORING

Sabana de la Mar

Sabana de la Mar is an isolated and rather uninspiring little fishing village, on the southern shore of Bahía de Samaná. Dominicans attempting to enter Puerto Rico illegally, and then continue on to the United States often depart from here. From the port, boats take visitors to the superb **Parque Nacional de los Haitises ★★**. However, departures are more frequent and better organized from Sanchez and Santa Barbara de Samaná, on the Samaná peninsula. A ferry goes to Santa Barbara de Samaná three times a day, but only pedestrians and motorcyclists are allowed on board, and the captain sometimes has difficulty mooring the ferry in Sabana de la Mar's port.

Higüey

Founded in 1502 by order of Nicolás de Ovando, the town of Higüey is one of the cradles of Spanish civilization in America. It became an important economic centre early in its history and, more importantly, the principal religious site in the country.

Even today, Dominicans come from all over the country to pay their respects to the sacred image of la Señora de la Altagracia, the country's patron saint, who is said to have performed several miracles. The basilica that houses the

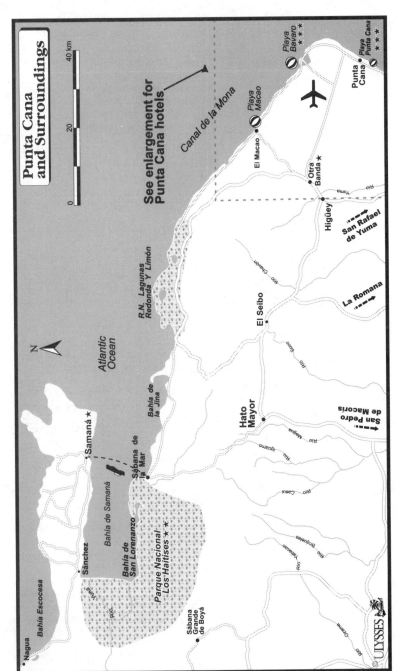

Punta Cana
and Surroundings

0   20   40 km

**See enlargement for
Punta Cana hotels**

Atlantic
Ocean

N

Nagua
Bahía Escocesa

Sánchez

Bahía de Samaná

Samaná ★

Bahía de
San Lorenzo

Sábana de
la Mar

Parque Nacional
Los Haitises ★★★

Sábana
Grande
de Boyá

Río Ozama

Río Yabacao

Río Brujuelas

Río Casuí

Río Iguamo

Río Maguá

Bahía de
la Jina

R.N. Lagunas
Redonda Y Limón

Canal de la Mona

El Macao

Otra
Banda ★

Higüey

Río Yuma

San Rafael
de Yuma

La Romana

El Seibo

Río Chavón

Río Soco

Hato
Mayor

San Pedro
de Macorís

Playa Bavaro ★★★

Playa
Punta Cana ★★

Punta
Cana

Playa
Macao

© ULYSSES

tiny painting is Higüey's focal point; without it, the place would be of little interest. A medium-sized town, Higüey is the capital of the province of Altagracia, and is at the centre of a large orange-producing area.

Higuey's basílica

The **Basílica de Nuestra Señora de la Altagracia** ★ *(right in the centre of town)* is striking from an architectural standpoint, with its 80-metre high arches. Construction of the church, built in honour of the patron saint of the region, began in 1954. The painting of the highly-venerated saint hangs inside. There is an impressive annual pilgrimage to the site each year on January 21. Visitors wearing shorts or miniskirts are not allowed inside.

Otra Banda ★

With its beautiful, pastel-coloured houses, the hamlet of Otra Banda, about 5 kilometres east of Higüey, is quite a sight. It is definitely one of the prettiest villages in the country. You'll come to a fork a few kilometres along

the road heading north from Otra Banda. Keep right to reach the Coconut Coast via Playa Macao. The left fork heads through beautiful scenery and isolated villages, where people on horseback are as common as those on motorcycles. The quickest way to the Coconut Coast, however, is to head southeast from Otra Banda.

The Coconut Coast ★★

Punta Cana, Playa Macao and Playa Bavaro ★★

An almost unbroken string of white-sand **beaches** ★★★ extends as far as the eye can see along the turquoise waters of the Canal de la Mona, which separates the Dominican Republic from Puerto Rico. Although a few of these beaches belong to large hotels, you won't have much trouble finding some wilder more scenic spots. As the name indicates, the vegetation of the region consists mostly of coconut palms. In fact, these trees line the entire strip of beaches, adding a certain idyllic cachet to the region. The area around Punta Cana has some of the most stunning beaches in the country. The local population is scattered amongst a few charming hamlets.

 PARKS

Parque Nacional de los Haitises ★★ is located at the southwestern extremity of Bahía de Samaná and covers an area of 208 square kilometres. Its very dense tropical vegetation blankets a gently undulating landscape that never rises more than 50 metres above sea level. The park hides innumerable treasures, such as grottos rich in pre-Columbian rock paintings, a bird sanctuary and large mangrove swamps. It is one of the most fascinating parks in the Dominican Republic. Boat trips to Los Haitises set out from Sanchez and Santa Barbara de Samaná, on the Samaná peninsula, and less frequently from Sabana de la Mar.

Maaita Park *(close to Playa Bavaro)* is a new conservation park that preserves the habitats of many winged species and other animals.

 BEACHES

The Coconut Coast boasts some of the most beautiful **beaches ★★★** in the country, if not in all the Caribbean. Whether it be Playa Macao, Playa Bavaro or Punta Cana, these endless stretches of fine white sand are lined with coconut palms. All of the hotel complexes in Playa Bavaro and Punta Cana offer direct access to the beach. More adventurous types can head off in search of countless deserted beaches lining the road between Playa Macao and Sabaná de la Mar.

 OUTDOOR ACTIVITIES

The big hotel complexes in Playa Bavaro and Punta Cana all organize activities. Because most of these hotels offer all-inclusive packages, these activities are usually offered to guests free of charge. Their prime locations mean that guests can enjoy scuba diving, snorkelling, sailing, windsurfing, horseback riding and many other sports, including tennis. There is only one golf course in the region, the one at the Hotel Bavaro.

 ACCOMMODATIONS

Higüey

The **Hotel San Juan** *($11 US; ⊗; at the corner of Colón and Juan Esquivel)* has a few good, clean, and fairly large rooms. The only (major) problem is that it is located right above a disco, making it very noisy on weekend nights. Find out precisely which nights the disco is open before booking a room here.

The **Topacio** *($30 US; ⊗, ℜ; at the corner of Duarte and Cambronal, ☎ 554-5892)* offers clean, quiet rooms, decorated with outrageously bad taste. This is nevertheless a very popular hotel, and it can be hard to get a room here on holidays and weekends. The restaurant on the ground floor is the preferred meeting place of prominent townsfolk.

Coconut Coast

If you plan to stay in one of the large hotel complexes in Punta Cana, Playa Macao and Playa Bavaro, reserve well in advance and do not arrive after nightfall, as you may be denied access. All of these establishments offer high-quality accommodation. Most offer all-inclusive packages, which include two or three meals a day and in some cases drinks and activities; such hotels include the mention "all-inclusive" after the price.

Those wishing to visit the region without the big hotel bill usually associated with it should try the **Hotel Cayacoa** *($32 US; ℜ, ⊗, ≈; Carretera Melia, ☎ 552-0622, ⊷ 552-0631)*, which offers clean, reasonably priced rooms. Located next to the road, the setting might not be the most enchanting, but it is still close enough to the beach (not far from the Melia Bavaro). The facilities are adequate and there is a pretty pool.

🦐 The **Melia Bavaro Resort** *($140 US all-inclusive; ≡, ≈, ℜ; Playa Bavaro,* ☎ *221-2311)* has 500 pleasantly furnished rooms in more than fifty beautiful little buildings surrounded by lush tropical vegetation. The huge grounds of the Bavaro Resort, part of the Spanish Melia chain, have been tastefully designed, and overlook an excellent beach. Visitors are greeted in a large, airy lobby graced with large pools of water. Not only can all water sports be enjoyed here, but the place also organizes a host of evening activities and regional excursions. Taxis wait by the entrance, making it very easy to explore on your own.

The **Riu** *(Playa Macao,* ☎ *221-2290 or 221-7515,* ≈ *221-1645)* hotels form an immense complex with four different luxury hotels all near a superb beach. A pleasant shopping street of pastel buildings has been built near by. The **Riu Taino** *($160 US all-inclusive; tv, ℜ, ⊗, ≡, ≈)* is the most affordable of the Riu hotels. It includes 90 small villas with four rooms each. The **Riu Naiboa** *($180 US all-inclusive; tv, ℜ, ⊗, ≡, ≈)* offers modern and comfortable rooms located in a large, uninspiring multistory building. The **Riu Melao** *($190 US all-inclusive; tv, ℜ, ⊗, ≡, ≈)* has 244 very pretty rooms set in quaint villas. The **Riu Palace Macao** *($210 US all-inclusive; tv, ℜ, ⊗, ≡, ≈)* is one of the prettiest hotels in the region. The rooms, set in one large building, are splendid. The lobby, with its rich wooden accents, the restaurants and the bars are magnificent.

The rooms at the **Fiesta Bavaro** *($200 US, all-inclusive; Playa Bavaro,* ☎ *221-8149)* are set up inside small pastel buildings, surrounded by lush vegetation. The pretty complex is located on huge grounds with direct access to the beach. As with the other hotels along the coast, swimming and other sports activities are offered as a means of enjoying the ocean's turquoise waters.

The **Caribbean Village Bavaro** *($200 US, all-inclusive; ℜ, ≈, ℝ, ≡; Playa Bavaro)* has 540 rooms spread throughout nine several-story buildings. The property is bordered by the superb Punta Cana beach. A whole slew of sporting activities are offered here, and shows are presented in the evening. Activities are organized especially for children.

The **Bavaro Beach Resort Hotel & Casino** *($200 US, all-inclusive; ≡, ≈, ℜ; Playa Bavaro,* ☎ *686-5797,* ≈ *682-2169)* is the largest hotel complex in the Dominican Republic. Capable of lodging 3,000 visitors, the Bavaro has four buildings (Hotel Beach, Hotel Garden, Aparthotel Golf, Hotel Casino) spread over an immense site, which is beautifully landscaped along a two-kilometre-long beach. No expense has been spared to offer guests a wide choice of sporting activities, including deep-sea fishing, scuba diving and golf on a superb 18-hole course. Guests can also choose between 15 bars, nine restaurants, three discos and seven pools. Do not arrive without reservations, as the guard at the entrance will probably make you wait for quite a while.

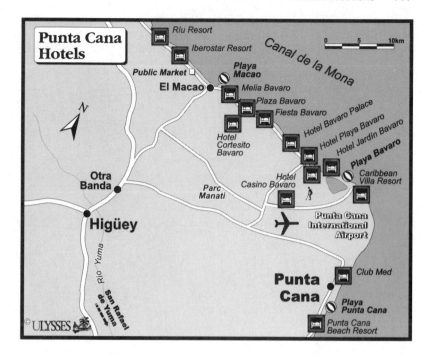

Punta Cana Hotels

Ríu Resort

Iberostar Resort

Public Market

Canal de la Mona

Playa Macao

El Macao

Melia Bavaro

Plaza Bavaro

Fiesta Bavaro

Hotel Bavaro Palace

Hotel Playa Bavaro

Hotel Jardín Bavaro

Playa Bavaro

Hotel Cortesito Bavaro

Parc Manati

Hotel Casino Bavaro

Caribbean Villa Resort

Otra Banda

Higüey

Río Yuma

San Rafael de Yuma

© ULYSSES

Punta Cana International Airport

Punta Cana

Playa Punta Cana

Club Med

Punta Cana Beach Resort

0   5   10km

The **Iberostar Hotel** *($280 US, all-inclusive; ℜ, ≈, ℝ, ≡; Punta Cana)* is a magnificent 750-room complex located on a vast property shaded by coconut trees and offering direct access to the superb Punta Cana beach. The rooms are tastefully decorated, and each one has either a balcony or terrace. Horses can be rented here as well.

The **Club Med** *($260 US, all-inclusive; ≡, ≈, ℜ; Punta Cana ☎ 687-2767, ≈ 687-2896)* is equipped with beautiful rooms in several three-floor buildings facing either the sea or a coconut grove. The key to Club Med's success is in the extensive choice of activities available from morning to night. As far as sports go, guests can try snorkelling, scuba diving, windsurfing, sailing, tennis and archery. They can even try their hands at circus acts, like the trapeze. Children are in for a special treat as well, since the Miniclub features an incredible variety of games and facilities. In the evening, you can take in live entertainment and dance at an open-air disco. The huge buffet meals prepared nightly by the chefs of the main restaurant are delicious. A second, quieter restaurant by the beach specializes in seafood. Though it is possible to stay for only one day, one- or two-week packages are a better value.

The **Punta Cana Beach Resort** *($160 all inclusive; ℜ, ⊗, ≡, ≈; Punta Cana, ☎ 541-2714, ≈ 547-2200)* is a little village unto itself spread out along the magnificent Punta Cana beach. The property is well laid out, with lots of flowers, plants and trees lending the place the feel of a tropical paradise. The rooms are large, prettily decorated and brightly painted. They are set in numerous small pavilions and a few large multi-storied buildings. The pack age deal includes two meals per day and access to all the activities offered on site. In the evening, there is fine dining at the excellent La Cana restaurant.

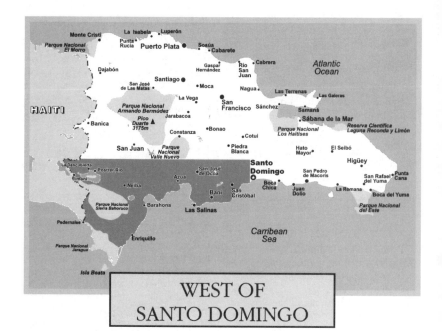

WEST OF SANTO DOMINGO

The southwestern region of the Dominican Republic includes the area along the Caribbean Sea between Santo Domingo and Barahona, as well as the point of land at the southwest extremity of the country, where Lago Enriquillo, the Bahoruco Valley and the Bahoruco mountain range are located. The vegetation varies widely from one part of the region to another, ranging from subtropical forest to desert. The change is visible as you move west, fields of sugar cane and palm groves give way to scrub growth and cacti. The sparse vegetation in this part of the Dominican Republic differs from that found elsewhere in the country, and creates a hauntingly desolate landscape of unique panoramas.

Because part of it is so arid, the southwest is a poor region. Compared to other parts of the country, the villages of thatched-roofed houses are bare and

drab and the vegetation, sparse. In contrast, the Bahoruco Valley is characterized by incredibly lush green fields. Coffee, sugar cane, grapes and bananas are all grown here in large quantities. The steep Caribbean coastline, with little coves nestled here and there, adds to the beauty of the region.

While the local tourism industry is still relatively undeveloped, the area has much to recommend it, including untouched beaches and interesting national parks. Some cities, such as Barahona, have begun to promote tourism, making it easier for visitors to explore the entire region. Among other things an airport has just been built. As yet there are no bustling resort towns like those on the northern coast (Sosúa, Cabarete), and so far only a handful of comfortable hotels have opened.

FINDING YOUR WAY AROUND

A fairly good highway links Santo Domingo and **Barahona**; it goes through **San Cristóbal**, **Baní** and **Azua**. Though there are only a few villages along the road, traffic is fairly heavy. There are gas stations in all the larger towns. Buses also make stops throughout the region.

San Cristóbal

To reach **San Cristóbal** from Santo Domingo, stay on the road that follows the water (Avenida George Washington). You will eventually end up on the highway that runs along the southern coast of the island and through San Cristóbal.

Bus station: buses heading west and elsewhere on the island stop on the way out of town.

Baní and Azua

The highway goes through both these towns.

Bus station (Baní): at the western edge of town, next to the market.

Bus station (Azua): buses heading east-west stop in front of the central park (Calles Emilio Prodan and Colón).

Barahona

The highway splits in two a few kilometres beyond Azua; to get to Barahona, keep left.

The highway from Santo Domingo becomes Calle Jaime Mota in Barahona. It crosses the whole town all the way to Calle Enriquillo along the sea, where all the hotels are located. This road provides access to the southern part of the peninsula.

Bus station: at the corner of Calles Padre Bellini and 30 de Marzo, a few steps from the central park.

Parque Nacional Isla Cabritos

If you go beyond Azua, where the highway splits in two, and follow the road to the right (when coming from Santo Domingo), you'll end up in the **Parque Nacional Isla Cabritos**, at the centre of Lago Enriquillo. To get there, head towards the northern shore of the lake. Take the turn-off after the village of Mella. Follow this road to Neiba and then head west. The entrance to the park is in the town of La Descubierta.

Haiti

To reach Haiti, take the highway to Jimaní, the main border crossing between the two countries.

PRACTICAL INFORMATION

San Cristóbal

The road from Santo Domingo goes through the centre of San Cristóbal.

The **Codetel** is at 14 Calle Palo Hincado.

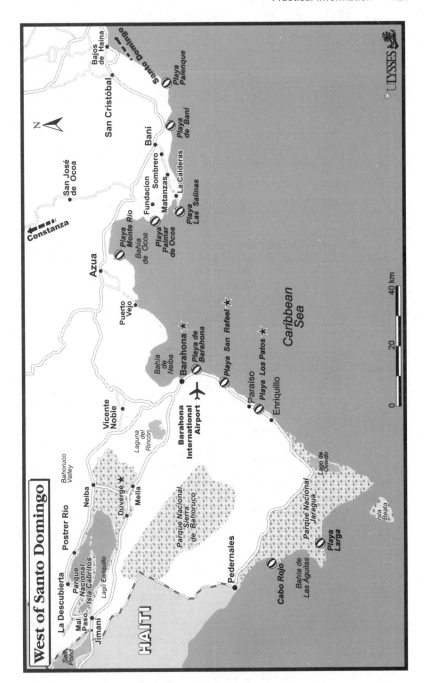

Baní

The highway leads directly to the downtown area, centred around Calles Padre Bellini and Mella. There are many shops and restaurants here. At the western edge of town, you'll find a market.

The **Codetel** is at 3 Calle Padre Bellini.

Azua

The highway passes through downtown Azua, which is bordered by Avenidas Emilio Prodan and Colón, around the park. There are a few banks and shops on Avenida Emilio Prodan, and some small restaurants near the park.

The **Codetel** is at 118 Calle 19 de Marzo.

Barahona

The downtown area is centred around the central park, on Calles Jaime Mota and Padre Bellini. There are several little shops and restaurants here. Most of the banks are on Calle Jaime Mota.

The **Codetel** is next to the central park at 36 Calle Nuestra Senora del Rosario.

Neiba

The road from Barahona leads directly to the centre of town.

The **Codetel** is on Calle Cambronal, at the corner of Calle Felipe Gonzales.

 EXPLORING

San Cristóbal ★

The history of San Cristóbal began in 1575 with arrival of colonists attracted by the discovery of gold in the Río Haina. The city was named after a fort that had been built in the region under the orders of Christopher Columbus. The city prospered and even played a part in Dominican history, as the site of the signing of the country's first constitution (November 6th, 1844). It is better known, however, as the birthplace of Trujillo, the Dominican Republic's terrible dictator (1891-1961). San Cristóbal is far from a haven of tranquillity, rather, it is a bustling urban centre with 140,000 inhabitants. It is therefore preferable to visit the city on day trips from Santo Domingo, which lies only about thirty kilometres away and has much more in the way of accommodations.

A number of magnificent buildings were erected in San Cristóbal in the first half of the 20th century, several of which belonged to President Trujillo. These buildings, now in ruins, reflect a tiny fraction of the wealth the dictator accumulated during his reign. Built in the 19th century, the **Iglesia de San Cristóbal**, facing the town's central park, houses Trujillo's tomb. The interior is attractive; the religious scenes painted in the choir are particularly striking.

On a hillside just outside the city is the **Castillo del Cerro**, formerly owned by President Trujillo — though he didn't like it and never lived here. This magnificent 1920s residence had six living rooms, each decorated in a different style. As the house is presently under renovation, it is difficult to get a true sense of its original beauty and opulence.

The **Casa Caoba**, or "mahogany house", located on the outskirts of town, was Trujillo's country house. It too sits atop a hill overlooking the city. The house has been abandoned and is in even worse shape than Castillo del Cerro. There are plans to restore it, but the work could take many years.

The Baní - Barahona Route ★

The section of highway between Baní and Barahona is over 100 kilometres long and crosses beautiful and often desolate countryside. The drier climate brings a gradual change in the vegetation; it becomes sparser and less verdant as scrub growth replaces luxuriant palm trees. Beyond Azua, huge stretches of dry earth and sandy hills dominate the landscape. The **Neiba Mountain Range** begins in this region, and the road becomes steeper. Before long, you'll start spotting cacti, which are plentiful in this area.

The region between Azua and Barahona is even more arid and consequently less populated. Villages along this virtually uninhabited road become increasingly far apart. The barren land produces so little that this is one of the poorest regions in the Dominican Republic. The contrast between the rest of the country and these modest villages, with their small huts of bleached dry wood and scraggy vegetation is striking. A startling and unexpected spectacle unfolds before your eyes as you weave your way through the bare hills. In fact, the road merits exploration simply for the beauty of the terrain through which it passes.

Baní

The province of Baní, whose name is a native word for "abundance of water", is a productive agricultural area where coffee, sugar cane and bananas grow in abundance. The region also prospers from natural riches in the form of large salt deposits, particularly those in Puerto Hermoso. The pretty town of Baní, capital of the province, suggests a certain affluence, due to the beautiful residences and buildings around **Parque Duarte**. Located in the centre of the city, the park is a pleasant verdant place to rest, as well as the hub of most of the local activity. Though its authenticity is appealing, the city has little to offer visitors.

South of Baní, beautiful wild beaches await those who prefer tranquillity to comfortable tourist resorts. There are three noteworthy beaches in the area: Palenque, Baní and Las Salinas (see p 129). Only about 60 kilometres from Santo Domingo, but far from the frenzy of tourist development, Baní is a charming place to pull off the road heading west.

From Baní, there are two options. Either continue west on the highway toward Azua, or take the little road to Las Salinas, which crosses the villages of Sombrero, Matanzas and Las Calderas.

Las Salinas

The town of Las Salinas developed on a long spit that projects into the Caribbean Sea. The location was propitious for a salt-works (hence the name of the town), and the ocean hid a million treasures. This certainly explains the size of the town, which is relatively large for this arid region of the country. Proving to be very authentic with its charming, brightly coloured houses, Las Salinas is mainly known today for its long, grey-sand beach, which is the pleasure of the many Dominicans who come to swim at it on Sundays.

Azua

Azua was founded in 1504 by Diego Velásquez on the shores of the Caribbean Sea. The town soon enjoyed a period of prosperity as a port city before being destroyed by an earthquake. Azua was rebuilt five kilometres away on its present site at the foot of the Ocoa mountains. The town's location, halfway between Santo Domingo and the border with Haiti, has been a source of trouble; several times in its early history, Azua was set on fire by French invaders. The main attractions, both survivors of this bygone era, are the **Puerto Viejo**, or old port, and the **ruins** of the old city.

Azua is the second biggest city on the road through southwestern Dominican Republic. It is located in a rich agricultural area where sugar cane, rice, coffee and fruit are the main crops. The economy of the region is also boosted by mining (mineral and precious stones) and lumbering. This busy city is not particularly charming or relaxing. While Azua offers all the conveniences one might need on a road trip, the town of Barahona, to the south, is a more enjoyable place to stop.

There are two wild beaches nearby, Monte Río and Blanca (see p 129).

The Southwestern Peninsula

Barahona is essentially the gateway to the peninsula; a large city, it serves as a departure point for travellers wishing to explore the southernmost tip of the Dominican Republic. Two roads leaving from Barahona provide access to the southwestern peninsula. The first one runs along the Caribbean, then heads over to Pedernales, on the Haitian border. The second crosses the northern part of the peninsula, passing Lago Enriquillo and going all the way to Jimaní, gateway to Haiti. Because of fluctuations in rainfall throughout the territory, there is a wide variety of plant life, and the landscape undergoes several transformations, ranging from desert zones around Lago Enriquillo to sub-tropical forests which cover part of the mountain chain. There are few historic relics or luxurious tourist developments on this peninsula, whose appeal lies instead in its varied and singular landscape.

Before arriving in Barahona, you'll notice many fields of sugar cane. During Trujillo's years as president, thousands of hectares of land around the city were seized for the cultivation of sugar cane. This was extremely difficult for the locals (who earned meagre wages in unbearable working conditions), but very profitable for the generalissimo.

Fishing is another important economic activity in this coastal region, and a relatively lucrative one as well. The waters around this point of the island are teeming with fish and shellfish, due to the shallow marine platform along the peninsula, which is ideal for the development of many species. A portion of the local population is thus able to live off the sea. You'll no doubt have a chance to visit one of the charming fishing villages along the coast, with a scattering of colourful little boats bobbing on the waves in the distance.

Barahona ★

Located on Bahía de Neiba, Barahona has a population of some 50,000, making it the largest urban centre in this arid landscape. It is nevertheless pleasant due to its enviable location on the Caribbean Sea, hemmed in on one side by a pretty bay and on the other by impressive cliffs.

The bustle and excitement of Barahona is countered by peaceful green spaces offering benches and shade. In fact, as with most towns in the country, the downtown area developed around a central park, where strollers can sit and take a break before continuing their exploration of the Creole cottages, little shops and restaurants that line the streets. There are no major attractions here but the town is typically Dominican. For a picturesque example of what this means, visit the lively public market near to the central park. Barahona also has a busy port that serves all the small neighbouring communities and therefore plays a central role in the region's economy. Follow Avenida Enriquillo if you want to check it out.

With a selection of good beaches located close by, Barahona seems poised to develop into one of the country's biggest tourist hubs. It has yet to become one of the Dominican Republic's

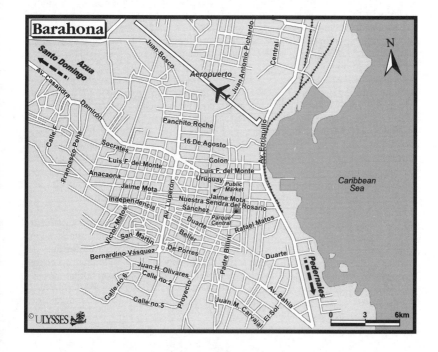

huge resort towns, like those on the northern coast, or to the east of Santo Domingo. Several modest hotels have been built to cater to visitors and the area's first major hotel complex was recently completed. The local tourism industry should therefore take off in the coming years, especially because an airport capable of receiving large planes has just been built here.

If you exit the city by Avenida Enriquillo, you'll follow the southern coast of the peninsula and pass by several beautiful sandy beaches, including Barahona, Los Patos and San Rafael.

The Barahona - Pedernales Route ★★

Leaving Barahona, the road heads south, passing through some of the most beautiful scenery in the Dominican Republic. A section of the road is flanked by the Bahoruco mountain range on one side and the Caribbean on the other. The ocean views along much of the road are stunning. In some places, the play of sunlight on vast stretches of open water creates distant mirages of shifting blue islands. Waves crash into steep cliffs that occasionally give way to little coves where, instead, waves wash up on golden sandy beaches perfect for swimming. Here and there, quaint villages spring up by the side of the road, reminding us that people live here. This region is less arid, with lush verdant vegetation. Continuing south, the road follows the shoreline to Enriquillo, the last seaside village. It then heads inland towards Pedernales, eventually following the Bahoruco mountains. Running along a hillside, the route is still charming, though the scenery is less impressive. The point of land farther south is part of Parque Nacional Jaragua.

The little village of **Paraíso** lies next to the beautiful Bahoruco beach. The village has little to offer besides its Caribbean charm. The beach, on the other hand, is a stunning ribbon of sand washed by refreshing and limpid waters.

The road across the peninsula ends at **Pedernales**, a little port city at the western extremity of the Dominican Republic, on the Haitian border. The town has little to recommend it, though there are some nice beaches in the area, including **Cabo Rojo**.

Around Lago Enriquillo

Another road runs through the northern part of the peninsula, from Barahona to Jimaní; it then heads back south, thus skirting around stunning Lago Enriquillo. A few modest, peaceful hamlets have sprouted up here and there, cut off from the frantic pace of life in the big, modern urban centres. The centrepiece of the trip, however, is Lago Enriquillo, an amazing stretch of salt water visible in the distance for a good part of the ride. Before setting out, take note that careful driving is a must the entire length of this little-used road, as many animals make their way across it, and parts of it are in poor condition.

Located in a region with particularly scraggly vegetation, **Neiba** is a small, dusty town made up mainly of modest little wooden houses. Life seems to move at a completely different tempo here than in the big modern towns: there are only a few stores in the centre of town, the main streets are lively in a quiet sort of way, and the residents go calmly about their business. The place offers quite a change of scenery, especially compared to the bustling villages elsewhere on the island, but that lends it a certain charm.

You'll also pass through **Postrer Río**, another simple little hamlet that seems untouched by time. Few visitors come here, and the place is not really

equipped to welcome travellers; some residents even seem hostile.

Lago Enriquillo, the largest lake in the Caribbean, is definitely one of the most impressive natural attractions in the region. It is located some 35 metres below sea level, and the concentration of salt in its waters is three times higher than that of the Caribbean. As there is little precipitation in this region, the shores of the lake are desert-like, especially to the west, where nothing but cacti and a few dwarf plants grow. There are three islands in the centre of the lake, **Barbarita**, **Islita** and **Cabritos**. Only Isla Cabritos and the remarkable wildlife that inhabits its shores are protected by a national park (see p 128).

Made up of small, wooden houses, the village of **La Descubierta** will delight visitors in search of picturesque spots that make them feel far from home, though there is nothing enchanting about the place itself. It is a sizeable village (the largest in the region), but has managed to retain a peaceful, rural atmosphere. La Descubierta has all the resources necessary to welcome visitors, who stop here mainly because the town is the starting point for excursions to the Isla Cabritos national park.

Trips to the **Parque Isla Cabritos** do not start in downtown La Descubierta, but rather at a small station a few kilometres east of the village, where boats set out to conquer Lago Enriquillo and its fascinating animal life. The only sign showing how to get there from the road is rusted and easy to miss.

Jimaní, located close to the Haitian border, is the last Dominican town on the highway leading westward to Port-au-Prince, the capital of the neighbouring country. Strolling down the main street on market days, it would be hard to ignore the Haitian presence in the air, as the fruit and vegetable stalls contain scores of handcrafted items from across the border.

The village of **Mal Paso** is set right on the Haitian border. In fact it looks more like an enormous market that a border-crossing because such numbers of Haitian craftspeople come here to sell, often at minuscule prices, their most beautiful pieces. This popular site is unique in the country and shoppers can choose from among thousands of finds.

The road that runs along the south shore of the lake leads back to Barahona. It is in excellent condition and offers a chance to contemplate more lovely, arid landscapes, with the perpetually calm waters of the lake off in the distance. It leads through several modest towns whose sole interest lies in their authenticity. The only food you'll be able to find here are fruits and vegetables displayed in a few forlorn stalls. Only one hamlet, **Duvergé**, is big enough to mention, though it has no attractions to speak of.

The road leads eastward to Barahona.

 PARKS

Parque Nacional Jaragua

Parque Nacional Jaragua, which encompasses the southern extremity of the southwest peninsula, is the largest national park in the Dominican Republic. It includes all the land on this part of the peninsula, some of the sea-bottom along the coast, and two islands, **Beata** and **Alto Velo**.

To date, no tour outfits offer excursions aimed at introducing visitors to the beauty of this vast, arid stretch of land covered with scraggly vegetation. The government's medium-term plan is to develop the region, but for the time being you'll have to settle for visiting the edge of the park; it is virtually impossible to make your way into the heart of this gigantic wild garden, as there are no marked trails leading through it. A trail on the west side of the peninsula does, however, make it possible to visit a tiny part of the park, including one of the loveliest beaches in the country, **Bahía de las Águilas ★**, where you can admire scores of tropical birds from afar, and also, if you're lucky, some flamingoes.

Parque Nacional Bahoruco

This park protects much of the Bahoruco mountain range. The vegetation varies with the altitude, and the large variety of orchids is particularly striking. The park holds much of interest to enthusiasts of tropical plant life; unfortunately, however, adequate facilities have not been developed for visitors.

Parque Nacional Isla Cabritos ★

Isla Cabritos is one of three islands in Lago Enriquillo, and the only one where the rich flora and fauna have been protected by the creation of a park. To reach the island, you must cross amazing Lago Enriquillo, the largest salt-water lake in the Caribbean and home to a number of fascinating wildlife

A few colourful cottages in the fishing village of Bayahibe – Michel Gagné

Pretty Iglesia Santa Barbara (Santo Domingo) - T.B.

species that can not be seen anywhere else in the country: American crocodiles up to two metres long, pink flamingoes, iguanas and rhinoceros. Excursions are organized to provide visitors with an opportunity to observe these fascinating animals that are otherwise very difficult to see. In fact the chances of seeing a crocodile are quite slim as they usually spend the day hidden under water lilies. The best time to spot them is early in the morning or as the sun sets. A visit is nevertheless quite something. If such an excursion doesn't interest you at least go to the lake shore where tropical birds, including pink flamingoes, can be seen.

A few kilometres before the village of La Descubierta, a rusted sign by the side of the road announces the entrance of Parque Isla Cabritos. The only building is a rundown wooden shack. Excursions to Parque Isla Cabritos start here, but you'll find the person who organizes them at the Brahamas restaurant, in the village of La Descubierta. It generally costs a minimum of 400 pesos to rent a boat (up to 10 people can share the cost), 50 pesos per person for a permit to enter the park and 80 pesos to get from the village to the starting point of the tour. If you get on well with the person in charge (at the restaurant), you shouldn't have to pay for anything else, but the price of the excursion should be determined before setting out and paid when you get back. It is possible to camp on the island, but to do so you have to get a government permit, issued by the park office in Santo Domingo (see p 69).

BEACHES

Baní

There are a several pretty beaches along the shore south of Baní, including **Palenque**, **Baní**, **Las Salinas** and **Palmar de Ocoa**. The **Las Salinas** beach is located about 20 kilometres south of Baní, beside the village of the same name. It runs along the west side of a strip of land that stretches out into the Caribbean, forming a small cove with calm waters that are perfect for swimming. Lined with shrubs, it boasts a pretty setting. Some people might be put off by the grey sand, which is nonetheless just as soft and clean as the golden sand of the other beaches in the country. If you are among these, or the lively atmosphere here does not appeal to you (on Sunday, the beach is overrun by fun-loving Dominicans) and you have an all-terrain vehicle, you can head to the more beautiful, unspoiled **Palmar de Ocoa** beach. To do so, follow the little road from the hamlet of Fundación. The ride is hardly relaxing, but the beach is worth it.

Azua

Around Azua, you'll have no trouble finding a few strips of golden sand where you can relax and soak up the sun. One of the more noteworthy of these is the **Monte Río** beach. To get there, take the dirt road on the way into town (2-3 kilometres); keep your eyes peeled, though, as the beach is only indicated by a small sign. You might also opt for the decidedly prettier **Blanca** beach, located west of town.

The Southwestern Peninsula

In **Barahona**, there is only one beach, itself of limited appeal; the poor quality of the water (due to the proximity of the port) and the resident jellyfishes detract considerably from its charm. On the way out of town, on the grounds of the Hotel Riviera, you'll find another part of the beach, which has lovely golden sand and is just fine as far as cleanliness is concerned. Still, the beaches south of Barahona have more to offer.

On the road to Pedernales, you'll pass several magnificent coves well suited to swimming or lounging about. You could start with the **San Rafael ★** beach, whose presence is indicated by a single, modest sign. To get there, take a very steep dirt road that runs through the hamlet, threading its way between the fishermen's shacks. At the end of the road, you'll find a superb beach covered with pebbles, in the heart of a magnificent bay surrounded by steep hills. A stream has created a small natural pool here. The only sign of development is a single little restaurant (which has grown over the years). On weekends and holidays, however, the peaceful atmosphere is somewhat disrupted by Dominican vacationers.

Continuing southward, you'll come to another lovely, untouched beach, the **Los Patos ★** beach, which is also covered with pebbles. A real little paradise for those who love solitude, the beach attracts very few visitors aside from the children from the neighbouring village, who come here to play.

 OUTDOOR ACTIVITIES

 Scuba Diving

Off the shores of Barahona and along the coast, there is a wealth of marine animal life, creating natural scenes of remarkable beauty. You can explore these outstanding underwater landscapes by taking part in a scuba diving or snorkelling expedition organized by the diving centre on the beach of the **Riviera** hotel in Barahona.

 Bird- and Crocodile-watching

Lago Enriquillo is the largest nature reserve for that most formidable of reptiles, the American crocodile. If you'd like to observe this ferocious animal in its natural habitat, you'll have to join an excursion (see p 128) to the centre of the lake, where the beasts can be seen in the early morning and late afternoon. This region is also wonderful for bird-watching, as the shores of the lake are home to scores of tropical birds, including flamingoes.

Parque Jaragua, which covers the entire southern portion of the southwest peninsula of the Dominican Republic, is another unparalleled refuge for all sorts of birds, and though it isn't really possible to make your way into the heart of this wild garden, avian species can be spotted all along the shore (if you take the trail south of Pedernales).

ACCOMMODATIONS

San Cristóbal

The choice of hotels in San Cristóbal is very limited; for this reason, we don't recommend spending the night here. It makes more sense to stay in Santo Domingo or even Boca Chica, where there are more pleasant hotels.

Baní

Located on the highway to Barahona, Baní has the necessary facilities to feed travellers, but the town just isn't interesting enough to spend more than a couple of hours here. Those who do choose to spend the night, however, will find some comfortable hotels. The **Hotel Alba** *($18 US; at the corner of Calles Padre Bellini and Mella)*, in a quiet part of the city, near the central park offers satisfactory rooms with simple furnishings.

Las Salinas

The **Salinas High Wind Center Hotel** *($US 35; ≡, ≈, ℛ; ☎ 223-7144)*, an ochre-coloured building on the way into Las Salinas, is the only hotel worth mentioning in this region. Though its name might lead you to think otherwise, it is a modest little hotel with a few decent rooms and a pool. It has the advantage of being built at the edge of a small beach.

Azua

Like Baní, Azua is not the tourist paradise you may be looking for, and has little to offer in the way of accommodation — no luxury hotels, and only a few modest bed and breakfasts. You can nevertheless stay inexpensively on Calle Colón, where various low-budget hotels are located.

Barahona

Barahona has the best selection of comfortable hotels. Budget travellers will also find simple but adequate rooms in one of the small hotels in the centre of town. The bigger more luxurious hotels are on Avenida Enriquillo, facing the sea.

The **Hotel Las Magnolias** *($16 US; ⊗, ≡; 13 Calle Uruguay at the corner of Le Cacique; ☎ 524-2244)* is conveniently located near the bus station. The rooms are well kept, and some have air conditioning. The service is courteous, and the rooms are simply decorated but comfortable enough for the price.

The **Guayocuya** *($20 US; ⊗; Avenida Enriquillo)* hotel is a pink building attractively located by the sea. Set back from the road, it offers a peaceful atmosphere. The rooms are clean, sparsely furnished and functional.

The **Hotel Caribe** *($20 US; ⊗, ℛ; Avenida Enriquillo)* is a modern white building located at the edge of town. It has spacious and comfortable but otherwise unspectacular rooms, each with a clean private bathroom. Good value.

The **Riviera Beach** *($US 75 bkfst incl.; ≡, ≈, ℜ; Calle Enriquillo, ☎ 524-5111)* is without question the loveliest and most comfortable hotel in town. Its two elegant white stucco buildings stand in the centre of a large piece of property giving onto the sea. Guests thus get to enjoy the most peaceful setting imaginable, a pretty beach and a lovely garden full of flowers, the perfect place to relax. Everything has been designed to ensure that your stay is a pleasant one: the pool is large, the restaurant serves delicious food and the spacious, airy rooms are attractively decorated with curtains in tropical hues and have a large balcony and big windows opening onto the garden.

South of Barahona

To relax in complete peace and quiet, go to the **Club Hotel El Quemaito** *($US 40; ≡, ≈, ℜ; 10 km south of Barahona, on the highway, ☎ 545-1496)*, located about 10 kilometres south of Barahona, atop a cliff that offers a splendid view of the shimmering water stretching to the horizon. Besides its magnificent site, it has about 15 spacious, well-kept rooms, an inviting garden and a small restaurant *($$)* with a varied menu.

La Descubierta

Those wishing to take an excursion on Lago Enriquillo can stay in Barahona and set out early in the morning (in order to arrive early enough to see the crocodiles) or spend the night in La Descubierta. The latter has a few small inns that could hardly be called charming, but offer a basic level of comfort that is fine for one night. One of these is the **Hostal del Lago** *($US 10; ⊗)*, a small wooden house with reasonably well-kept rooms.

RESTAURANTS

Baní

It's hard to miss **Pollo Rey** *($; Calle Bellini; the restaurant has a second location near the market, on the west edge of town)*, since there are signs for it along the highway for at least five kilometres before the city. This busy fast-food restaurant serves decent breaded chicken for a few pesos. Since buses often stop here, meal-times can bring long line-ups. There is another **Pollo Rey** *(Calle Billini)* in the centre of town, on a quieter street. The dining room there is a little more comfortable.

There are many little restaurants near the central park. As well, you can buy fresh fruits and vegetables from the market at the western edge of the city.

Barahona

Restaurants and food stalls line Calle Enriquillo, which runs along the sea. These places are easy to find, and usually have nice terraces.

La Rocca Restaurant *($$; adjacent to the Hotel Caribe)* is a long wooden building that opens onto the street. Beneath a roof made of palm fronds, you can enjoy delicious local fish and seafood dishes in a peaceful, friendly atmosphere.

The **Brisas del Caribe** *($$-$$$; Avenida Enriquillo)* has a large terrace that looks out onto Avenida Enriquillo and is decorated with wooden furniture, a very pleasant place to have dinner. This restaurant is sure to appeal to visitors who like lots of choice, as the menu is extremely varied, ranging from Chinese food to pizza, and including meat, chicken, fish and seafood dishes. The only letdown is that the meat is not always top quality.

Melo's Café *($; Calle Anacaona)* is a friendly spot facing the Las Magnolias hotel. Just a few tables make up the decor. Delicious breakfasts are served as well as snacks during the day. The service is friendly.

The restaurant in the **Hotel Riviera** *($$-$$$; Calle Enriquillo,* ☎ *524-5111)* has one big advantage: it is air conditioned. You can thus spend a cool, comfortable evening in a lovely dining room, without having to battle any mosquitoes (there are a lot of them in this area). The menu, which changes daily, is short, but the food is always good and served in generous portions.

La Descubierta

Excursions to Isla Cabritos park start at the **Brahamas** restaurant *($; in the centre of town)*, where you can also grab a bite to eat. The menu includes *pica pollo* dishes.

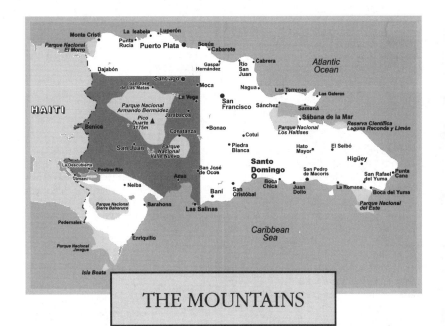

THE MOUNTAINS

Most visitors who stay in seaside resorts cannot imagine that this country, primarily known for the splendour of its beaches, also conceals a mountainous landscape of exceptional beauty. There can be no doubt, however, that the mountains of the Cordillera Centrale are one of the most eloquent testimonies to the stunning geographical diversity that is the Dominican Republic.

Starting from the vast plains of the Cibao valley or the southwestern part of the country, winding roads climb up to this wild region where high, verdant summits succeed one another, stretching out as far as the eye can see. With the exception of a few rare agglomerations nestled in the hollows of valleys or along narrow plateaus, the biggest of these being Jarabacoa and Constanza, the Cordillera Centrale is huge, virgin territory. These "Dominican Alps", as the Cordillera Centrale is wont to be called here, form the most impressive chain of mountains in the Caribbean. Indeed, lost among the clouds, its highest peak, the Pico Duarte (3,175 metres), surpasses all other summits in the country as well as those of the West Indies.

For several years now, the Cordillera Centrale has been a popular holiday resort, though it was once known only to Dominicans themselves who came mostly during the summer months to take advantage of its cool temperatures, play golf or go horseback riding. The growing infatuation with outdoor activities now attracts an increasing number of foreign visitors to the region; leaving from large coastal tourism complexes, excursions are now organized on a regular basis, as the cordillera's main cities have improved their facilities remarkably.

FINDING YOUR WAY AROUND

Travellers can reach this region from the southwestern part of the country (the Barahona region) or from the Cibao valley.

From the southwestern part of the country: the road between San José de Ocoa and Constanza can seem very attractive, as it shortens the trip by several dozen kilometres and allows travellers to avoid Santo Domingo. However, this rocky trail, which runs for approximately 80 kilometres, is in very bad condition and if travelling by car, chances of experiencing mechanical breakdowns are considerable; there are no mechanics between the two cities, of course. Four-wheel drive vehicles generally make it through alright. The average driving speed on this road is about 30 kph. Travellers take note: some recent maps show a road between Padre Las Casas and Constanza. In reality, this is nothing more than a path that can only be travelled on horseback.

From Cibao valley: from the motorway that links Santo Domingo to Santiago, excellent roads run to Constanza (the road begins between Bonao and La Vega) and to Jarabacoa (the road begins just north of La Vega). The road to San José de Las Matas is in good condition; it starts from Santiago's western periphery.

San José de Ocoa

An excellent road breaks off from the highway about 20 kilometres west of Baní, allowing travellers to reach San José de Ocoa. For those who decide to continue on to Constanza, San José's service station is the last one on the road.

Constanza

The city of Constanza is located halfway up the magnificent mountain road. It is easily reached from the highway, between Bonao and La Vega; the interesting journey from San José de Ocoa, however, is far more perilous and takes approximately three hours.

Jarabacoa

Approximately 10 kilometres north of La Vega, a road heads west to Jarabacoa, passing several hotel complexes on the outskirts of the city. It is also possible to reach Jarabacoa from Constanza. The road is unpaved half the way, but it is passable by car.

San José de Las Matas

From downtown Santiago, take the new bridge over the Río Yaque del Norte. Shortly thereafter, turn left onto the well-maintained but winding road to San José de Las Matas (pay attention, there are very few signs).

EXPLORING

San José de Ocoa

A thriving little village, San José de Ocoa draws its principal sources of income from market gardening and trade. It is built across small valleys at

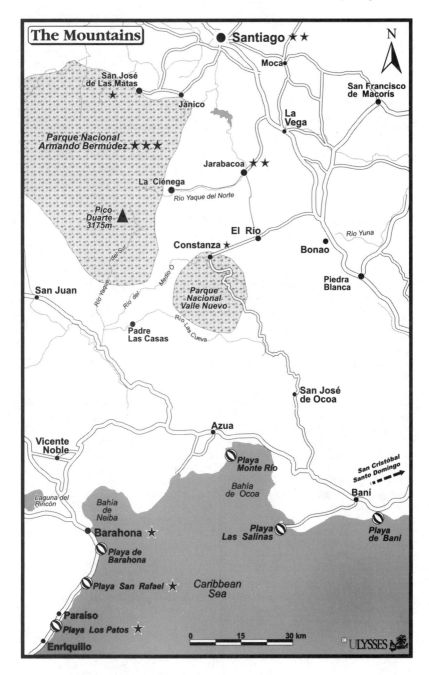

the foot of the magnificent Cordillera Centrale and constitutes the point of departure of the magnificent mountain road to Constanza. There are restaurants and a few modest hotels here as well. For over twenty years now, Father King, of Canadian origin, has been one of San José de Ocoa's most respected figures. Since his arrival, Father King has become involved in and poured a lot of energy into improving the financial condition of the community. Through his efforts, San José de Ocoa is quite frequently host to aid workers or Canadian students.

Constanza ★

The little town of Constanza is situated on a picturesque plain encircled by the mountains of the Cordillera Centrale. The fertile land in this region is the only place on the island where "exotic" fruit, such as raspberries, strawberries, peaches, pears and apples are grown. Coniferous trees are plentiful in certain areas as well, which is unusual at such a southern latitude. In fact, climatic conditions in Constanza make it something of an anomaly in the Caribbean; though summer temperatures are not that much lower than in the rest of the country, winter temperatures can drop to below freezing. Costanza thus has a charm all its own, and the magnificent mountain landscapes nearby make it a place for adventure and discovery.

The **Salto de Agua Blanca** ★ *(approximately 20 kilometres in the direction of San José de Ocoa, in Valle Nuevo's national reserve)* is a magnificent waterfall, standing about 30 metres tall. Not easily accessible, the area is much less developed than the falls of the Jarabacoa region.

Jarabacoa ★★

Located in the mountains of the Cordillera Centrale, at an altitude of more than 500 metres, Jarabacoa is blessed with pleasant temperatures all year long. Many wealthy Dominicans have their second home here, and the attractive houses that line the streets give the city an affluent look. The lively downtown area features an attractive little park, beside which stands an elegant colonial-style church.

While the city has its appeal, visitors and artists are more often attracted to the rolling countryside surrounding it. The region is also renowned for horse breeding, and equestrian sports are very popular here. Golf, swimming at the foot of waterfalls and in *balnearios*, as well as a host of other sports activities (river rafting, rock climbing, hiking, mountain biking) visitors can practise in the region, make Jarabacoa an increasingly popular holiday resort.

El Salto de Jimenoa ★★ *($1 US; 10 km from Jarabacoa on the way to La Vega, near the Alpes Dominicanos hotel, a road about 5 km long leads to the entrance to the site, from there it is a 5 min walk)* is one of the most beautiful waterfalls in the country. The water cascades down about 30 metres into a natural pool, where you can go swimming. The setting is idyllic. Footbridges lead up the river to the falls, and there is a little café that sells refreshments.

El Salto de Bayagate ★ *(free admission; heading to Constanza, take the third road to the right after the Pinar Dorada*

The Mountain Routes

San José de Ocoa to Constanza ★★★

Exceptionally beautiful mountain scenery unfolds all along the road between San José de Ocoa and Constanza. Lush coffee plantations hugging the slopes of verdant mountains quickly give way to narrow valleys with rivers raging through them. The spectacular panoramas encountered on this mountain pass through the region known locally as the Dominican Alps, are unequalled anywhere else in the country or even the Caribbean. In some completely uninhabited regions, the vegetation changes, consisting solely of coniferous trees. The only problem with this dirt road is its pitiable condition. Seasoned drivers can venture here by car, but will rarely be able to go faster than 30 kph. Expect this extraordinary and memorable drive to take at least five hours, and remember to fill up with gas, because there is no station between San José de Ocoa and Constanza. Also, the road is very poorly marked, so avoid driving it after dark. Despite all of this, the singular wild beauty of this mountainous and isolated region is worth the adventure.

Constanza to Jarabacoa ★★

Jarabacoa may be reached by crossing the mountainous landscape of Cordillera Centrale. Drive about 20 kilometres from Constanza towards La Vega, until you see a road branching off to the left, in the direction of Jarabacoa. This dirt road continues for another 30 kilometres to Jarabacoa, affording stunning panoramas along the way. Although not in very good shape, it is passable for cars, except in the days following heavy rains.

Santiago to San José de Las Matas ★

The road between Santiago and San José de Las Matas is in excellent condition, but tortuous and very steep in some places, both uphill and downhill. It offers a chance to admire a superb mountain landscape dominated by coffee plantations.

hotel, after a few kilometres, you'll see a parking lot, from there it's a 10-min walk) is not as spectacular a waterfall as the former, but is nonetheless very pretty. It, too, is about 30 metres high, with a natural pool at its base. The area, however, is less developed than Salto de Jimenoa.

The **Balneario de la Confluencia** (at the end of Calle Norberto Tiburcio), at the confluence of the Jimenoa and Yaque del Norte rivers, is a tumultuous whirl-pool where you can go swimming. There is a small park beside the *balneario*.

The **Balneario de la Guazaras** (take Calle Norberto Tiburcio, then turn left on the third road after the fork), near the centre of Jarabacoa, is a waterfall and a popular swimming spot with the city's younger population.

Jarabacoa is the ideal place from which to undertake an expedition to the summit of **Pico Duarte** ★★★ (see "Hiking" below), since the tourist information bureau here can work out a lot of the logistics for you. Rancho Baiguate *(Jarabacoa; ☎ 696-0318, 563-8005 or 574-4840, ≠ 574-4940)* also organizes expeditions to Pico Duarte. The hike begins in the village of La Cienega, 30 kilometres from Jarabacoa and accessible by car. At 3,175 metres, Pico Duarte is the highest mountain in the Caribbean.

San José de las Matas ★

San José de las Matas is a peaceful little town nestled among pine-covered mountains. It is a popular resort area with wealthy Dominicans. Throughout the year, the temperature is slightly cooler here than it is in Santiago or on the coast. San José is a charming and visibly prosperous town. Though there isn't much to do, the beautiful road that leads here makes the excursion worthwhile.

 PARKS

The **Parque Nacional Armando Bermudes** ★★★ is the largest park in the country. It protects the plants and wildlife of the untouched Cordillera Centrale. Unfortunately, the park is hard to get to and has very few facilities for visitors. Most people come just to climb Pico Duarte.

The **Parque Nacional Valle Nuevo**★ *(just south of Constanza)* spreads over

409 square kilometres. It shelters several conifers as well as cypresses growing in this area, trees that can be found practically nowhere else in the country. Approximately 250 species of plants and 65 species of birds have been counted on this reserve. The Valle Nuevo consists of a high plateau rising some 2,200 metres in altitude. From a hydrological point of view, the Valle Nuevo is very important because it is the source of two among four of the country's principal rivers: the Yuna and Nizao rivers.

 OUTDOOR ACTIVITIES

 Hiking

Climbing **Pico Duarte** ★★★, the highest mountain in the Caribbean (3,175 metres), is a challenge best taken on by hardy, well-equipped adventurers. Before embarking on such an excursion, visit the tourist information office in Jarabacoa, which can help you plan the long hike. It takes three days to cover the 46 kilometres (return) between the last village, La Cienega, and the top of Pico Duarte. You will need a sleeping bag (there are a few rudimentary huts along the way) warm clothes and food for three days. You must obtain a permit at the entrance of the park or at the tourist information office in Jarabacoa, and be accompanied by a guide. The **Rancho Baiguate** *(Jarabacoa, ☎ 696-0318, 563-8005 or 574-4840, ≠ 574-4940)* also organizes expeditions to Pico Duarte. There are a multitude of other hiking possibilities in the Jarabacoa region.

Horseback Riding

Horseback riding is the most popular sport in Jarabacoa. Horses can be rented in Parque La Confluencia, near the Salto de Bayagete, at the Pinar Dorado hotel and at Rancho Baiguate *(1 km past the hotel Pinar Dorado, ☎ 696-0318, 563-8005 or 574-4840, ↪ 574-4940).*

 Golf

There is a small nine-hole golf course just outside of Jarabacoa, near the Alpes Dominicanos hotel.

 River Rafting

River rafting has just recently become a very popular sports activity in the Jarabacoa region. Aboard a rubber dinghy large enough to transport a dozen people, the descents generally take place on the Río Yaque del Norte. The **Rancho Baiguate** *(1 km past Pinar Dorado, ☎ 696-0318, 563-8005 or 574-4840, ↪ 574-4940)* is one of the enterprises that organizes this type of activity.

Other Outdoor Activities

For the last few years, the **Rancho Baiguate** *(first road on the left after the Pinar Dorado hotel, ☎ 696-0318, 563-8005 or 574-4840, ↪ 574-4940)* has been specializing in organizing a host of outdoor activities: besides horseback riding, hikes and river rafting, visitors can practise such sports as mountain biking, rock climbing and hang-gliding.

 ACCOMMODATIONS

Constanza

Despite its somewhat uninviting appearance, the **El Gran** *($10 US; ⊗; on the way into the city)* hotel, has perfectly decent rooms on the second floor and quiet, wooded and relaxing surroundings.

Located on a quiet street, the **Mi Casa** *($10 US; ⊗; Calle Sanchez)* is a friendly family-run establishment. The guest rooms are not very big, but are nevertheless clean and pleasant. There is a restaurant on the ground floor.

The recently built **Mi Cabana Resort** *($25 US; K, ≈, ⊗; 1 km from downtown, ☎ 539-2930, ↪ 539-2929)* is a small residential complex that rents and sells small two-floor accommodations with a lovely view of Constanza. The place can seem isolated, especially since the complex is virtually unoccupied most of the time. To get there, take the road towards San José de Ocoa for about one kilometre.

Right next door, the **Nueva Suiza Hotel** should open for business soon, after many years of renovation. Perched on a hillside, it offers a striking view of Constanza.

Right in the vicinity of Constanza, the **Altocerro** *($30 US; ⊗; Colonia Kennedy, ☎ 686-0202)* is comprised of approximately 20 villas with one, two or three rooms, as well as ten hotel rooms. Though not very luxurious, the rooms are adequate. Camping sites are also available.

Jarabacoa

Jarabacoa has the greatest number of hotel rooms in the region. The least expensive are in the *cabañas* located at the city's entrance.

The **Hotel Hogar** *($20 US; ⊗, ℜ; downtown)* offers rooms with very basic furnishings. The interior courtyard, however, is peaceful and charming. This is the perfect place to meet locals or young Dominicans on vacation.

For a long time, the **Montana** *($20 US; ⊗, ≈, ℜ; on the highway, a few kilometres before Jarabacoa, ☎ 682-8181)* was the meeting place of illustrious Dominicans. Trujillo even had his own personal suite. Nowadays it seems to have fallen out of favour with rich Dominicans and is usually empty. The large rooms, however, are still quite pleasant, and boast an unobstructed view of the mountains.

Located in a pleasant area on the outskirts of town, the **Pinar Dorado** *($50 US all-inclusive; ⊗, ≈, tv, ℜ; just outside of town on the way to Constanza, ☎ 594-2820)* is a friendly hotel with comfortable, modern and spacious rooms, a big pool, a restaurant and beautiful gardens. Horseback riding excursions are organized here as well.

Located on a large, beautiful property, the **Alpes Dominicanos** *($50 US; ⊗, ≈, ℜ; on the highway, a few kilometres before Jarabacoa, ☎ 581-1462, ≈ 689-3703)* consists of ten small buildings. Nevertheless, the site is occupied mostly by luxurious private houses. The atmosphere is friendly and

relaxing, and the restaurant serves excellent cuisine (see p 143).

Somewhat removed from the city, deep in the country, the **Rancho Baiguate** *($52 US; ℜ, ⊗; first road on the left after the Pinar Dorado hotel, ☎ 696-0318, 563-8005 or 574-4840, ≈ 574-4940)* rents rooms that are very clean, though somewhat rudimentary for the price. Sports enthusiasts will undoubtedly find it advantageous to stay here, for the Rancho Baiguate is primarily known for the numerous outdoor activities it organizes.

San José de Las Matas

San José has a few inexpensive hotels. Downtown, you'll find the **Oasis** *($11 US; ℜ, ⊗; facing the Parque Central)*, whose rooms are pretty basic. You might also opt for the **Hotel Las Samanás***($11 US; ℜ, ⊗; Avenida Santiago, ☎ 578-8316)*, in the same category, located on the way into town.

The charming, comfortable **Hotel La Mansion** *($45 US; ℜ, ≈, ≡; near the village, ☎ 581-0395)* is ideally located in a large park overlooking San José. Guests have the choice between hotel rooms and cottages.

RESTAURANTS

Constanza

As in all small Dominican towns, the streets of Constanza are lined with cafes and restaurants that serve varied and inexpensive food. For a more elaborate meal, try the **Lorenzo** *($$; Calle El Conde)*. Its decor and four television screens are sure to please sports fans. As for the food, the *creolla* steak is particularly good. The restaurant is air-conditioned and serves less expensive meals during the day.

Jarabacoa

The **Jarabacoa Deli-Bar-B-Q** *($; Avenida Independencia on the way into town)* is a pleasant restaurant that serves grilled chicken in a family atmosphere.

The **Don Luis** *($$; next to Parque Duarte)* is well-located right in the heart of town, near Parque Duarte. It is a pleasant spot, but can get noisy. The menu consists mainly of steak and chicken prepared in a variety of ways. Great ice cream is available next door. The restaurant in the **Alpes Dominicanos Hotel** *($$$)* is worth a try for its refined Dominican and international cuisine and excellent service. The restaurant is in a small building near the swimming pool.

San José de las Matas

La Caoba *($-$$; Fernando Valerio, ☎ 578-8141)* is a pleasant restaurant that serves a variety of local dishes, including good grilled chicken. The host of this small, quiet spot makes every effort to provide service worthy of the best restaurants in Santo Domingo.

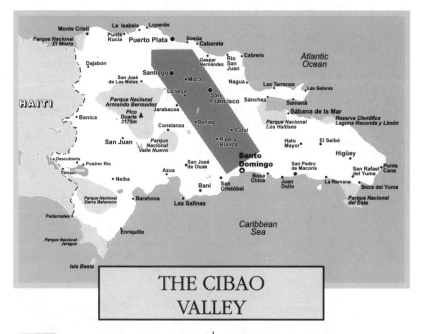

THE CIBAO
VALLEY

This vast region of the Dominican Republic encompasses the Cibao valley and the Cordillera Septentrionale mountain range, which isolates it from the Atlantic coast. The one common denominator is the quality of the arable land. An astonishing variety of agricultural products grow in these remarkably fertile lands, which also provide pasture for nearly all of the Dominican Republic's livestock. The fact that the Dominican Republic is one of the only islands that can produce most of its foodstuffs locally is above all due to the formidable agricultural potential of this region.

The natural riches of the central region have been coveted for many years. Christopher Columbus wrote enthusiastically in his logbook about the area's enormous potential. From the start of colonization, the Spaniards set out to tap its resources, cultivating the Cibao valley, though many were initially attracted here by the rich gold deposits discovered there. Some of the first European settlements in the New World began as fortifications built to protect gold mining operations. A number of these have grown into the most prosperous and important cities in the country. The Cibao valley is the most densely populated part of the Dominican Republic after the Santo Domingo region. The valley is home to the city of Santiago de los Caballeros, the second largest city in the Dominican Republic.

FINDING YOUR WAY AROUND

The highway that links Santo Domingo to Santiago de los Caballeros is the main trunk road crossing the Cibao valley. In the course of the last few years, major government funding has allowed for this arterial road to be widened. The highway now has two lanes in each direction for most of the length of the journey. Traffic, therefore, moves along much faster now, and the risk of accidents has been greatly reduced. This highway transects the cities of Bonao, La Vega and Santiago. Another major road allows drivers to quickly reach the Samaná peninsula from Santo Domingo. This road leaves the Santo Domingo-Santiago highway in Piedra Blanca, a small town approximately 60 kilometres north of Santo Domingo. It then goes through the city of Cotui, leading to Nagua on the Atlantic coast. Drivers can also easily reach the mountainous region, notably in Constanza and Jarabacoa, from the Cibao valley.

Santiago de Los Caballeros

If you are coming from La Vega and want to avoid the downtown area, turn right at the traffic circle in front of the Monumento. Several downtown arteries are one-way, including Calle del Sol, which goes from Parque Duarte towards the Monumento, and Calle Las Cabreras, which runs in the opposite direction.

The city's airport is less than two kilometres from downtown, near the highway leading to Monte Cristi.

Several car rental companies have offices in Santiago, including Budget ☎ 575-9230.

The Metro bus station is on Calle Maimón, at the corner of Avenida Duarte.

Moca

Several well-maintained roads lead to Moca from the highway that links Santiago to Santo Domingo. It is also possible to reach Moca from the tiny town of Sabaneta, just a few kilometres east of Cabarete on the Atlantic coast.

Cotui

From Santo Domingo, drivers can travel north on the highway leading to Santiago until reaching the small town of Piedra Blanca. From there, a road heading east leads straight to Cotui.

San Francisco de Macorís

From Cotui, continuing toward the northwestern part of the country, drivers can reach San Francisco by taking a left at the turn-off that suddenly appears a little after the small town of Pimentel. Conversely, the road on the right leads to Nagua, then to the Samaná peninsula. In other respects, for travellers coming from Santiago, San Francisco is a necessary crossing point on the way to the peninsula.

 PRACTICAL INFORMATION

Santiago de Los Caballeros

The downtown area extends around Parque Duarte and onto Calle del Sol, which is lined with a series of shops, banks and restaurants.

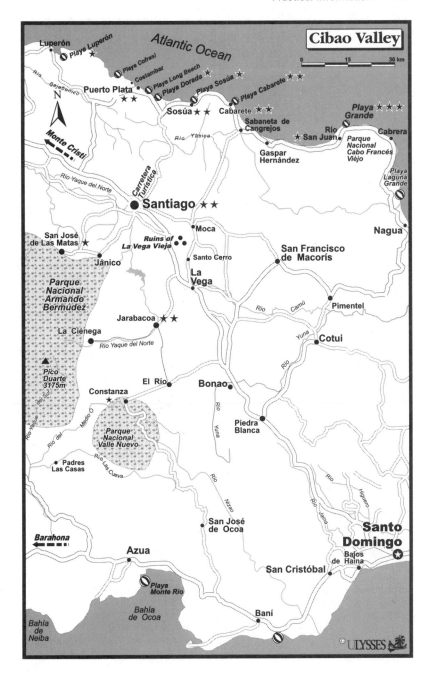

A **Codetel** can be found at 21 Avenida Circunvalación.

Moca

The **Codetel** is located on Nuestra Señora del Rosario, at the corner of Calle Duvergé.

San Francisco de Macorís

The downtown area and its numerous shops are concentrated around the central park (Avenida Castillo).

The **Codetel** is located at 54 Avenida 27 de Febrero.

 EXPLORING

Bonao

The highway from Santo Domingo practically passes right through the middle of Bonao.

Once a fort erected on Admiral Christopher Columbus' orders, in 1493, Bonao was one of the country's very first settlements. Today, it is a peaceful little town in the hollow of the Cibao valley. Though lacking any particular charm, it affords a view of the lovely landscape of mountains in its vicinity. Bonao draws its prosperity from agriculture, but also, to a great extent, from the mining of rich nickel deposits found in the region. The Dominican Republic is the seventh largest producer of nickel in the world and the second in the Americas. Bonao's nickel deposits are mined by Falconbridge, a Canadian multinational corporation.

La Vega

La Vega's downtown area is on the west side of the highway (well indicated).

The history of La Vega began in the 15th century when Christopher Columbus ordered a fort built here to protect the region's bountiful gold mines. Within a few years, La Vega had become one of the most important cities on the island, as well as the summer residence of Viceroy Diego Columbus, his father's successor. However, this prosperity came to an abrupt end in 1562, when the city was completely destroyed by an earthquake. La Vega was rebuilt the next year on the banks of the Río Camu, its present location, but did not regain its former economic and political stature until it was linked to the coast by rail during the 19th century. It is now a rather noisy, crowded city of moderate size, whose economy is closely linked to the fertile agricultural land surrounding it. La Vega is known for its carnival masks (depicting devils). The carnival takes place at the end of February.

To get to Santo Cerro from La Vega, take the highway heading north for a short distance until you reach a turn-off on the right. After approximately four kilometres along this narrow road, a rocky trail will appear on the left, climbing up to the convent.

Santo Cerro *(about 5 km northeast of the city)* is a small hill topped by a church built in the 1880s, which houses a portrait of La Virgen de las Mercedes (Our Lady of Mercy). Christopher Columbus ordered the construction of a large wooden cross at the summit of Santo Cerro, or holy hill, in

1495 (the first crucifix erected in the New World), after the Virgin Mary was said to have appeared there and helped the Spanish win a decisive victory over the natives. Each year on March 25th, pilgrims from all over gather at this spot. The site offers an excellent view of the Cibao valley.

To reach the ruins of La Vega Vieja, continue along the same road for about two kilometres.

The archaeological site of the ruins of **La Vega Vieja** *(2 km farther on the same road)* is one of the largest in the country. Visitors can see vestiges of a Franciscan monastery (1512) and a fortress (1495).

Santiago de Los Caballeros

To get to Parque Duarte (downtown), take the road skirting the Monumento on the right (Las Cabreras), then turn left onto Calle 30 de Marzo.

In 1494, Christopher Columbus ordered a fort built on the banks of the Río Yaque del Norte river, once again to protect gold mining operations in the region. Some years later, in 1503, one of the first waves of Spanish agricultural workers chose to settle in this village. As the group was made up of about thirty *caballeros* (gentlemen) belonging to the Order of St-James (El Orden de Santiago), the new colony was called Santiago de Los Caballeros.

Destroyed in 1562 by a strong earthquake, the city was rebuilt the next year on its present site, a few kilometres from the former location. Later, its strategic position in the centre of the rich Cibao valley allowed it to prosper and to play an important role in the

history of the country. As shown by the many monuments throughout the city, it played a crucial role during the War of Independence (1844) and the Restoration of the Republic (1865). Santiago is also the proud birthplace of most of the country's presidents.

With a population of over 400,000, Santiago is the second largest city in the country after Santo Domingo. It is generally quieter than the capital, though downtown traffic is heavy and **Calle del Sol** is one of the liveliest commercial streets in the country. Like its rum and tobacco production, the *merengue*, which supposedly originated here, has earned local residents a reputation for their vitality.

The best time to visit Santiago is during **Carnival**, which takes place in February. This tradition originated in the last century, and is marked by colourful parades and celebrations and by a competition between residents of the Los Pepines and La Joya neighbourhoods, who are easily identifiable by the shape of their respective carnival masks.

El Monumento de los Héroes de la Restauración de la República ★ *(free admission; on the road from Santo Domingo)* was erected in the 1940s under the dictator Trujillo and served as a monument to himself; it was originally known as the Trujillo peace monument. The 67-metre-high marble structure, visible throughout the city, has since been dedicated to the heroes of the Restoration. It presently houses a museum displaying works by Spanish painter Vela Zannetti. There is an excellent view of Santiago and the Cibao valley from its top.

The Carnival

Twice a year, in February and August, the carnival is in full swing in the Dominican Republic. The days leading up to and following this popular festival are animated with parades, large gatherings and dancing. The highlight of these wild festivities, however, is unquestionably the carnival characters, dressed in brightly-coloured costumes and masks, which are often endowed with huge horns. Whether *diablos cojuelos* from Santo Domingo or La Vega, *lechones* from Santiago, *toros y civiles* from Monte Cristi, *papeluses* from San Francisco or *buyolas* from San Pedro de Macorís, these amusing devils roam the streets in search of sinners. Some of the masks are on display in the Museo del Hombre Dominicano in Santo Domingo (see p 78).

The carnival's origins are obscure, but celebrations such as these take place in a good number of Latin countries. They may be derived from a pagan ritual that once honoured the coming of spring and the rejuvenation of nature, or perhaps even from an ancient Roman festival. The fact remains that this celebration has come down through the ages and has adapted to each country's customs and traditions.

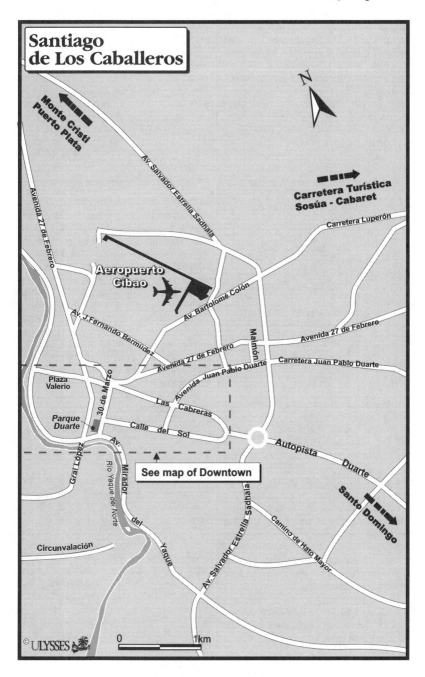

Santiago de Los Caballeros

Parque Duarte *(at the corner of Calle del Sol and Calle 30 de Marzo)* is an oasis of peace in the heart of the bustling city centre. It encloses an elegant Victorian-style pavilion and a monument to the heroes of the Restoration. Carriage drivers wait near the park, offering tours of the city *($8 US)*. Nearby Calle del Sol is one of the most vibrant commercial streets in the country.

The **Catedral de Santiago Apostol** *(free admission; facing Parque Duarte)*, built between 1868 and 1895, has neoclassic and republican architectural features. It contains the tombs of the dictator Ulysses Heureaux and several Restoration heroes. The beautiful stained-glass windows are the work of the Dominican artist Rincón Mora.

The **Palacio Consistorial** *(free admission; facing Parque Duarte)* was the city hall for a good part of the 19th century. It now houses the Santiago Museum, which exhibits old and recent works by local artists.

The **Museo del Tabaco** *(free admission; facing Parque Duarte)* houses an exhibit on the history of the tobacco industry and its importance to Santiago's and the country's economies. The exhibit may not be spectacular, but it is nonetheless interesting. The museum's staff can tell you which cigar manufacturers in Santiago allow visits. One that offers impromptu tours is just a few streets from the museum. Visitors will see workers, sitting side by side, some in charge of the drying of the leaves, others of rolling the delicate leaves into fine and handsome cigars.

The **Centro de la Cultura** *(free admission; 100 m north of the park on Calle del Sol)* regularly puts on interesting exhibits of works by Dominican painters.

The **Thomas Morel Folkloric Museum** *(free admission; Mon to Fri 8:30am to 1:30pm; Calle Restauración)* houses a private collection of popular art pieces as well as articles related to Santiago's carnival.

Moca

Located in the mountains of the Cordillera Septentrionale range, the town of Moca is the hub of a major coffee growing region. Plantations abound on the slopes of the nearby mountains, lending a touch of green to the surrounding landscape. The town itself is peaceful and appealing. At its centre stands a monument to Ramón Caceres, who assassinated the terrible dictator Ulysses Heureaux on July 25, 1899. Its main streets are lined with buildings, including the beautiful **Iglesia del Sagrado Corazón de Jesús** and the **Iglesia del Rosado**. The town also has a small **zoo**, whose interest lies mostly in its luxuriant gardens.

Cotui

Passing through the city of Cotui is necessary for those who wish to get to Santo Domingo in the Samaná peninsula.

Cotui is a peaceful, charming little town that, like many of the Cibao valley's agglomerations, was established at the very onset of colonization on Christopher Columbus' orders. Today, a central park, some restaurants and a few rather modest hotels can be found here. Known for its major agricultural

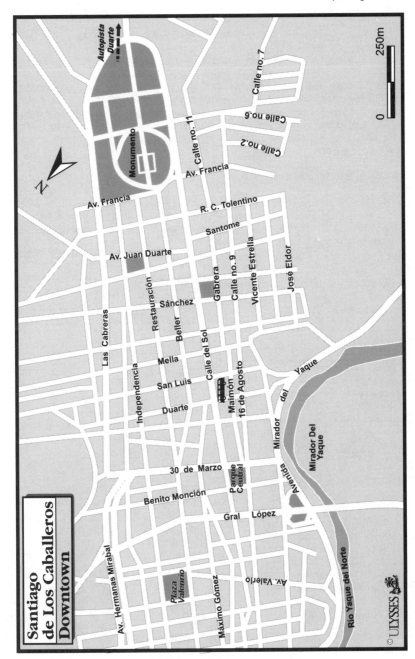

Santiago
de Los Caballeros
Downtown

Av. Hermanas Mirabal

Máximo Gómez

Plaza
Valerrio

Av. Valerio

Gral López

Benito Monción

30 de Marzo

Parque
Central

Mirador Del
Yaque

Avenida

Río Yaque del Norte

Independencia

Las Cabreras

Restauración

Sánchez

Beller

Mella

San Luis

Duarte

Calle del Sol

Maimón

16 de Agosto

Mirador del

Yaque

Av. Juan Duarte

Gabrera

Calle no. 9

Vicente Estrella

José Eldor

Santome

R. C. Tolentino

Av. Francia

Av. Francia

Monumento

Autopista
Duarte

Calle no. 11

Calle no. 2

Calle no.6

Calle no. 7

0   250m

© ULYSSES

The Valley Routes

The Carratera Turística: Santiago to Sosúa ★

The Carratera Turística provides a quick link between the Atlantic coast and Santiago, through the majestic landscape of the Cordillera Septentrionale in the centre of the country. The road is in excellent condition, and traffic moves quite fast, since weight limits are enforced. It takes about an hour to reach Santiago from the Atlantic coast. The road starts on the coast between Sosúa and Puerto Plata.

Moca to the Atlantic Coast ★

The road from Moca to the Atlantic coast has recently been repaved. It, too, runs through mountainous landscapes of the Cordillera Septentrionale, offering magnificent views of the Cibao valley. This road begins on the Atlantic coast in the village of Sabaneta, near Sosúa.

---

production, the Cotui region can also be counted among the country's large mining centres.

San Francisco de Macorís

Covering an area of several square kilometres at the foot of the Cordillera Septentrionale, San Francisco de Macorís is one of the largest urban areas in the country. The fertile land nearby, used primarily for grazing and growing rice, contributes significantly to the economy of the city. San Francisco de Macorís has few attractions to speak of, except its **Parque Central**, located on Avenida Castillo and flanked by two imposing churches, a university building and several restaurants and small businesses. For most travellers, San Francisco de Macorís is just a stop along the way between Santo Domingo and the Samaná peninsula.

 ACCOMMODATIONS

La Vega

A few hotels along the highway to the north offer adequate, but very basic and noisy rooms. Warning: if you are looking for accommodation that is even the least bit comfortable and quaint, then avoid La Vega.

On a calm street in the heart of town, the **Hotel San Pedro** *($8 US; ⊗; Avenida De Carceres)* has quiet, simply furnished rooms. The **Hotel Astral** *($15 US; ⊗; Avenida De Carceres)*, right across the street, offers rooms only slightly nicer than those at the San Pedro.

Santiago de Los Caballeros

Most of the inexpensive hotels are clustered around the Plaza Valerio.

Among these, the **Santiago Plaza** *($9 US, ⊗; Plaza Valerio)* offers very basic rooms. The **El Gallo de Oro** *($10 US; ⊗; Plaza Valerio)*, in the same area, has several clean but completely bare rooms.

The **Hotel Mercedes** *($25 US; ⊗; 18 Calle 30 de Marzo, ☎ 583-1171)* is a charming old building, considered to be part of the city's architectural heritage. A pleasant, traditional atmosphere prevails here, though the rooms are simple, noisy and not always well kept. The hotel is located right at the heart of the downtown area.

The **Hotel Ambar** *($25 US; tv, ≡, ℜ; Avenida Estrella Sadhala, outside the downtown area, ☎ 575-4811)* offers plainly decorated but clean rooms. It is quite far from the city centre in an uninteresting area, near the airport which probably explains its low rates.

The **Matum** *($30 US; ≡, ℜ; facing the Monumento, ☎ 581-5454)* has a stately air about it, but it has clearly seen better days. Although not very luxurious, the rooms are large and clean. The Matum is well-located near downtown Santiago.

The **Hotel Don Diego** *($40 US; ≡, ≈, ℜ; Avenida Estrella Sadhala, outside the city centre, ☎ 575-4186)* has 40 decent, comfortable rooms. It is a bit far from downtown, but the price is reasonable for what you get. Like the Ambar, the Don Diego is next to the highway heading to the northern part of the island.

The **Santiago Camino Real** *($50 US; tv, ≡, ℜ; at the corner of Calle del Sol and Calle Mella, ☎ 581-7000, ⋈ 582-4566)* is centrally located on the liveliest street in the city, close to the main

sights. Modern and comfortable, this hotel has a piano bar, a disco and a restaurant with a good reputation. The Camino Real is one of Santiago's institutions; it has recently undergone some renovations.

The **Aloha Sol** hotel *($55 US; ≡, ℜ; Calle del Sol. ☎ 583-0090 or 581-9283, ⋈ 583-0950)* is practically new. It is a beautiful hotel with comfortable rooms that, since its recent opening, has given the Camino Real, located right nearby, some stiff competition.

Recently built, the **Gran Almirante** *($80 US; ≡, ℜ, ≈, ♣; Avenida Estrella Sadhala, on the periphery of the downtown area, ☎ 580-1992, ⋈ 241-1492)* is Santiago's most luxurious hotel. The rooms are spacious and well-tended. The hotel has a casino.

 RESTAURANTS

Santiago de Los Caballeros

A good choice of restaurants with outside terraces can be found on the streets around the Monumento de los Héroes de la Restauración de la República. The atmosphere in this part of town, like downtown Santiago, especially along Calle del Sol, is often very lively in the evening.

Caldero Feliz *($; lunch only; at the corner of Calles San Luiz and Beller)* is a cafeteria, which prepares inexpensive, copious servings of Dominican family cooking. Workers in the area meet here at noon to enjoy a quick meal in a friendly atmosphere, and you should join them!

Panchito *($; at the corner of Calles Restauración and Duarte)* is fast-food Dominican-style! Sandwiches, ice cream and pizza are among the very inexpensive offerings.

A variety of inexpensive sandwiches can be enjoyed in the friendly and laid-back atmosphere of the **Cafeteria Digna** *($; at the corner of Calles Maximo Gomez and Benito Mancion)*. Breakfast service begins in the wee hours of the morning. This is something of a meeting place for locals.

The **Olympus** *($$-$$$; Calle del Sol, Camino Real Hotel, ☎ 581-4566)* prepares international specialties, as well as a selection of fine Dominican dishes. Diners can enjoy a wonderful view of the city from the terrace on the top floor of the Camino Real.

Cotui

Facing the parque central, and opening onto the street, is the **El Río** *($-$$)* restaurant, where visitors can have a bite to eat. Sandwiches, pizza, and several Dominican fish and meat dishes are served here.

San Francisco de Macorís

There are several restaurants in the downtown area, but also on the way out of town heading toward the middle of the country.

 ENTERTAINMENT

Santiago de Los Caballeros

Rather trendy and resolutely oriented toward North America, **Francofol Café** *(Calle del Sol, practically facing Parque Duarte)* is a bar with modern decor perfect for having a drink in the heart of Santiago.

Those who wish to try their luck can head to the **Gran Almirante** hotel's **casino** *(Avenida Estrella Sadhala, on the periphery of the downtown area, ☎ 580-1992)*.

 SHOPPING

Santiago de Los Caballeros

Calle del Sol is the shopping mecca of Santiago. All kinds of shops are to be found here, particularly clothing stores. Cigars can be purchased in a number of grocery stores, at the tobacco museum as well as in the city's various factories.

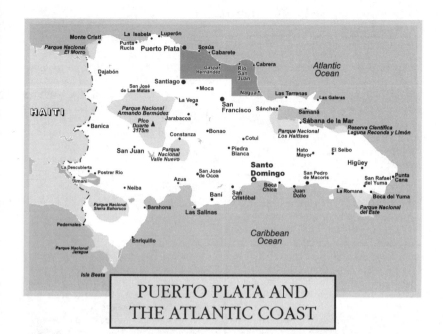

PUERTO PLATA AND THE ATLANTIC COAST

Travelling from Puerto Plata to the Samaná peninsula, a formidable 150-kilometre-long seafront, takes you through one of the best known regions of the Dominican Republic. More than anywhere else in the country, the development of tourism has been particularly intense over the last 20 years, and many of the region's towns and villages have become major resort areas. Following Puerto Plata, Sosúa and Cabarete, development of the superb beaches has now moved further east, to the region of Río San Juan and Playa Grande.

However, despite the ever-increasing popularity of this coast, the daily lives of its inhabitants still revolve around the traditional economic activities they always have, that is fishing and farming. With a relatively low population, these vast expanses remain untamed in many spots, and countless splendours await discovery by adventurous travellers.

 FINDING YOUR WAY AROUND

Highway 5 links the coastal cities from Puerto Plata to the Samaná peninsula. Most of the road is in excellent condition. Several roads branch off of Highway 5 and head across the magnificent Cordillera Septentrionale toward the centre of the country. One of the most picturesque and useful is the **Carretera Turistica**, which provides a quick link between Santiago de los Caballeros and the coast. The advantage of this lovely mountain road is that trucks are not allowed on it, so traffic moves a lot faster.

Puerto Plata International Airport

The Puerto Plata International Airport is only 18 kilometres east of the city and 8 kilometres west of Sosúa. It is the point of arrival for most visitors to the Atlantic Coast, and is the second largest airport in the country after Santo Domingo's. The recently enlarged airport is well laid-out, and includes waiting rooms. The personnel is generally quite efficient. A taxi from the airport costs around $14 US to Puerto Plata, $7 US to Sosúa and $20 US to Cabarete. A considerable number of taxis wait outside the airport. There is no regular bus service (*guaguas*) from the airport to the city. However, *guaguas* and collective taxis stop on the highway, which is only about a ten-minute walk from the airport. The bus fare is about $1 US to Puerto Plata or Sosúa and $2 US to Cabarete. *Guaguas* and collective taxis are not very comfortable. They stop frequently to let passengers on and off, and are always packed. However, both modes of transportation are very economical, offer frequent service and provide an interesting way to meet the locals.

Renting a Car

The international car rental agencies have offices in Puerto Plata and at the airport. National rental companies occasionally have offices in the other urban areas along the coast. These companies rarely offer better rates, and their vehicles are more likely to be in poor condition. In any case, before renting a car, compare prices and insurance policies carefully, as they can vary greatly from one agency to another, and make sure the car is in good condition. The following agencies can be contacted by telephone: Budget ☎ 586-4480, Hertz ☎ 586-0200, Thrifty ☎ 586-0242. Budget's rates are often less expensive. It is possible to rent a car in advance by contacting the international reservation service offered by the major rental agencies. The roads in the Puerto Plata region and along the Atlantic coast are generally in good condition, and traffic is not too heavy. Nevertheless, avoid driving at night, and drive slowly in urban areas.

Puerto Plata

There is only one main road into Puerto Plata. It crosses the city from west to east, where it becomes Avenida Circunvalación Sur. Running parallel, Avenida Circunvalación Norte (which becomes Avenida Luperón) follows the ocean from Long Beach to the San Felipe fortress. These two main roads are linked to the west by Avenida Colón and to the east by Avenida Mirabal. The four avenues form a rectangle around the city, making it easy to find your way around. Most of the hotels in Puerto Plata are located on the east side of town, facing Long Beach, or along Avenida Mirabal.

If you haven't got a car, it is easy to get around by hailing a motorcycle, locals are used to picking up passengers and will take you from one end of the city to the other for about $1 US.

Bus and *Guagua* Stops

The following two companies offer inexpensive and direct long-distance bus service aboard air-conditioned vehicles: Métro *(Calle Beller,* ☎ *586-6556)* and Caribe Tours *(Calle 12 de Julio,* ☎ *586-4544)*. If you don't mind

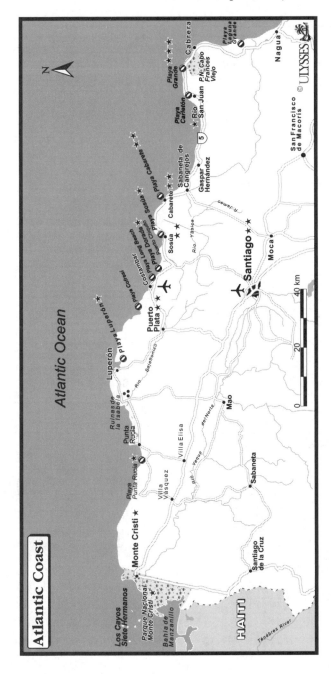

a bit of discomfort, an even cheaper option is to take one of the public buses, or *guaguas*, from Puerto Plata to towns along the coast and elsewhere in the country.

Guaguas to and from the western part of the island or Santo Domingo stop on Avenida Imbert (the continuation of Avenida Circonvalación Sur), about 500 metres west of Avenida Colón. For destinations east of Puerto Plata, buses stop in front of the hospital.

Taxi

It is possible to get from Puerto Plata to other resort towns by private taxi. The prices are always clearly marked in front of taxi stands. In Puerto Plata, there is a taxi stand next to the central park and another in the hotel zone across from Long Beach.

Sosúa

The company Caribe Tours stops at the edge of Los Charamicos, a few hundred metres from the beach. Public buses (*guaguas*), heading east or west, stop along the main road. Service is frequent in both directions.

Cabarete

To catch a public bus (*guagua*) heading east or west, just wait along the main street, which is part of the Atlantic coast highway.

PRACTICAL INFORMATION

Puerto Plata

The parque central *(at the corner of Beller and Separacíon)* is right in the heart of town. The **Codetel** and a bank are right beside.

Sosúa

Several shops, a bank and the **Codetel** are all located around Plaza Maxim, on Calle Alejo Martínez.

Cabarete

The better part of the town is spread on either side of the highway. You'll find shops, an exchange office and a small bank. The **Codetel** is on the highway, about one kilometre in the direction of Sosúa.

EXPLORING

For some, it is the magnificent beaches, among the most beautiful in the Caribbean and lined with resort villages offering accommodation for every taste and budget, that draws them here; others prefer the splendid mountain scenery and lush vegetation of the Cordillera Septentrionale. Whatever the reason, this region has plenty to please all types of travellers.

Sunset over Playa Bonita - T.B.

Escape to the tropics - D. Staquet

The beach at Punta Cana, deliciously shaded by coconut palms - Philippe Renault

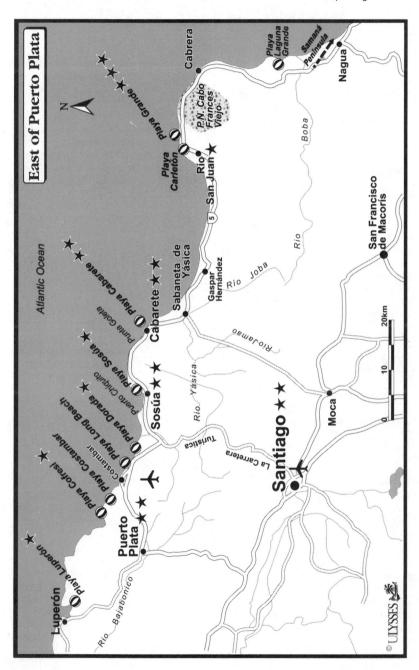

Puerto Plata ★★

Puerto Plata was founded in the early days of Spanish colonization (1502) by Nicolás de Ovando, in order to give the Spanish fleet a port on the northern coast of the island. Its first years were prosperous, but with the discovery of riches elsewhere in the Americas, the port of Puerto Plata became less important to the Spanish Crown. To make up for the lack of activity in their city, the residents of Puerto Plata began dealing in contraband with the French and English. To reaffirm its power and put a stop to smuggling in the area, the crown ordered that the city of Puerto Plata be destroyed and abandoned a century after it was founded. The city was not rebuilt until 1742, when a few Spanish families arrived from the Canary Islands. Once again, the city became an important seaport used for shipping out natural resources and agricultural products from the centre of the country. Today Puerto Plata is a lively, medium-sized urban centre with the busiest seaport on the northern coast.

The city's beautiful location, nestled between the Atlantic Ocean and the Cordillera Septentrionale mountain range, adds to its allure. Despite the constant development in Puerto Plata, its downtown has remained largely unchanged, retaining its typical Caribbean flavour. A number of Victorian and Republican buildings from the last century still line the avenues near the Parque Duarte, where most of the commercial activity takes place. The main tourist facilities in Puerto Plata are located on the east side of the city, near **Long Beach** and its pleasant promenade. Since Long Beach is not very good for swimming, many visitors head for the beaches just outside Puerto Plata.

The **Fortaleza San Felipe de Puerto Plata ★** *($1 US; at the western end of the Malecón)* is located on a point of land that juts into the ocean at the western edge of the city. Built in the 16th century to defend the port against pirates, this massive fortress is the only remnant of Puerto Plata's first period of colonization. At several points in its history the fort served not only to defend the city but also as a penitentiary. Visitors will find a small military museum, as well as the cell that held the great hero of the country's war of independence, Juan Pablo Duarte, in 1844. The site has a good view of the city, the ocean and the mountains. To get there, walk to the end of the **Malecón**, the long promenade that runs alongside the ocean for several kilometres. In the evening, the Malecón is a popular meeting place for Dominican families and couples, and countless stalls selling snacks and drinks line the sidewalks.

The **central park ★** *(at the corner of Calles Beller and Separacíon)* is one of the busiest areas in the city. On the lively neighbouring streets you will find restaurants, market stalls and stores, while the park itself is surrounded by Victorian buildings. The **Iglesia San Felipe**, an Art Deco church with a very sober interior, also stands on the south side of the park.

The **Museo del Ámbar ★★** *($2.50 US; Mon to Sat 9am to 6pm; at the corner of Calles Prudhomme and Duarte, ☎ 586-2848)* contains a small but beautiful collection of amber, the fossilized resin found throughout the Dominican Republic. Amber is hardened resin from a type of pine tree that has long since

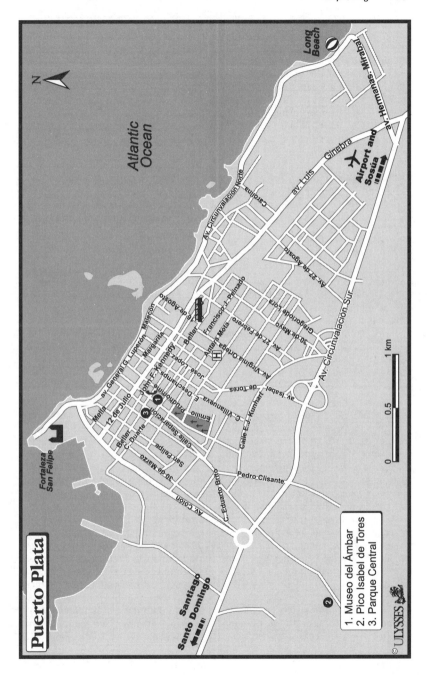

Puerto Plata

Atlantic Ocean

Long Beach

Airport and Sosúa

Santiago
Santo Domingo

Fortaleza San Felipe

1. Museo del Ámbar
2. Pico Isabel de Tores
3. Parque Central

© ULYSSES

0   0.5   1 km

Making Rum

Sugar cane has been grown in the Dominican Republic for centuries, long requiring hard labour on the part of local men and women, especially at harvest time. The men were responsible for cutting each plant down to the soil, stripping off the leaves (for fodder) and cutting each cane into one-metre-long pieces. The women followed, tying up the pieces into bundles of 10 to 12 pieces. This work required a lot of manpower and was carried out in the hot sun. Although harvesting sugar cane is somewhat easier today, thanks to modern instruments, it is still an arduous task.

After being tide into bundles, the sugar cane is taken to the factory so that its juice can be extracted. When pressed the first time, it produces a substantial quantity of juice. To collect the remaining liquid, the cane is moistened with water, and then pressed a second time. The crushed fibres, the bagasse, become fuel for the mill, while the sweet juice is used to make a variety of other products, notable sugar and rum.

The sweet juice (molasses) is fermented to produce a liquid with an alcohol content of 95%, which is then diluted with distilled water in copper barrels. The alcohol is then decanted into another set of copper barrels and sometimes mixed with almonds or caramel to give it its chatacteristic flavour and colour. This blend is decanted yet again, this time into wooden barrels and aged for one to 25 years. Afterward, it is filtered and sampled, then left to settle for 15 days in copper barrels to make sure there will be no sediment in the finished product. Finally, the rum is bottled, thus becoming the favourite companion in both joy and sorrow of the Dominican population.

---

disappeared. The oldest pieces date from tens of millions of years ago, and some are so transparent that insects or other animals can be seen trapped inside. Because of the American science fiction film *Jurassic Park*, people the world over now know about this kind of resin. In this fantastical story, scientists are able to breed Prehistoric creatures from animal cells preserved in pieces of amber. Since the release of the film, the price of amber has risen considerably, as has attendance at this museum. The little shop below the museum has a good selection of souvenirs, including jewellery made of amber and *larimar* a pretty blue stone, also found in the Dominican Republic.

For a look at an old Dominican house with period decor and furnishings, visit the **Hotel Jimesson** *(free admission; Calle Kennedy, ☎ 586-2177)*.

One of the most popular attractions in town for a long time now, the cable car up to the summit of **Pico Isabel de Torres ★★** *($2 US; about 500 m out of town to the west, a well-marked 500-m trail leads to the cable car)* was unfortunately undergoing renovations at press time. Be sure to check on the progression of the work before heading all the way there. From its highest point, at 793 metres above sea-level, the Pico Isabel de Torres provides an exceptional view of Puerto Plata and the surrounding beaches, mountains and towns. At the summit there is an impressive statue of Christ the Redeemer and trails leading through the flowering gardens.

If you are curious to know how rum is made, tours are offered at the **Brugal Rum Distillery** *(free guided tours; Mon to Fri 9am to noon and 2pm to 4pm; 500 m outside of town on the east side, buildings are visible from the road)*. This small, modern distillery produces about 1,300,000 litres of white and dark rum a year, 95% of which is consumed in the Dominican Republic. The tour of the premises is short, amounting to little more than a look at the bottling process. However, the guides can provide a wealth of information on the rum industry. There is also a small kiosk that sells souvenirs sporting the Brugal logo, as well as the different varieties of the famous rum at a slight discount.

Baseball fans will be happy to learn that it is almost certain that the next baseball team in the Dominican Republic professional league will be in Puerto Plata.

Costambar

Costambar is located three kilometres west of Puerto Plata. From there (there is a sign), a dirt road leads to Costambar after one kilometre.

Costambar lies alongside of the first small **beach** west of Puerto Plata. It is a peaceful, fairly undeveloped area with few hotels, but a fair number of villas belonging to foreigners or wealthy Dominicans. A nine-hole golf course is located nearby, while a few restaurants, a motorcycle rental shop and some markets round out the facilities on site. Few vacationers end up staying here, most come for the golf course or the beach.

Playa Cofresi

Still on the main highway, but a few kilometres west of Costambar, a well-marked road branches off and leads directly to Playa Cofresi after about one kilometre.

Recent years have seen considerable growth in Playa Cofresi, due mainly to the opening of the large Hacienda Resorts complex, which regroups several hotels. The site also includes many private villas, fine restaurants, grocery stores and various other businesses. The main reason for coming here, the pretty, little white-sand beach ★, remains unchanged.

Playa Dorada ★

From Costambar or Playa Cofresi you'll have to retrace your steps and go through Puerto Plata to reach Playa Dorada. It is about three kilometres east of Puerto Plata on the main road.

This is neither a village nor a town that became touristy, but rather a few square kilometres of buildings erected solely for tourism. It has about a dozen luxury hotels offering a wide range of services and activities. The area is very pleasantly landscaped with lovely gardens, hibiscus bushes, a few ponds, a superb 18-hole golf course designed by Robert Trent Jones and a beautiful long white-sand **beach** ★. Visitors can enjoy a wide range of water sports, set off on excursions and adventures into the surrounding region or simply relax with a drink on one of the many terraces. For many years now, Playa Dorada has been the most popular of the large resort areas. It is perfect for travellers looking for a beautiful, safe seaside resort with luxury hotels and all the modern comforts. Those in search of more of an introduction to the Dominican culture and way of life, however, will be somewhat disappointed. Playa Dorada is accessible from Highway 5, which follows the northern coast.

Puerto Chiquito

Continue along Highway 5 for about 20 kilometres. About 1.5 kilometres before Sosúa, a large colourful sign clearly marks the road to Puerto Chiquito. The village lies less than a kilometre away.

Located a bit more than one kilometre west of Sosúa, Puerto Chiquito lies alongside a pretty little bay surrounded by towering rocky cliffs. The setting is definitely worth a look, especially from the terrace of the Sand Castle hotel, which offers a stunning panoramic view of the ocean. The white-sand **beach**, divided in two by the Río Sosúa, is several hundred metres long. It is used mostly by guests of the Sand Castle, who enjoy all manner of water sports in the calm waters of the bay. The water here is unfortunately not very clean.

Sosúa ★★

The city of Sosúa consists of the Los Charamicos and El Batey neighbourhoods. These two areas are separated by a long, sandy beach. When coming from Puerto Plata, you'll pass by Los Charamicos first, then El Batey, about one kilometre farther along, where most of the hotels are located.

Sosúa was little more than a small banana-growing centre when a group of European Jews took refuge here in the 1940s. The president at the time, the dictator Trujillo, agreed to welcome these refugees in an effort to improve his poor international reputation. The new arrivals were to have a significant impact on the development of Sosúa, especially its economy, by setting up the prosperous dairy and livestock farms for which the region is known. A number of these refugees and their descendants still live in the area. However, the city they helped build seems to have escaped them, lost to the ever-increasing throngs of tourists; their synagogue, for example, looks out of place among the restaurants, bars, discotheques and hotels, as if it belonged to another era and another civilization. In fact, with the exception of Puerto Plata, Sosúa has undergone more tourist development than any other area on the coast, and the general appearance of the city has unfortunately suffered as a result. Little remains of its traditional architecture, and large parts of the city are devoted completely to commerce. The ambience has also changed considerably; vendors of all sorts have become pushier, and prostitution is flourishing (the government intervened in 1996 in an attempt to ban prostitution and return a certain respectability to the city).

Nevertheless, Sosúa can still be a pleasant place to stay, due to its abundance of restaurants, hotels and outdoor diversions. The jagged coastline makes for some beautiful landscapes, and the bay's waters are always

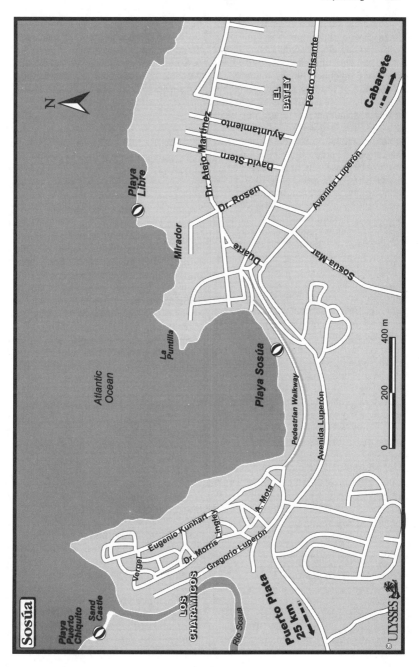

Sosúa

crystal-clear. Sosúa has two beaches: **Playa Sosúa** ★, about one kilometre long and always crowded, and **Playa Libre**, smaller but also much calmer. The two neighbourhoods located on either side of the bay are separated by Playa Sosúa. Most of the hotels and touristy development is on the east side, in the **El Batey** neighbourhood, which is also home to several beautiful residences. The **Los Charamicos** neighbourhood has remained essentially residential, thus preserving a typical small-town Dominican atmosphere.

Sosúa's **Sinagoga** *(Alejo Martinez)* is a small, modest-looking building still used as a place of worship by the city's Jewish community. Right next door is the **Museo de Sosúa** *(free admission; 6pm to 11pm; Alejo Martinez)*, whose mission is to inform visitors about the city's history. Historical documents and personal objects belonging to Sosúa's first Jewish settlers are on display.

From the outskirts of Sosúa, visitors can enjoy beautiful excursions to the Cordillera Septentrionale on the **Carretera Turistica**. This highway is closed to big trucks and offers magnificent **views** ★ of the mountainous landscape of the Cordillera all the way to Santiago de los Caballeros in the centre of the country. The Carretera Turistica starts along the main road midway between Sosúa and Puerto Plata. The drive to Santiago takes about an hour.

Punta Goleta

To reach Punta Goleta from Sosúa, follow the highway for about ten kilometres.

The pretty, sandy **beach** of Punta Goleta runs along the ocean for a few hundred metres and is an extension of the superb Playa Cabarete. The beach is not particularly crowded, as there are few big hotels nearby. Pretty thatched parasols have been set up on the sand for shade.

Cabarete ★★

Continue east on the highway to get to Cabarete.

Cabarete is considered the windsurfing capital of the country, and with good reason. The conditions for this sport are excellent, especially on windy summer days. Cabarete has actually become somewhat famous; each June windsurfing professionals gather here to take part in an international competition. Windsurfing is not the only reason to go to Cabarete, however. Its magnificent **beach** ★★ stretches nearly three kilometres, making it perfect for long walks. Contrary to the beach at Sosúa, for example, Cabarete's beach is large enough that you don't feel hemmed in on all sides by hotels and sunbathers. Though tourism has become the mainstay of the village's economy, Cabarete has retained a pleasant, casual atmosphere and also offers a good selection of hotels, generally small or medium-sized, as well as several restaurants. Those who choose to stay will also find themselves well situated for excursions along the Atlantic coast.

Behind the village, there is an interesting **lagoon**, where the comings-and-goings of several species of birds, including the pelican, can be observed.

To visit Cabarete's **caves** ★ *($12 US; take the road near the Codetel, on the west side of Cabarete, for 1 km to the Cabarete Adventure Park)*, you must be accompanied by a guide from the Cabarete Adventure Park, the only outfit with the rights to market this place. The three-hour guided tour leads through the countryside and a tropical forest, but unfortunately includes several uninteresting stops along the way. Once at the caves, however, you are allowed to look around and swim in one of the natural pools. The caves are interesting, but the rest of the tour is uninspiring, and the guides and owner of the place are downright unpleasant.

Gaspar Hernández

An unremarkable but always busy little coastal town, Gaspar Hernández is a little more than 15 kilometres from Cabarete on the road to Río San Juan and Samaná. The town has a few banks and gas stations, a Codetel, and some small, inexpensive hotels of dubious quality.

Río San Juan ★

Río San Juan is about 30 kilometres east of Gaspar Hernández. To reach the beach of the Bahía Blanca hotel, follow the lagoon shore to the left.

Río San Juan is a pleasant fishing village in an area known for farming and dairy production, where life still revolves around the sea. Some of the village streets, with their small houses painted in pastel shades, correspond to the romantic images people often have of small Caribbean towns. Although most visitors come here to visit the famous Laguna Gri-Gri and its striking stands of tangled, tropical mangrove trees, Río San Juan has enough to offer to make a longer stay worthwhile. The region is full of enchanting landscapes, and beautiful sandy **beaches** line the shore in front of the friendly little Bahía Blanca hotel. There are several other small beaches, virtually deserted most of the time, around the lagoon. And finally, about two kilometres west of Río San Juan, is **Playa Carleton**, accessible either by boat from the Laguna Gri-Gri, or by foot from the road towards Cabrera.

Gri-Gri lagoon is accessible from the highway by following Calle Duarte, the main road in Río San Juan.

Boats are always available for visits to the **Laguna Gri-Gri ★★** *($17 US per boatload of up to 15 people; departure from the end of Calle Duarte, at the corner of Calle Sanchez).* The tour leads around the lagoon all the way to the ocean, through a magnificent mangrove forest where a variety of tropical bird species can be observed at close range. The excursion continues along the coastline to a small inlet called **La Piscina**, whose crystalline waters are perfect for swimming. You will also stop at **Playa Carleton** long enough for another swim before returning to the lagoon. Those who would like to spend more time bird-watching around the lagoon can get there on foot by following the Bahía Blanca's road to the end. Early morning is the best time to observe and photograph birds.

El Barrio Acapulco *(near the ocean on the west side of town)* is a working-class neighbourhood where most of the fishermen in Río San Juan live. Those interested in boat-building and fishing will appreciate a visit to this unfortunately very poor area.

Red Mangrove

Playa Grande

About eight kilometres from Río San Juan is **Playa Grande ★★★**, without a doubt one of the most impressive beaches in the country. This wide ribbon of white sand extends for more than one kilometre between a splendid bay and a string palm trees. The surrounding scenery is lovely, and the good-sized waves delight swimmers and surfers alike. The large Caribbean Village hotel complex opened near the beach in 1994; fortunately, it has not marred the beautiful setting. Most beach-goers here are either guests at this hotel, or part of organized tours from Playa Dorada, Sosúa, Cabarete or elsewhere. Nevertheless, Playa Grande is still the least crowded beach of this calibre in the western part of the country.

Cabrera

A few kilometres further along, the highway passes along the outskirts of Cabrera. To reach Cabrera from the highway, you must follow a small road on the left side. Watch carefully because it is poorly marked and located in a curve in the road.

Cabrera is a typical Dominican coastal town pleasantly located on a small cape. While it has no major attractions, the view of the ocean and the cliffs nearby is spectacular. A good spot to take in this beautiful seaside panorama is **Parque Nacional Cabo Frances Viejo** *(about 2 km before the village, accessible by a dirt road)*. This small and pleasant park is always quiet. There are a number of interesting undeveloped beaches close by, but most are hard to get to. You'll need a good map and directions from the locals to find them.

A visit to the brand new **Amazone 2** *($US 3; east of Cabrera)* ecological park offers a chance to take an interesting 20-minute walk in a dense forest, where you can see some of the plants typical of this region and learn about certain aspects of the local geology. Before setting out, you will be given a small map indicating the various points of interest in the park (marsh plant zone, fern valley, bat cave, etc.). Visitors will also find a gigantic canvas aviary containing a variety of birds, and another, smaller one sheltering scores of pretty butterflies.

The Palm Tree Route

For more than ten kilometres the road between Cabrera and Nagua runs alongside the ocean through a striking palm grove. After cutting across the palm grove to the shore, you'll find some superb wild beaches. If you decide to swim, be very careful, because the current and undertow can be very strong here.

Nagua

Highway 5 passes through the town of Nagua. The road forks here, with one side (to the left) heading to the Samaná peninsula, and the other (to the right) to San Francisco de Macorís.

Nagua is a medium-sized town at the intersection of the roads from Puerto Plata and San Francisco de Macorís, and anyone on their way to the magnificent Samaná peninsula must inevitably pass through here. It has a number of commercial streets, gas stations, and a **Parque Central** *(Calle Duarte)*, where several restaurants can be found. As the town is of little interest, few visitors passing through decide to stay. There are, however, a few lovely, undeveloped beaches farther south, between Nagua and the Samaná peninsula, with a few small hotels nearby.

 PARKS

Parque Nacional Cabo Frances Viejo *(2 km before Cabrera)* is a small, protected area along the coast. It is a quiet, virtually deserted spot, where you can observe the waves crashing into the surrounding cliffs. This is a good place for a picnic.

 BEACHES

Long Beach extends over several kilometres, lining Puerto Plata's seascape. Unfortunately, this sandy beach is poorly maintained and located much too close to the road to make it a very enjoyable place to swim.

Playa Costambar is relatively quiet during the week. This rather narrow strip of sand is a few hundred metres long.

Playa Cofresi ★ is a lovely white-sand beach. Since the opening of the Hacienda Resorts it has become quite busy.

Playa Dorada ★ is a long band of golden sand washed by calm waters where you can swim to your heart's content. Most of the beach is lined with the large hotels of this popular resort area, so a comfortable terrace for a drink or quick bite is never far away. The beach can get very crowded in winter, when most of the hotel rooms are rented. The prettiest section of the beach is to the west, in front of Jack Tar Village. The waves are also rougher here.

Playa Puerto Chiquito, near Sosúa, is a long ribbon of white sand divided in half by the Río Sosúa. The bay's waters are calm, and the surrounding scenery is very pretty, as the beach is flanked on both sides by small cliffs. Unfortunately, the waters of the bay are not always that clean.

There are two beaches in Sosúa: Playa Sosúa and Playa Libre. **Playa Sosúa** is a beautiful fine-sand beach about one kilometre long and washed by the crystal-clear waters of the bay. The setting is beautiful, but hardly relaxing as the beach is always overrun with tourists and vendors. Restaurants, bars and stands selling souvenirs have been built all along it. It is a noisy place, and the vendors can be very pushy. This is a shame, because the beach is definitely one of the best on the coast. **Playa Libre** *(El Batey neighbourhood)* is another option for swimming. This small beach, lined with quality hotels, is quieter and the vendors are less conspicuous here. Less than one kilometre to the east are a few small stretches of sand where you can swim.

A few kilometres before Cabarete, a sign on the left indicates the way to **Playa Punta Goleta**. This beach is pretty and fairly quiet, with a few hotels here and there.

Playa Cabarete ★★ is one of the best beaches on the Atlantic coast. It stretches more than three kilometres, making it great for long walks in peace and quiet. The waves can be quite high, and windsurfing is very popular here. There are restaurants and terraces close by, and vendors wander about selling their wares.

The seashore of **Río San Juan** is graced with a few beaches. Those near the Bahía Blanca hotel are pretty and have showers. Small stretches of wild, deserted beach can also be found near

the Laguna Gri-Gri. Furthermore, about two kilometres east of Río San Juan, there is a sign for **Playa Carleton**, which is about a 10-minute walk from the small parking lot by the side of the road. It is also accessible by boat from the Laguna Gri-Gri. This pretty little beach is washed by calm turquoise waters. A few vendors walk about selling food and drinks.

Playa Grande ★★★, among the most spectacular beaches in the country, is remarkable for the sheer length and width of its ribbon of fine sand. Lined with coconut palms from one end to the other, Playa Grande extends more than one kilometre. This is an excellent place to go swimming, despite the occasionally heavy surf. The Caribbean Village hotel complex sits nearby on the western side. Its architects had the good sense not to construct the hotel right on the beach, thereby preserving the harmony of the landscape. There is, however, a small pub on the beach reserved for guests of the Caribbean Village. For those who are not staying at the hotel, vendors rent beach chairs and sell food and drinks on the east side of the beach.

Wild beaches dot the coastline between **Cabrera** and **Nagua**. You can swim here but be careful, the undertow can be very strong and just may carry you out to sea.

 OUTDOOR ACTIVITIES

Everything has been thought of to make the Atlantic coast a great place for outdoor activities. One of the main advantages of this part of the country is that visitors can enjoy just about every water sport here, plus all sorts of other activities, including golf, horseback riding, bicycling, tennis, etc.

 Windsurfing

Cabarete

Although it is possible to go windsurfing in many places along the coast, Cabarete is without a doubt the best spot. Cabarete is not called the "windsurfing capital" for nothing. Its strong winds and protected bay make it one of the top ten places in the world for this sport. The necessary equipment can be rented on site at more than a half-dozen specialized shops. Rates vary little from one place to the next: about $15 US an hour, $45 US a day and $150 US a week. Courses for beginners are also available for $25 US an hour. If you have your own equipment, expect to pay about $25 US a week for storage.

 Scuba Diving

Playa Dorada, Sosúa and Río San Juan are the principal places along the northern coast that offer diving excursions. Deep-sea dives are available at each place, as are courses for beginners. Scuba diving can be a dangerous sport, so be sure to check that the diving centre you sign up with follows all safety guidelines (see p 58).

Sosúa

Swiss Dive in Sosúa respects these guidelines. The **Aquario Diving Center** *($35 US;* ☎ *571-2868)* offers courses and excursions for those who have never dived before.

Río San Juan

Gri-Gri Divers *(☎ 589-2671)* in Río San Juan also respects safety regulations.

 Snorkelling

Snorkelling equipment can be rented at all the resorts along the coast, either from hotels or specialized shops. In many cases, excursions out on the high seas are offered. Sosúa is the most popular place along the coast for this activity.

 Deep-sea Fishing

Deep-sea fishing excursions are not offered in all tourist centres. Sosúa and Playa Dorada are usually the departure points for these outings.

 Water Slides

Next to the road between Sosúa and Cabarete, the **Colombus Aqua Parque** *(☎ 571-2642)* has just opened.

 Golf

Playa Dorada

Real golfers know that the best place to play is in Playa Dorada, even though there are two other small nine-hole courses on the Atlantic coast. This exquisite 18-hole course was designed by Robert Jones Trent. It, along with the course at Casa de Campo on the south side of the island, are the best golf courses in the Dominican Republic. Clubs and balls can be rented on the premises.

Horseback Riding

The Atlantic coast of the country is an ideal place for excursions on horseback. There is the Cordillera Septentrionale to explore, as well as the coast and countryside. Most of the big hotels offer either half-day or full-day rides.

 Tennis

The only tennis courts, besides those in the hotel complexes, are in Cabarete, near the Las Orquideas hotel. Rackets and balls can be rented at the courts in Cabarete; private lessons are also available. In Playa Dorada, Jack Tar Village and Playa Naco are the two most popular hotels with tennis-players.

 Bird-watching

Numerous species of birds can be seen along the Atlantic coast, be it on the beaches, in the forests or in the countryside: cattle egrets, hummingbirds, turtledoves and pelicans especially. One spot guaranteed to have some winged activity is the **Laguna Gri-Gri**, in Río San Juan, the nesting grounds of many species. The birds can be observed during a boat tour of the lagoon, or by reaching the lagoon on foot *(easy access from the end of the Bahía Blanca hotel road)*.

 ACCOMMODATIONS

Puerto Plata

Puerto Plata has a fairly large network of accommodations. However, visitors wishing to stay near a beautiful beach often choose hotels outside of town, in Playa Dorada or in one of the many other resorts in the area. Keep in mind, though, that the big hotels in Puerto Plata often offer lower rates than those in Playa Dorada, and also provide efficient transportation to the best beaches in the region.

Several hotels downtown and near Long Beach offer accommodation suitable for those on a tight budget. Even so, Puerto Plata is not the best place on the northern coast for inexpensive lodging; Sosúa and Cabarete have a much better selection of hotels in this category. If decide to stay in Puerto Plata anyway, you may want to try the **Beach Hotel** *($13 US; ⊗, ℜ; across from Long Beach)*. The hotel has a wonderful ocean-side location, but the rooms leave quite a bit to be desired. The **Hotel Dilone** *($13 US; ⊗; 96 Calle 30 de Marzo)* is similar in both price and comfort, but located in downtown Puerto Plata.

The **El Indio** *($22 US; ⊗, ℜ; 94 Calle 30 de Marzo)* hotel has a few rooms that are much quieter and better maintained than those of the two aforementioned hotels. It is located on a quiet street in the heart of the town, and has a pleasant tropical garden. With no pool or beach nearby, and no beach shuttle, this hotel is best suited to travellers with their own means of transportation. You can try negotiating the price of your room with the German-born owner.

The **Latin Quarter** *($US 40; ℜ, ≈, ≡, ⊗; on the Malecón, ☎ 586-2588, ⚑ 586-1828)* is a brand-new hotel on the Malecón. At first sight, this little place is hardly charming, but its attractive garden, secluded from all the action, makes it a pleasant place to stay. The rooms are pretty, too.

The **Puerto Plata Beach and Casino Resort** *($90 US; ≡, ≈, tv, ℜ, ⊛, ♣; Malecón, ☎ 320-4243)* is by far the most luxurious hotel complex in the city. Its excellent restaurants, beautiful gardens, casino, swimming pools and host of activities make it a wonderful place for a vacation. The nicely decorated rooms are clustered in small, pastel-coloured buildings, and they all have balconies. Shows are presented in the evenings, and everyday there is a shuttle to and from the main beaches of the area. It is best to reserve ahead of time during the winter months.

The **Montemar Hotel** *($130 US all-inclusive; ≡, ≈, ℜ, tv; ☎ 586-2800, ⚑ 586-2009)* offers a package deal, including three meals a day and locally produced beverages. Though its rooms still are very comfortable, the Montemar, an enormous, uninspiring white building, hasn't been touched up at all since it was built. There is a shuttle service to Playa Dorada and local casinos for hotel guests.

Costambar

The **Villas Marlena** *($25 US; ⊗, ≈, ℜ; ☎ 586-5393, ⚑ 586-5373)* is a mid-range hotel complex best-suited to visitors who are looking to get away from the big resort areas, and don't mind staying in rooms that provide only the basics in comfort. Hotel rooms and apartments are both available; there is no transportation service to other areas.

Playa Cofresi

⚓ The newest of the Dominican Republic's big hotel complexes stands at the edge of Playa Cofresi, just west of Puerto Plata. A veritable tourist village, the **Hacienda Resorts** *(all-inclusive; ☎ 320-8303, ⚑ 320-0222)* are a cluster of no fewer than five hotels, each with its own distinctive features, designed to satisfy the widest possible range of expectations. **The Garden Club** *(ℜ, ⊗)* is made up of pretty buildings that are more like simple, comfortable little cottages than modern hotel rooms, lending this part of the complex an intimate atmosphere. **The Elizabeth** *(≈, ⊗, ≡, ℜ)*, for its part, will appeal to visitors looking to stay in a lovely hotel that is small but still offers a high level of comfort and has a large, attractive garden. It is distinguished by its vaguely Spanish-style building, which has only 18 rooms and is quite charming. The more modern-looking **Andrea** *(≈, ⊗, ≡, ℜ)* has two beautiful pools. The chicest of the five hotels, the **Tropical** *(≈, ⊗, ≡, ℜ)*, stands next to the beach. In addition to its splendid rooms and outstanding swimming pool, it boasts a lovely garden that opens onto Playa Cofresi. Finally, the **Villas de Luxe** *(≈, ⊗, ≡, K)* is not really a hotel, but rather a heavenly little village with magnificent houses scattered across a vast, rolling stretch of land. The developers truly outdid themselves; the place has been designed so that each little house is isolated enough to ensure its occupants' privacy. As the villas have only a few rooms each, a family can rent an entire one for themselves. Each has its own terrace with a magnificent view, a kitchenette and a private pool. A great deal of care has been taken with another important aspect of these all-inclusive hotels: the restaurants, which always serve a buffet with a good selection of delicious dishes. One last plus: all guests have access to lovely Playa Cofresi.

Playa Dorada

All the hotels in Playa Dorada meet international standards. All have comfortable air-conditioned rooms, at least one pool, restaurants and dining rooms, bars and nightclubs, shops and sometimes a casino. Prices do not vary much from one hotel to the next, the most affordable being the Heavens, and the most expensive, the Jack Tar Village. Many hotels offer all-inclusive packages, which include three meals a day, all local beverages (Dominican beer, rum, etc.), taxes and service charges. If you arrive in Playa Dorada without a reservation, expect to pay an average of $110 US per night (a bit less in the low season), or even more if you want to stay in a studio or deluxe apartment.

For stays of one week or longer, it is often much more economical to make reservations from home through a travel agent, as they often have discounts. Finally, remember that during the winter season there is always a risk that all of the hotels will be full.

The **Flamenco Beach Resort** (all-inclusive; ≡, ≈, ⊗, ℜ; ☎ 320-6319, ↦ 320-6319) is a large complex whose architecture has a certain Spanish feel to it. Guests stay in a series of white villas, with large balconies. The service

is attentive and the fine woodwork in the lobby, bar, restaurant and elsewhere creates a warm, welcoming atmosphere. Guests have access to the beach.

The **Heavens** (all-inclusive; ≡, ≈, ℜ, ⊗; ☎ 562-7475, ↦ 566-2436 or 566-2354) hotel complex consists of two groups of buildings evidently built at different times. This is a pleasant place, even though some of the buildings are bunched together. The complex is near the golf course, and at a reasonable distance from the beach, which is accessible by way of a small path.

The **Jack Tar Village** (all-inclusive; ≡, ≈, ℜ, ⊗; ☎ 320-3800 or 1-800-999-9182, ↦ 320-4161) occupies a large, well-maintained property. The rooms are set in charming villas arranged, like the name suggests, into a little village. The Jack Tar is especially popular with tennis players, as it has a large number of courts; it is also close to a golf course and the beach. Many consider this the most luxurious hotel complex in Playa Dorada. Renovations were scheduled for summer 1997.

🏅 **The Paradise Beach Club and Casino** (all-inclusive; ≡, ≈, ℜ, ⊗, ♣; ☎ 1-800-752-9236, ↦ 586-4858) has a total of 436 units in several buildings decorated with attractive woodwork. The hotel's designers went to great lengths to make it visually pleasing; the impressive grounds feature luxurious gardens, waterfalls, ponds and swimming pools in interesting shapes. This unique and friendly resort offers comfortable rooms and lies right on the beach.

The **Playa Dorada Hotel** (all-inclusive; ≡, ≈, ℜ, ⊗, ♣; ☎ 320-3988 or

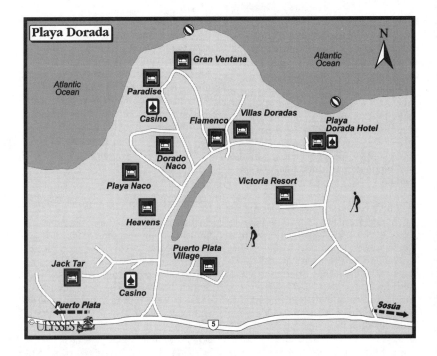

1-800-423-6902, ≈ 320-1190) has 254 pleasantly decorated rooms, some with a clear view of the ocean. The nondescript older buildings of the hotel are located right on the beach. Guests will also find a casino, restaurants, a pleasant café and a piano-bar.

The **Playa Naco Golf and Tennis Resort** *(all-inclusive; ≡, ≈, ℜ, ⊗; ☎ 320-6226, ≈ 320-6225)* is graced with an imposing colonnaded façade and a monumental lobby overlooking a very large pool. The comfortable rooms are located in the building that surrounds the pool, where all the action takes place, and in various other structures scattered throughout the vast property. The Naco has several tennis courts, among other things.

The **Puerto Plata Village** *(all-inclusive; ≡, ≈, ℜ, ⊗; ☎ 320-4012, ≈ 320-5113)* is made up of charming little houses, some painted in pastel colours, others in bright colours, and all equipped with balconies or terraces. The complex is pleasantly located in a large and airy garden, near the golf course and not too far from the beach. The service is excellent.

The **Villas Doradas** *(all-inclusive; ≡, ≈, ℜ, ⊗; ☎ 320-3000, ≈ 320-4790)* consists of a grouping of several-story buildings, each housing a few rooms with a balcony overlooking a large tropical garden. The lobby includes a relaxing open-air space with rattan chairs. A trail leads through a thicket, past a pond and on to the beach.

The newest hotel in Playa Dorada, the **Gran Ventana** *(all-inclusive; ≈, ≡, ℜ; ☎ 412-2525, ↬ 412-2526)* is a vast hotel complex whose buildings, all in warm hues, stand on a large piece of property by the sea. In the centre of this little village lies a huge swimming pool, the focal point of most of the day's activities. Great care has been taken with the decor, so all the rooms are spacious, have big picture windows and are adorned with lovely tropical colours.

If you have no desire to spend your vacation in a place with a perpetually lively atmosphere, opt for the **Victoria** *(all-inclusive; ≈, ≡, ℜ; ☎ 320-1200, ↬ 320-4862)*. This hotel cannot boast a seaside location, but offers a peaceful setting alongside a golf course. The building itself is sober-looking, as if to emphasize the establishment's desire to provide a tranquil atmosphere. Finally, many people claim that the food served here is among the best of any hotel in Playa Dorada.

Puerto Chiquito

The **Coral Beach Resort** *($40 US; ⊗, ℜ; on the road to the Sand Castle, ☎ 571-2577, ↬ 571-2194)* offers clean and adequate accommodation. The buildings housing the rooms are grouped around a pleasant lounge area where guests can relax. The Coral Beach Resort was built in a somewhat desolate spot, void of any vegetation, about 500 metres from Playa Puerto Chiquito. There is, however, a daily transportation service to the beach in Sosúa.

The **Sand Castle Hotel** *($85 US; ≡, ≈, ℜ, tv; ☎ 571-2420 or 1-800-448-8355,*

↬ 571-2000) boasts a spectacular location atop a small rocky cliff overlooking a beautiful sandy beach, where the poor quality of the water unfortunately rules out swimming. Excellent views of the little bay and the ocean can be enjoyed from its many terraces. In fact, this beige stucco building was designed to offer views from almost every room. The Sand Castle is not as well maintained as in previous years.

Sosúa

Sosúa, which lives and breathes by tourism, offers accommodation for all budgets and tastes. Most of the hotels in the city are located in the El Batey neighbourhood, east of Playa Sosúa. None of these have direct access to Playa Sosúa, but they are all within walking distance. Some hotels, however, face right onto smaller Playa Libre. Lodging is also available on the outskirts of Sosúa, in a few large complexes to the east and west of the city, along the ocean. During the summer, which is the off-season, when none of the hotels are filled to capacity, don't hesitate to negotiate for a better rate.

Koch's Guest House *($25 US; ≡, K; close to Calle Martinez, El Batey, ☎ 571-2284)* rents out clean *cabañas*, each with a kitchenette. The *cabañas* are scattered throughout a narrow well-maintained property, which ends at the ocean. The place may not be very luxurious, but it does offer reasonable rates and lots of peace and quiet, despite being located a few steps from the city's busiest streets. The owner can be a bit surly at times.

The **Pension Anneliese** *($30 US; ⊗, ℝ, ≈; Calle Dr. Rosen, El Batey,*

☎ *571-2208)* is a good, inexpensive little place with ten spotless rooms, each with a balcony and a refrigerator. The rooms at the front boast a pretty view of the ocean, which is just a few metres away. The location is quiet, even though it's close to the heart of Sosúa. There is a pleasant pool in the little garden out back. Hearty and tasty breakfasts are served each morning *(starting at $3 US)*. The Pension Anneliese is run by a German couple who has lived in Sosúa for over 15 years.

Outside the centre of town, about 500 metres from the last buildings along Playa Libre, there are several inexpensive, well-kept and quiet hotels. One of these is the **Voramar** *($US 30; ℜ, ≈, ⊛, ≡; at the east end of Sosúa,* ☎ *571-3910, ⌨ 571-3076)*, which has large, comfortable rooms, each with a balcony. A few hotels in the same category are located near by, as are some narrow, sandy beaches. The Sosúa beach is just a few minutes' drive away.

The **Waterfront Hotel** *($40 US; ⊛, ≈, ℜ, ℝ; 1 Calle Dr. Rosen, El Batey,* ☎ *571-2670, ⌨ 571-3586)*, also known as Charlie's Cabañas, rents out small white stucco cottages set in a garden by the ocean. Without being luxurious, this place is quaint and comfortable, and features a pleasant restaurant, a bar and a small pool. It is located right next to the Pension Anneliese and enjoys the same quiet atmosphere.

The **Sosúa Hotel** *($45 US, bkfst incl.; ≡, ≈, ℝ, ℜ, tv; Alejo Martinez,* ☎ *571-2683 or 571-3530, ⌨ 571-2180)* is in a modern building located on a relatively calm street in the centre of Sosúa. The rooms are

pleasant and are equipped with a balcony or terrace.

The **Yaroa Hotel** *($45 US; ≡, ≈, ℜ; Calle Dr. Rosen,* ☎ *571-2651, ⌨ 571-3814)* offers comfortable lodging just a few steps from Sosúa's bustling streets.

The **Club Marina** *($60 US all-inclusive; ≡, ≈, ℜ, tv; Alejo Martinez,* ☎ *571-3939, ⌨ 571-3110)* is a pretty hotel with thirty comfortable, modern rooms and a swimming pool. This quiet place lies right next to Playa Libre, and just a few minutes' walk from Playa Sosúa.

The **Sosúa by the Sea** *($60 US; ≡, ≈, ℜ, tv; Playa Libre, El Batey,* ☎ *571-3222, ⌨ 571-3020)* is a comfortable, attractively decorated hotel complex overlooking a classic tropical garden, a pool and a restaurant with a beautiful view of the ocean. A wooden staircase leads down to the pretty Playa Libre, which is often much more relaxing than Playa Sosúa. The centre of Sosúa is only a few minutes away by foot.

Among the most comfortable establishments in Sosúa, the **Casa Marina Beach Club** *($70 US; ≡, ≈, ℜ; Playa Libre, El Batey,* ☎ *571-3690, 571-3691 or 571-3692, ⌨ 571-3110)* offers direct access to Playa Libre as well as well-maintained rooms, several of which boast ocean views. These are spread throughout a large complex consisting of several pastel-coloured buildings. The service is particularly attentive and professional. The Casa Marina is often booked solid in the winter; during the rest of the year, however, it is possible to negotiate the room rates.

The **Marco Polo Club** *($US 80; ℜ, ≈, ⊗, ≡; at the end of Calle Alejo Martinez, ☎ 571-3128, ⇌ 571-3233)*, which boasts an unimpeded view of the Sosúa bay, is a pretty little hotel built on a well laid-out piece of property on the side of a cliff. Though located almost right in the centre of town, it feels far from all the hubbub. The rooms are not very luxurious, but are charmingly decorated. Some even have a lovely view of the sea. Last, but certainly not least, the hotel restaurant serves delicious meals.

Also with direct access Playa Libre, the **Larimar Beach Resort** *($110 US all-inclusive; ≡, ≈, ℜ, pb, tv; Playa Libre, El Batey, ☎ 571-2868, ⇌ 571-3381)* is a comfortable, modern hotel complex offering a range of services. Its several tall buildings are surrounded by a large garden of tropical plants and trees. Most rooms have a balcony or terrace.

A few kilometres east of Sosúa, the **Sol de Plata Beach Resort** *($120 US all-inclusive; ≡, ≈, ℜ, tv; east of Sosúa, ☎ 571-3600, ⇌ 571-3380)* is an immense hotel complex where you can rent a room, a suite or a villa. The modern buildings face onto a private beach. A wide range of sports activities are organized here along with evening shows, and a shuttle takes guests to Sosúa and Cabarete.

Punta Goleta

The **Playa de Oro** *($60 US; ≡, ≈, ℜ, tv; ☎ 571-0880, ⇌ 571-0871)* offers accommodation in comfortable, more than adequate rooms. The hotel stands on the beautiful white-sand beach between Cabarete and Sosúa.

The **Punta Goleta Beach Resort** *($80 US; ≡, ≈, ℜ; ☎ 571-0700, ⇌ 571-0707)* is a large, somewhat isolated hotel complex on the road between Sosúa and Cabarete. It offers all of the services one would expect from a luxury hotel — multiple restaurants and bars, a pool, sports and activities, shows, etc. The hotel is very well maintained, but unfortunately on the wrong side of the road, which you must cross to get to the beach.

Right next to the Playa de Oro, in the same category, the **Bella Vista** *($90 US, all-inclusive; ≈, ℜ, ≡; on the way to Cabarete, ☎ 571-1878, ⇌ 571-0767)* offers all-inclusive packages. The rooms each equipped with a balcony, are located inside two rows of rather simple-looking buildings. The back of the hotel looks right out onto the white-sand beach.

Cabarete

Due to its growing popularity, Cabarete now offers a good selection of accommodation. Most of the hotels are of good quality, without being too luxurious. If you visit Cabarete during the summer months, don't hesitate to look at several hotels and negotiate for the best price before making your choice.

Las Orquideas de Cabarete *($35 US; ⊗, ≈, ℜ; east of Cabarete, ☎ 571-0787, ⇌ 571-0853)* offers reasonably priced, perfectly adequate accommodation in clean and comfortable rooms. Hidden behind is a beautiful tropical garden filled with lush vegetation and encircling a swimming pool. Though the beach is only a short walk away, the setting is surprisingly quiet and will please those in search of tranquil surroundings. To get there follow the little street a few hundred metres beyond the east end of the city. Suites with kitchenettes are also available.

The **Caribe Surf Hotel** *($US 36; ≈, ⊗, ℜ; ☎ 571-0788, ⇒ 571-3346)* is built right on the beach, but at the east end of town, in the heart of a small residential neighbourhood removed from all the tourist activity. This is not a big, luxurious hotel complex, but rather a pleasant little inn with a great holiday-by-the-sea atmosphere. The rooms are very simply decorated but well kept and perfectly comfortable.

The **Windsurf Apart Hotel** *($50 US; ⊗, ≈, ℜ, ℝ, K; in the centre of town, ☎ 571-0718, ⇒ 571-0710)* rents out fully-equipped apartments. Those on the first floor were recently renovated and are perfect for medium to long stays. Weekly rates are available. The grounds include a pool, where all sorts of activities are organized. The best apartments start at $25 US a night during the summer.

One of the first establishments on the way into Cabarete, the **Albatros** *($50 US; ≡, ≈; on the way into town from the west, ☎ 571-0841)* is a pretty hotel with a lovely tropical garden, in the middle of which lies a well-maintained pool. The rooms are well equipped, and complemented by natural lighting and a balcony or terrace. The Albatros was built quite recently.

The **Apart Hotel Cita del Sol** *($55 US; ≈, K, ⊗; in the centre of town, ☎ 571-0720, ⇒ 571-0795)* rents out clean but rather nondescript apartments which are spacious enough for families.

The **Casa Laguna Hotel & Resort** *($112 US all-inclusive; ≡, ≈, ℜ; in the centre of town, ☎ 571-0725, ⇒ 571-0704)* offers very comfortable modern studios, each complemented by a balcony or terrace. It is one of the more luxurious places in Cabarete, and despite its central location, boasts a lovely natural ambience. Reserving in advance, especially in winter, is strongly recommended.

Río San Juan

The cheapest place to stay in Río San Juan is the **Apart-Hotel San José** *($14 US; ⊗; facing the lagoon)*, whose rooms are very basic.

The **Río San Juan** *($30 US; ≡, ≈, ℜ; Calle Duarte, ☎ 589-2379 or 589-2211, ⇒ 589-2534)* hotel stands on a large property right in the heart of town. The use of woodwork in the hotel's decor creates a warm atmosphere, and the gardens and the restaurant in the rear are lovely. The rooms, while clean, are a bit stark. The Río San Juan has seen better days.

The **Bahía Blanca** *($35 US; ⊗, ℜ; Calle G.F. Deligne, ☎ 589-2563, ⇒ 589-2528)* is a veritable tropical paradise, and the choicest spot for a peaceful stay in Río San Juan. It is located on a quiet street just outside the centre of town, next to several small beaches. The beautiful design of the Bahía Blanca allows for exceptional views of the ocean from the lobby, the restaurant and the terraces. Rooms are perfectly adequate. Because this is a small hotel, it is very peaceful, and a convivial atmosphere prevails. Upon request, the hotel's staff can organize all sorts of excursions, like horseback riding and cave tours, to help guests explore the region.

The **Bahía Principe** *(140 $US all-inclusive; ℜ, ≈, ≡, ⊗)* stands at the edge of a magnificent, golden, sandy beach, which it has all to itself. Particular care has been taken with the layout, so not only do the rooms have all the comforts, but the setting is magnificent as well, making this a real little Caribbean paradise. The buildings are well maintained, the tropical garden is abloom with hundreds of flowers and guests receive a warm welcome. Even the little shopping gallery displays a remarkable attention to detail, with each shop set up inside a charming, brightly coloured little Creole cottage. The place is truly gorgeous.

Playa Grande

The **Caribbean Village** *($160 US all-inclusive; ≈, ≡, ℜ;* ☎ *582-1170,* ⌨ *582-6094)* is a large hotel complex located near the superb Playa Grande, one of the most idyllic beaches in the country. Several large buildings house the comfortable, modern and spacious rooms, each of which has a balcony. Those at the back boast a magnificent view of the ocean. The Caribbean has tennis courts, a lovely pool, restaurants, bars and a discotheque, and guests can enjoy a variety of sports activities, excursions and evening shows. A stairway leads from the complex to the beach, where a pleasant bar-restaurant has been built. The all-inclusive package offered by the Caribbean Village includes three meals and all local drinks.

Cabrera

Set back a bit from the road to Cabrera, on a hillside with a far-off view of the ocean, is **La Catalina** *($62 US; ⊗, ℜ, ≈; towards Cabrera,* ☎ *589-7700,* ⌨ *589-7550)*, a wonderful inn surrounded by magnificent tropical gardens. Beautiful vistas and a refreshing breeze create an enchanting ambience on the terrace of the dining room, which serves first-class cuisine. This elegant little complex offers well-maintained and beautifully furnished rooms, as well as one- and two-bedroom apartments. Guest can reach the neighbouring beaches and villages by taxi.

Nagua

Nagua has a limited choice of accommodations, so if you decide to spend more than a day in the region, it is better to stay on the outskirts of town, on the road towards the Samaná peninsula. The **Hotel Carib Caban** *($25 US; ⊗, ℜ; less than 10 km from Nagua on the way to Samaná,* ☎ *543-6420,* ⌨ *584-3145)* has small, fairly well-kept rooms and villas overlooking a quiet, undeveloped beach.

 RESTAURANTS

Puerto Plata

Puerto Plata has a wide selection of restaurants to suit all budgets and all palates. The best ones are found mainly in the hotel zone. There are, however, a host of small restaurants in the downtown area that serve simple, inexpensive food. In the evening, the promenade along the ocean is lined with food stalls selling light meals and sweets.

For a refreshing break while strolling through the streets of Puerto Plata, ice cream is just the thing, and **Helado Bon** *($; at the corner of Calles Separación and Beller)* located right in front of Parque Duarte, is just the place to get it. This neighbourhood also has several other little restaurants.

A small restaurant with a pleasant atmosphere, the **Plaza Cafe** *($; on Calle 30 de Marzo near Calle Beller)*, specializes in *pica pollo* and fish. It has an open-air terrace alongside a quiet street.

Sam's Bar and Grill *($-$$)* is a delightful little restaurant in the heart of all the hustle and bustle in Puerto Plata. People come here for simple meals (burgers, steak, etc.) in a young unpretentious atmosphere.

The **Portofino** *($$; Avenida Mirabal)*, located in the hotel zone, is an attractive restaurant ensconced in greenery. The menu consists essentially of pizzas and other well-prepared Italian dishes. There is an outdoor terrace looking onto the street, as well as an indoor dining room.

The **Neptune** *($$$; inside the Puerto Plata Beach and Casino Resort hotel complex)* is the most popular restaurant in Puerto Plata for fish and seafood. The atmosphere is relaxed and cosy, and the service, excellent.

Playa Dorada

The vast majority of restaurants in Playa Dorada are located in the hotels.

A wide variety of international cuisine is available, as well as excellent local dishes. Make sure to try the Dominican cuisine, which is generally delicious and only mildly spicy. Light, inexpensive dishes can be found at the Playa Dorada Plaza, and at the snack bars in most hotels.

Outside the hotels, there are very few restaurants in Playa Dorada. For burgers, steaks, fajitas, pasta, salads and other simple fare, head to **Hemingway's Café** *($-$$; Plaza Dorada, ☎ 320-2230)*, which has a young, convivial atmosphere. On weekends, in the evening, you can dine to the sounds of live pop music.

Sosúa

Over the years, Sosúa has seen the opening of a plethora of restaurants for all tastes and budgets. If you want a quick bite to eat, countless stalls up and down the beach sell refreshments and fish and chicken snacks, plus a variety of other simple dishes. There are also several little restaurants on Calle Dr. Rosen in the El Batey neighbourhood, which, like those in the hotels, offer affordable international cuisine for the most part.

Ideally located on the way to the beach, **Yogen Fruz** *($; near the shopping arcade)* serves refreshing frozen yoghurt.

A number of hotels in Sosúa offer rooms equipped with kitchenettes. If you stay in one of these, you can stock up on fresh pasta and sauce at the **Reina de la Pasta** *(Alejo Martinez)*.

La Crêpe Bretonne *($-$$; Calle Dr. Rosen)* serves a selection of dinner and dessert crepes. This little place, with about ten tables under a palm-thatched roof, is good for a quick snack or a light evening meal.

You'll feel more like you are in the United States than the Caribbean at **PJ's** *($-$$; Pedro Glissante)*, but this is still a neat place for an evening drink and a burger or some other American fast food specialty. The atmosphere is friendly, and the decor does have a certain something.

If you are one of those people who think that there's nothing like a good cold beer after a day in the sun, head to the **Britania Pub** *($$; Pedro Glissante)*, where they also serve good steak and shrimp.

🦐 The menu at the **Waterfront** *($$; Calle Dr. Rosen, in the Waterfront Hotel)* includes both light and more elaborate meals, plus local and international specialties. Once a week, there is an inexpensive all-you-can-eat barbecue. This is a pleasant spot with a beautiful ocean view. It becomes a quiet bar towards the end of the evening.

The **Restaurante Cristóbal Colón** *($$; 6 Calle Dr. Rosen)* specializes in Spanish cuisine, which it serves in a cosy yet elegant atmosphere. Of course, paella gets top billing on the menu. The restaurant is located in a quiet area, slightly removed from the busiest streets.

The menu at the **El Coral** *($$; at the end of Calle Alejo Martinez)* places special emphasis on Dominican specialties and seafood. Hearty servings of tropical fruit are served for breakfast, and at lunch there is a selection of simple dishes. The terrace, located atop a promontory, offers a striking view of the bay of Sosúa.

The **Neuva Sol** *($$; Pedro Glissante)*, which specializes in fish and seafood, offers a fixed price menu every evening for less than $15 US. The restaurant has a terrace looking out onto the street and a quieter dining room at the back.

🦐 Every visitor should dine at the **La Puntilla de Pierfiorgo** *($$-$$$; 1 Calle La Puntilla, ☎ 571-2215)* at least once. It has been one of the most prestigious establishments in Sosúa for several years, known not only for its excellent Italian cuisine, but also for its splendid location. Its multi-level balconies overhanging the waves offer the most spectacular view in Sosúa. The dishes, mostly Italian and seafood, are all finely-prepared and delicious. To enjoy the breathtaking setting at its best, try to arrive just before sunset.

Cabarete

Cabarete has a vast array of restaurants in all price ranges. A good number of restaurants on the beach offer inexpensive meals, perhaps because so many young windsurfers come to Cabarete. There are some more elaborate dining possibilities here as well, however.

The **Rendez-vous Café** *($; in the centre of town)* is a friendly place to relax for a drink or a light meal.

Leandra's *($; in the centre of town)* is a simple restaurant with just a few tables and a pleasant atmosphere. The menu consists primarily of Dominican dishes. Good breakfasts can be had here for about $2 US.

The **El Pirate** *($; in the centre of town, facing the ocean)* is known first and foremost for its delicious choice of desserts, especially its chocolate crepes and banana flambé.

The menu of the **Blue Paradise** *($)* is made up of North American fare like hot chicken sandwiches, hamburgers and hot dogs. This friendly place is a good bet for breakfast, though, as the dishes are copious and very nourishing.

The **Basilic** *($$; adjoining the Las Orquideas hotel)* offers a varied menu including Dominican, French and German dishes. The excellent service, subdued atmosphere and delicious cuisine make for a fine meal and a pleasant evening.

The **Luci Mar** *($$; in the centre of town)* is a lively place that serves excellent and hearty dishes, including brochettes, chicken and fish. Its terrace overlooks the ocean.

Facing right onto the beach, the **Lobster House** *($$)* is a modest-looking place that serves good fish and seafood dishes. At lunch time, a lighter menu is also available.

If you'd like a change from the local cuisine and are craving a hearty, nourishing meal, try the German restaurant **Zur Pfanne** *($$)*. Located on the way out of town, it has a terrace that looks out onto the street but is nonetheless fairly quiet. You can also eat in the dining room, which is a little cozier.

The menu at the **Casa del Pescador** *($$-$$$; on the main Street)* naturally headlines fish and seafood. The food is

exquisite and the charming beach-side location is propitious to long relaxed meals. Be sure to try the daily special.

Río San Juan

Most of the restaurants in Río San Juan are on Calle Duarte and along the shores of the lagoon. Generally the cuisine is simple and good. For more sophisticated fare, try the restaurants in the hotels.

Located in a pretty little pastel-coloured house, the **Casona Rapida Comida** *($; Calle Duarte, opposite the Brigandina)* serves fast-food, including great *empanadas* (less than $1 US).

Well-located, in front of the lagoon, the **Deli Quesos** *($; facing the lagoon)* is a small eatery serving sandwiches and other simple dishes, that are ideal after a boat trip.

The dining room in the **Hotel Bahía Blanca** *($$; Calle G.F. Deligne, ☎589-2563)* is an idyllic spot to enjoy a good meal while taking in the sunset from the terrace overlooking the ocean. The menu includes meat, fish and seafood prepared according to local and international recipes. Professional service.

The restaurant in the **Río San Juan Hotel** *($$$, Calle Duarte, ☎589-2211)* enjoys an excellent reputation in the area for its local cuisine. A footbridge leads to the restaurant, which stands on stilts overlooking a garden. Evening shows are presented occasionally.

Cabrera

 Whether you are staying in town or just passing through, be sure to stop for a bite at the restaurant in the **La Catalina** *($$-$$$; before Cabrera)* inn. Savoury and well-presented light meals are served at lunchtime, while a gourmet French menu is offered in the evening. The setting is enchanting and boasts a lovely view of the ocean.

 ENTERTAINMENT

Playa Dorada

Playa Dorada has an active and varied nightlife centred around the big hotels, almost all of which have at least one bar and often a disco and a casino as well. Local performers and groups often perform at the hotels. As the schedules and type of entertainment vary, it's best to check what's on when you arrive.

If the evenings seem a little long to you, you can go to the Plaza Dorada cinema, which shows movies in English every night.

Sosúa

The choice of bars and cafes is never-ending in Sosúa, and includes the pleasant and friendly **Waterfront** *(in the hotel of the same name)*, where you can listen to some jazz while imbibing local or imported drinks. Another pleasant spot is, the **Tall Tree**, on crowded, noisy Calle Pedro Glissante. Most of the restaurants in Sosúa become terrace bars as the evening wears on; one of the liveliest is always **PJ's** *(Calle Pedro Glissante)*. If you feel like dancing, most of the discotheques are located at the heart of Sosúa on Calles Pedro Glissante and Dr. Rosen.

Cabarete

Several of the restaurants in town, like the Lobster House or Luci Mar, open onto the beach, and are pleasant spots for an after-dinner drink.

Río San Juan

The little **discotheque** on Calle Sanchez, right near the lagoon, is generally open weekend evenings. The ambience varies from one night to the next. The **Mega Disco** *(Calle Mella)* is the latest hot spot for getting down and kicking up your heels. For a quieter evening, try the **Hotel Río San Juan piano bar**, which has regular shows in the evenings.

$ SHOPPING

Puerto Plata

In addition to the shops in the large hotels, many places downtown sell souvenirs, jewellery and clothing. The busiest commercial streets are Calles J.F. Kennedy and 12 de Julio, near the central park. One of the best places to buy local crafts and jewellery is the gift shop at the **Museo del Ámbar** *(at the corner of Prudhomme and Duarte)*.

Playa Dorada

The Plaza Dorada has all sorts of little shops selling rum, cigars, bathing suits and beachwear. The merchandise is generally of good quality, but the prices are a tad higher than elsewhere in the country. Boutiques can also be found inside many of the hotels.

Sosúa

Stores are certainly not what is missing in Sosúa, both downtown, mostly on Calles Pedro Glissante and Alejo Martinez, and along the beach, which is lined with shops of all kinds. You'll find souvenirs, clothing, local and Haitian paintings, sculptures, etc. Prices are negotiable in many of these places. The **Family Jewel Shop** on Pedro Glissante is a good place for jewellery, and also sells pieces of amber at reasonable prices.

Cabarete

If you're in the market for lovely local handicrafts or pretty jewellery, **Atlantis** is one of the best shops in town.

For great cotton beachwear that will keep you comfortable under the hot tropical sun, head to **Island Clothes.**

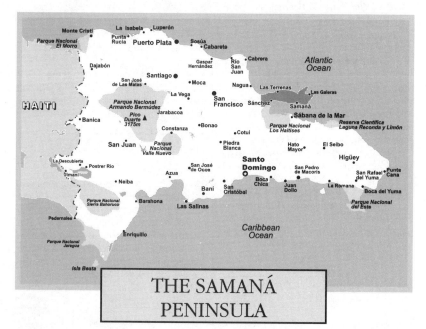

THE SAMANÁ PENINSULA

Rich in spellbinding and picturesque landscapes, this long peninsula covers an area of almost 1,000 square kilometres and is undeniably one of the most beautiful regions in the Dominican Republic. The area is crossed from east to west by the Cordillera de Samaná, a chain of mountains whose rounded peaks reach heights of more than 500 metres. At various points, these mountains plunge abruptly into the blue waters of the ocean or the Bahía de Samaná, adding greatly to the charm of the region. Their slopes, furthermore shelter a wonderful variety of lush vegetation. Mountains give way to magnificent beaches of white sand, extending for kilometres in some places along the northern and southern coasts of the peninsula, and on the shores of nearby islands. In fact, such a harmonious blend of mountains and beaches, towns and villages is rarely found elsewhere in the country. The Samaná peninsula is washed to the north by the waters of the Atlantic Ocean, and to the south by those of the Bahía de Samaná. Its main cities are Santa Barbara de Samaná, generally known as Samaná; Sanchez, the gateway to the peninsula, and Las Terrenas, the only one of the three located on the Atlantic coast of the peninsula.

From the beginning of colonization, the Samaná peninsula was coveted by the Spanish conquistadors for its strategic location at the extreme northeast end of the island. It was in fact the site of the first battle between Europeans and the indigenous peoples of the Americas, January 12th, 1493. The conflict unfolded on a beach, since then evocatively named Las Flechas (The Arrows). It was during his first voyage to the New World that Christopher Columbus encountered Caribs on this beach, just a few kilometres from the present site of Santa Barbara de

Samaná. The Caribs were much less docile that the Tainos, who lived inland, and it would take several decades before the Spanish were able to "pacify" them and build a series of forts all along the coast to maintain Spanish control of the area. Even Napoleon Bonaparte, who took over the eastern part of Hispaniola in the early 19th century, acknowledged the strategic position of the peninsula, and chose it as the site of the future colonial capital, a plan that never materialized. A few years later, in the 1820s, African slaves who had fled the United States settled in Samaná. The old Protestant church in Santa Barbara was built by their descendants.

FINDING YOUR WAY AROUND

It takes about two and a half hours to drive the 210 kilometres between Puerto Plata and the town of Santa Barbara de Samaná, the largest urban centre on the peninsula. The road is in generally good condition. From Santo Domingo, take the excellent road that passes through San Francisco de Macorís and Nagua. This trip takes about four hours by car.

The main roads on the peninsula are in good condition, though they pass regularly through mountainous regions. Some dirt roads can prove difficult for cars, especially after heavy rain. This is particularly true of the road between El Limón falls and the city of Samaná.

When travelling by *guagua*, remember to be patient, as service here is less frequent than in more populated parts of the country.

Taxis can be found in front of the big hotels; they travel all over the peninsula and even beyond. The fares to various destinations are clearly posted.

Motorcyclists provide another means of getting around, in exchange for a small fee. Finally, motorbikes and cars can be rented in Las Terrenas and Samaná.

Samaná Airport

Located between Samaná and Sanchez, this airport receives flights from airports throughout the country; travellers can therefore reach Samaná or leave the peninsula by means of small planes. The runway is presently too short to accommodate large carriers, but the Dominican government may soon invest in turning it into an international airport.

Sanchez

The road from Nagua crosses the outskirts of Sanchez. Turn right to get downtown, or keep going straight for Samaná. To reach Las Terrenas, head uphill on the little road to the left at the east edge of Sanchez (next to the gas station). Keep an eye out, because the sign is easy to miss. To get to the departure dock for visits to Parque Nacional Los Haïtises, turn right on the first street, on your way into Sanchez, and continue to the old port. **Codetel:** 4 Calle Duarte.

Las Terrenas

The road for Las Terrenas starts about one kilometre east of Sanchez (right next to the gas station). It is in good condition, but very narrow and winding. It takes a little less than half an hour to drive the 17 kilometres from

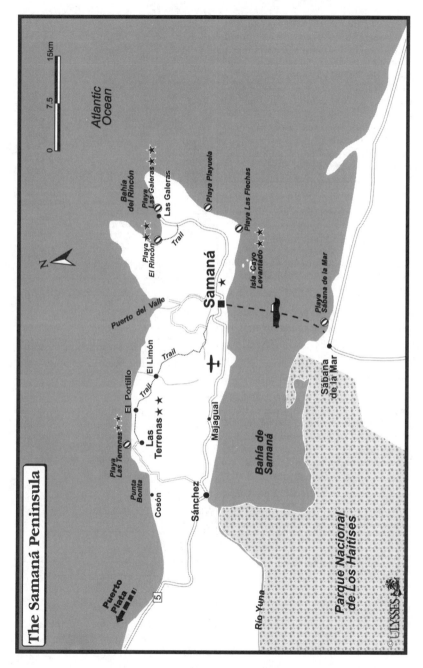

The Samaná Peninsula

Atlantic Ocean

Bahía del Rincón

Playa Las Galeras ★★★

Las Galeras

Playa El Rincón ★★

Trail

Playa Playuela

Playa Las Flechas

Samaná ★

Isla Cayo Levantado ★★★

Puerto del Valle

Playa Sábana de la Mar

Trail El Limón

El Portillo

Trail

Las Terrenas ★

Majagual

Bahía de Samaná

Sábana de la Mar

Playa Las Terrenas ★★★

Punta Bonita

Cosón

Sánchez

Puerto Plata

5

Parque Nacional de Los Haitises

Río Yuna

N

0   7.5   15km

© ULYSSES

Sanchez to Las Terrenas. In Las Terrenas, the road goes through town and ends at the ocean. Turn left and continue about five kilometres to reach Playa Bonita. If you turn right, you'll reach El Portillo after about eight kilometres. A bad road leads from El Portillo to the village of El Limón, departure point for hikes to the El Limón falls. A dirt road runs from the village of El Limón to the city of Samaná. This road, which links Las Terrenas, El Portillo, El Limón and Samaná, is supposed to be paved soon.

Samaná

Highway 5 goes through the city of Sanchez, then continues east toward Samaná.

Samaná has a **Baribe Tours** and a **Metro Bus** (on the Malecón) bus terminal.

Cayo Levantado

Small crafts shuttling back and forth between Samaná and Cayo Levantado leave from the port of Samaná. Count on spending approximately $30 US for a boat able to accommodate up to 10 people. Departures are every day at 9am, 10am and 11am.

Las Galeras

To get to Las Galeras, travellers should take the road skirting the bay and continue east.

Sabaná de la Mar

A ferry runs three times a day between the city of Samaná and Sabaná de la Mar, on the south side of the bay. There are two departures in the morning (9am and 11am) and a third toward the middle of the afternoon (3pm). Return trips generally leave an hour later. The ferry is only available to pedestrians and motorcyclists, however.

 PRACTICAL INFORMATION

Las Terrenas

The **Codetel** is located at 4 Calle Duarte.

The downtown area is concentrated along the main street, where visitors will find a bank, a grocery store and shops.

Samaná

To exchange American money, go to the bank on Calle Sanchez, next to the traffic circle.

Visitors can make phone calls at the **Codetel**, on the Malecón.

 EXPLORING

Sanchez

The road from Nagua goes through Sanchez's immediate periphery. Turn

The beach and the thrill of water sports – Herb Zulpier

Modest craft of a Dominican fisherman – P.R.

En route to the quaint town of Samaná - P.R.

Saiboat at anchor in the bay of Samaná - P.R.

right to get downtown or continue straight ahead to reach Samaná. To get to the port of embarkation whence tours of the Parque Nacional Los Haïtises depart, take the first road on the right upon entering Sanchez and continue until you reach the old port.

Today, farming and fishing, especially for shrimp, are the bread and butter of Sanchez, a little town beautifully located at the foot of the mountains, facing the Bahía de Samaná. But a stroll through its streets, which are lined with old Victorian residences, offers a glimpse of a much more prosperous past. In fact, from the end of the last century up until only a few decades ago, Sanchez was one of the country's major sea ports. It was linked to La Vega by the country's only railroad, and so all produce from the fertile Cibao valley destined for exportation had to pass through Sanchez, generating significant financial and economic activity there. Sanchez's port slowed down considerably in the seventies, because trucks had superseded rail transportation and ocean liners were too big to enter the port. Port activity shifted to areas around Samaná, and the port and train station of Sanchez were abandoned.

Sanchez is an excellent departure point for a visit to **Parque Nacional Los Haïtises** ★★ (see p 196). Excursions start every day at 10am at the Las Malvinas restaurant *(about $30 US; near the old port, ☎ 552-7593)*, last about four hours and include a boat trip alongside a magnificent bird sanctuary and up through a lagoon bordered by mangroves, as well as tours of the park's most interesting caves. The price includes a meal. Excursions up the Río Yuna are also arranged once a week. Prices are similar; check the departure

schedule at the Las Malvinas restaurant. These trips are organized by the owners of the restaurant.

Las Terrenas ★★

A road cuts through the city, leading right to the ocean. Most hotels are therefore in the immediate vicinity. To get to Playa Bonita, take a left turn approximately one kilometre before reaching the beach (you will see signs).

From Sanchez, you'll have to cross the Cordillera de Samaná to reach Las Terrenas on the Atlantic coast of the peninsula. The 15-kilometre stretch of winding road linking the two towns climbs to an altitude of 450 metres before heading down into Las Terrenas. On the way, it passes through several little hamlets and offers some magnificent **views** ★★ of Bahía de Samaná and the region's mountainous landscape. Until recently, Las Terrenas was a small, hard-to-reach village, somewhat cut off from the rest of the peninsula. Its inhabitants live on farming and fishing, as well as tourism, which is becoming more and more important to the community, for many people view Las Terrenas as a paradise lost. The area boasts several kilometres of magnificent white-sand **beaches** ★★ (see p 196) lined with coconut palms and perfect for exploring on foot or horseback. Heading west along the water from Las Terrenas, the beach extends for about 10 kilometres, passing by Punta Bonita and running all the way to Cosson. To the east the long ribbon of sand stretches all the way to the little town of El Portillo, about 8 kilometres away. All of these often untouched beaches are good places to swim, while some of the country's best scuba diving sites lie offshore. Many hotels, inns, restaurants and bars have sprung up along the ocean over the years, but happily they have yet to detract from the tranquil beauty of the setting.

The **El Limón Falls** ★★ are accessible from Las Terrenas. A poorly maintained dirt road leads from El Portillo to the village of El Limón about 10 kilometres away. From the village, you must continue on foot for about an hour over rough terrain, or you can rent a horse in El Limón or Las Terrenas. Either way, the 50-metre-high spectacle of crashing water is worth the effort, and you can cool off in the natural pool at the base of the falls. The dirt road from El Limón leads to Santa Barbara de Samaná after about 15 kilometres.

Samaná ★
(Santa Barbara de Samaná)

After crossing the city of Samaná, the road continues all the way to the promenade skirting the bay. The port is located at the eastern extremity of the promenade.

Samaná has a distinctly more modern and airy feel about it than most Dominican towns and cities. There is a simple reason for this: although its origins date far back, the town was rebuilt after having been completely destroyed by fire in 1946. Today, wide avenues, traffic circles and recently constructed buildings give it a very distinctive look, which is not without its charms. Samaná's location, sheltered by mountains and overlooking the magnificent Bahía de Samaná, with its fishing boats and yachts, adds greatly to the appeal of the town.

Samaná was founded by order of the king of Spain in 1756, as a stronghold against French and English privateers and bandits. Though it is commonly called Samaná, the town was christened Santa Barbara de Samaná in honour of Barbara de Bracance, wife of King Fernando VI. During the French occupation, from 1795 to 1809, the city was to be the capital of the island and was renamed Fort Napoléon; an ambitious urbanization plan was drawn up but never realized (the plans can be seen at the Museo del Hombre Dominicano, in Santo Domingo). During the following decades under Haitian control, Samaná became a haven for escaped black slaves from the United States. This influx of people left its mark, perceptible today in the local language, place names and religious practices. Since Samaná has no nice beach, many visitors skip over it altogether. This city does, however, boast a pretty little **port**, one of the most colourful **public markets** in the country, a few hotels of varying quality and several good restaurants. It is also a departure point for visits to the famous **Cayo Levantado** ★★ (see p 195), and **Parque Los Haïtises** ★★ (see p 196). Winter **whale-watching excursions** ★★ (see p 198) also set out from here. Samaná's geographic location allows for easy access to the rest of the peninsula.

The structure known as **La Churcha** *(downtown Samaná)* was transported from England in 1820. Originally a Methodist church, it is now the Evangelical Church of Samaná.

The little island of **Cayo Vigia** is accessible by a long footbridge just behind the Hotel Cayacoa (if you are not a guest there, be discreet, and nobody will mind if you explore). Though the island is no longer maintained, it bears witness to more prosperous times. The

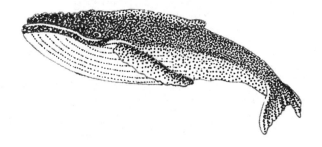

Humpback whale

view ★, however, is still striking, encompassing Samaná, the port, and the bay. You can swim here, although the little beaches are not very inviting. It takes at least a half-hour to walk to the island and back.

Excursions to **Parque Nacional Los Haïtises ★★** (see p 196) are organized from the port of Samaná. Trips leave Samaná at around 8am and last about six hours. The cost is about $40 US per person. Note that trips also leave from Sanchez, which is closer to the park.

From January to March, **humpback whale-watching excursions ★★** *(about $30 US; WhalesMarine, on Avenida le Malecón, one trip in the morning and one in the afternoon, ☎ 538-2494)* are organized from Samaná (see p 198).

You can take a ferry to **Sabana de la Mar** *($2 US; departure from port at 9am, 11am and 3pm)*, on the other side of the Bahía de Samaná. Although it makes for a pleasant stroll, there is not much to see in the village.

Cayo Levantado ★★

There are daily trips to the magnificent island of **Cayo Levantado ★★** *(about $30 US for a 10-passenger boat; departure from port of Samaná everyday 9am, 10am, 11am; departures also from the small village of Las Flechas, about 8 km east of Samaná; arrive early to be able to share a boat)*. This island paradise off the shores of Samaná is one of the peninsula's most precious treasures. Luxuriant vegetation, featuring a harmonious blend of beautiful gardens and virgin tropical forest, covers the rolling landscape. Well-maintained trails lead to the southern point of the island, where a promontory offers an excellent view of the bay and the coastline. Cayo Levantado is best known for the magnificent **beaches ★★★** (see p 197) that circle the island. The beach on the west coast, tucked inside a bay with turquoise waters and lined with palm trees, is a particularly idyllic spot. From sunrise until around 11am, when the first tourists begin to trickle in, this beach seems like a forgotten paradise. Quality accommodation is available in the one hotel on the island (see p 201).

Las Flechas

On January 13, 1493, a beautiful sandy beach about eight kilometres from Samaná was the site of the first battle between Europeans and the indigenous people of the Americas. The beach was named Las Flechas (The Arrows) in reference to the hostile greeting that Christopher Columbus and his crew received here during their first voyage to the New World. A few hundred metres beyond lies the beautiful Gran Bahía hotel, one of the most luxurious on the island.

El Rincón

To the left of Las Flechas, a dirt road in very poor condition leads to **Playa El Rincón** ★★ (see p 197). This magnificent white-sand beach stretches a full kilometre, and is lined from one end to the other by a palm grove. Hidden along the shores of a calm and beautiful bay, the beach is often empty.

Las Galeras ★

Las Galeras has managed to retain the quiet charm and atmosphere of a little fishing village despite the push of tourism. Located on the eastern tip of the peninsula, it overlooks a large bay with calm waters perfect for swimming and snorkelling. Facing the village, **wild beaches** ★★(see p 197) stretch several kilometres beckoning to wanderers.

Tourism development is recent in Las Galeras, but there are already a few excellent hotels.

 PARKS

Parque Nacional Los Haïtises ★★ *($40 US; departure at 8am; boat trips depart from Sanchez and Samaná)* (see also p 114), at the southwestern extremity of the Bahía de Samaná, covers an area of 208 square kilometres. Dense tropical vegetation blankets the gently rolling terrain. Hidden within the park are caves that once served as dwellings and religious meeting places for natives before the arrival of the Europeans. Some cave walls are covered with pre-Columbian sculptures and drawings. The park also contains a remarkable bird sanctuary and large expanses of mangrove swamp. Los Haïtises is definitely one of the most interesting parks in the country.

 BEACHES

Las Terrenas

Las Terrenas and its immediate region are adorned with several kilometres of golden **beaches** ★★, among the most spectacular in the country. Coconut palms provide welcome shade while exploring on foot or on horseback. Starting in **Las Terrenas** and heading west, the beach continues for 10 kilometres, passing **Punta Bonita** beach and then **Playa Cosón**, a veritable splendour. Indeed, it extends over several kilometres and one often has the beach all to oneself. Visitors can reach the beach by either continuing further west, past Punta Bonita, or by taking a left turn at the junction leading to Punta Bonita from Las Terrenas. Heading east, the long strip of sand extends to the small town of El Portillo, about eight kilometres away. This is an ideal area for swimming, and the nearby coral reefs make for interesting scuba diving.

Cayo Levantado

Cayo Levantado has at least three superb white-sand **beaches ★★★**. The prettiest is on the west side of the island; lined with palm trees, it is washed by the turquoise waters of a lovely bay. This spot is remarkably beautiful, especially early in the morning before the beach is overrun with tourists. Wandering vendors sell snacks and drinks along the beach.

El Rincón

Playa El Rincón ★★ is a magnificent white-sand beach about one kilometre long. Bordered by a palm grove, it is nestled inside a pretty bay with calm waters. Chances are fairly good that you will find yourself completely alone. There are no businesses close by, but the local children will probably try to sell you some coconut.

Las Galeras

Opposite Las Galeras, and in the immediate surroundings, **wild beaches ★★** stretching several kilometres just waiting to be explored. Their waters are great for swimming and scuba diving. The half-dozen hotels in Las Galeras all have restaurants in case you get hungry.

OUTDOOR ACTIVITIES

 ### Scuba Diving

Scuba diving is the sport par excellence in **Las Terrenas,** which has the best dive sites in the country. The necessary equipment can be rented on site. Excursions on the open sea are offered, as well as introductory classes (for around $50, beginners can take a course that includes initiation in a swimming pool followed by a forty-minute dive in the ocean). There are four schools in the immediate vicinity of Las Terrenas: the Tropical Diving Center *(Tropic Banana hotel, Las Terrenas;* ☎ *240-6110)*, the Acaya Diving Center *(Acaya hotel, Punta Bonita)*, Cacao Beach *(Cacao Beach hotel, Las Terrenas)*, and right nearby, Divebold. There are also a few diving centres in **Las Galeras.**

 ### Snorkelling

Snorkelling does not require much equipment and can be practised near the beach. Most hotels and diving centres in Las Terrenas, Las Galeras and Cayo Levantado have equipment and can indicate the best spots to try out this sport.

Horseback Riding

Horseback riding is a popular sport in **Las Terrenas**, besides being a pleasant and easy way to explore the region. Visitors can take part in excursions into the mountains, along the beaches and to the surrounding villages. Two companies in Las Terrenas offer courses, organize outings and rent horses:

Rancho de Las Terrenas and Casa Colón. You can also go riding at the Rancho Thikis *(Casa Blanca hotel)* in Las Galeras. One particularly interesting option is to ride out to the magnificent El Limón falls (horses can be rented in El Limón or Las Terrenas).

 Golf

The only golf course on the peninsula lies near the Gran Bahía hotel *(Las Flechas, about 8 km east of Samaná, ☎ 538-3111)*. The nine-hole course is nice, but not quite up to par with the splendid courses at Casa de Campo, near La Romana, or at Playa Dorado near Puerto Plata. An 18-hole course is planned for the vicinity of Las Terrenas.

 Hiking

Cayo Levantado

About a kilometre of trails has been cleared near the very pretty Cayo Levantado. They pass through tropical gardens on their way to beaches and lookout points offering splendid views of Bahía de Samaná.

El Limón

Another, more difficult hike starts in the village of El Limón, in the vicinity of Las Terrenas, and leads to the El Limón falls. The freshwater pool at the base of the falls is the perfect spot to cool off. The trip there and back takes about two hours. Finally, there are endless outings to be enjoyed along the beaches of Las Galeras and Las Terrenas.

 Bird-watching

Parque Nacional Los Haïtises is a wonderful place to go bird-watching. Boat rides through the park usually include a trip up a river lined with mangroves, where various species of birds nest, as well as a tour of the bird sanctuary, home to frigate birds and pelicans. Some of the park's caves, moreover, are inhabited by bats.

 Whale-watching

From January to March, **humpback whale-watching excursions ★★** *(about $30 US; WhalesMarine, on Avenida le Malecón, one trip in the morning, another in the afternoon, ☎ 538-2494)* are organized out of **Samaná**. During the winter months, humpbacks from the North Atlantic come to give birth (the gestation period is about 12 months) in the warm waters of the Caribbean Sea. About 1,000 to 2,000 of the total population of 6,000 choose the Bahía de Samaná and its surroundings. Excursions provide glimpses of these spectacular mammals, which when fully-grown measure an average of 14 metres in length and weigh 35 tons. Several companies offer trips; the one that organizes the most interesting and the safest excursions for both you and the whales is WhalesMarine. It is extremely inadvisable to head out in fishing boats, which are too unstable for this kind of activity.

ACCOMMODATIONS

Las Terrenas

The Las Terrenas region, including Punta Bonita and El Portillo, has about twenty hotels in all price ranges. All of the hotels in the area are situated along beautiful beaches facing the ocean.

Set in a wooden building vaguely resembling a Swiss chalet and shaded by large trees, **Los Pinos** *($24 US; ⊗; on the beach in Las Terrenas,* ☎ *240-6168)* offers some of the cheapest rooms in Las Terrenas. The atmosphere is friendly, and the place well maintained. More luxurious rooms are also available.

The **Casa Grande Beach Hotel** *($30 US; ℜ, ⊗; on Punta Bonita beach;* ☎ *240-6349,* ⇌ *240-6349)* is comprised of a few rooms distributed throughout a single building. The rooms are modest but clean. A room for four can be had for $40 US.

 The **Araya** *($40 US; ℜ, ⊗; on Punta Bonita beach,* ☎ *240-6161,* ⇌ *240-6166)* is a lovely little hotel with a very convivial atmosphere. The rooms are clean, sufficiently large, ventilated and all equipped with a terrace or balcony. The upstairs rooms are particularly pleasant. Moreover, the palm-roofed restaurant adjacent to the hotel has an excellent and varied cuisine.

 The **Tropic Banana** *($50 US; ⊗, ≈, ℜ; on the beach in Las Terrenas,* ☎ *240-6010,* ⇌ *240-6112)* is a small hotel complex with about twenty rooms in pretty little houses shaded by palm trees. Visitors soon feel at ease in this charming place. At cocktail time, guests can enjoy a drink in the small, palm-roofed bar's relaxing atmosphere, play a game of pool or bowls. The Tropic Banana was one of the very first hotels to open in Las Terrenas and has retained a loyal clientele ever since. A scuba diving centre awaits guests on the hotel's grounds.

The **Atlantis** *($50 US; ℜ, ≈, ⊗; on Punta Bonita beach,* ☎ *240-6111,* ⇌ *240-6205)* is a charming little hotel housed in rococo-style buildings. Reception is friendly. The 18 rooms and common rooms have been carefully decorated. The bigger rooms cost about $20 more.

The **Aglio Beach Hotel** *($100 US including two meals; ℜ, ≡, ≈; on Las Terrenas beach,* ☎ *240-6255,* ⇌ *240-6169)* is a very lovely complex built under the shade of palm trees. The very charming rooms are spread throughout a few, storied buildings. Like many hotels in the region, the Aglio has a scuba diving school.

The **El Portillo Beach Resort** *($120 US all inclusive; ℜ, ≈, ≡; El Portillo,* ☎ *240-6100,* ⇌ *240-6104)* is a few kilometres east of Las Terrenas, close to the little village of El Portillo, along a magnificent beach. It is a very large and fairly isolated complex, which offers all-inclusive deals that, besides the room, include meals, local drinks, most sports activities and evening entertainment. There is a scuba diving school on site. This friendly spot has French owners.

Atlantis *($60 US; ℜ, ≈, ⊗; on the beach in Punta Bonita,* ☎ *240-6111,* ⇌ *240-6101)* is an adorable little hotel with rococo-style buildings.

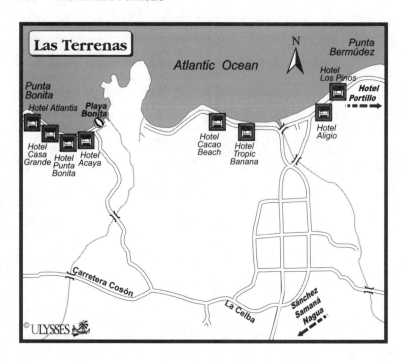

Las Terrenas

Atlantic Ocean

N

Punta Bermúdez

Hotel Los Pinos

Hotel Portillo

Punta Bonita

Hotel Atlantis

Playa Bonita

Hotel Aligio

Hotel Casa Grande

Hotel Punta Bonita

Hotel Acaya

Hotel Cacao Beach

Hotel Tropic Banana

Carretera Cosón

La Ceiba

Sánchez Samaná Nagua

© ULYSSES

Guests can choose between comfortable hotel rooms or cottages with kitchenettes at the large beachside **Punta Bonita Resort** *($122 US including 2 meals; ℜ, ≈; Punta Bonita, ☎ 240-6082, ≈ 240-6012)*, located a few kilometres west of Las Terrenas. This hotel complex is the biggest in Punta Bonita and one of the largest in the region. The buildings are dispersed throughout a large garden.

The **Cacao Beach** *($125 US all-inclusive; ≡, ≈, ℜ; on the beach in Las Terrenas, ☎ 530-5817)* is the largest hotel complex in Las Terrenas, with several restaurants, nearly 150 rooms in cottages and a large swimming pool. All sorts of activities are organized for guests.

Samaná

The most inexpensive rooms in town are generally those in the smaller hotels on Samaná's main street. The **King** hotel *($14 US; ⊗, ℜ; downtown, on the road to Sanchez, ☎ 538-2353)* is one of these. It offers very simple rooms, in a relatively noisy part of town. The building is tall and narrow, offering a lovely view of the city and the bay.

The **Cotubanana** *($22 US; ⊗, ℜ; downtown, ☎ 538-2557)* is clean and fairly comfortable, but unremarkable. Check out a few rooms before settling on one, because while some are adequate, others are unbelievably tiny and have no windows. All guests have access to a common balcony overlooking the bay.

The owner has a bit of a rough personality, but his restaurant serves good food and his bar is a pleasant little spot.

More like a small inn than a hotel, the **Tropical Lodge** *($40 US; ⊗, ℜ; Avenida Marina, at the eastern edge of town, ☎ 538-2480, ↔ 538-2068)* offers decent, well-kept rooms in a peaceful atmosphere. There is an excellent view of the bay from the front rooms, the lounge and the breakfast room. Built on a hillside just east of downtown Samaná, the Tropical Lodge is ensconced in a beautiful tropical garden.

The **Cayacoa** *($160 US, all-inclusive; ≡, ≈, ℜ; take the little street on the right before the promenade, ☎ 538-3131, ↔ 538-2985)* boasts an excellent location on a hill overlooking the bay just outside the downtown area. Quality rooms and *cabañas* are both available. The Cayacoa has a pool, as well as its own private beach. In addition, a small footbridge leads out to the little island of Cayo Vigia. The hotel organizes various sports activities and tours of the area, including excursions to Cayo Levantado.

The **Gran Bahía** *($160 US; ≡, ≈, ℜ; 8 km west of the city, on the road to Las Galeras, ☎ 538-3111, ↔ 538-2764)* is considered one of the best hotels in the Dominican Republic. Located on the side of a cliff, it offers a clear view of the Bahía de Samaná and Cayo Levantado. Indeed, the layout of the hotel makes the most of this enchanting spot, for a large and beautiful terrace allows visitors to relax comfortably while admiring the water. Moreover, the rooms also offer a view of this wondrous sight of the ocean as far as the eye can see. The hotel is beautiful, and takes full advantage of its enchanting location. The rooms are well furnished, and the service impeccable; a serene, relaxed atmosphere prevails at the Gran Bahía. Guests are offered a wide selection of activities, including excursions to Cayo Levantado and all sorts of sports, such as tennis, golf (nine-hole course), scuba diving, horseback riding, etc.

Cayo Levantado

The long-awaited **Cayo Levantado Hotel** *($90 US all inclusive; ℜ, ⊗; Cayo Levantado, ☎ 538-2426 or 558-3131)* recently opened its doors. Set in an enchanting location, it offers the level of comfort one would expect from the Occidental Hoteles chain. There are close to 30 rooms and 10 *cabañas*. Guests at this hotel will enjoy the early mornings and late afternoons on the virtually deserted beaches of Cayo Levantado.

Las Galeras

Until recently, the **Moorea Beach** *($30 US; ⊗, ℜ; 200 m left of the main street, ↔ 538-2545 or 689-4105)* was the only hotel in Las Galeras. This small, two-story building has 12 rooms, as well as a bar and a restaurant looking onto a beautiful tropical garden. The French owner knows the region very well.

On the way into Las Galeras, you'll spot the cottages of **Paradiso Bungalow** *($30 US; ⊗; at the edge of Las Galeras, ☎ 696-0292, ↔ 538-2545)* on the left. They are quite rudimentary, but can accommodate up to four people. The beach is close by.

The beautiful Victorian building housing the **Todo Blanco** *($60 US; ℜ, ℝ, ≈, ≡; on the beach, ☎ and ♯ 223-0049)* hotel is right on the beach in Las Galeras. The rooms are spacious and comfortable, and several have balconies and small sitting rooms. The hotel's restaurant serves Italian cuisine.

The **Club Bonito** *($84 US; ℜ, ≡, ≈; ☎ 696-0082, ♯ 638-2545)* is the latest hotel to open in Las Galeras. The Club boasts a rather bold and unique decor. The rooms are pleasant and well-tended. The establishment looks directly onto the beach, in the middle of the village.

The **Villa Serena** *($90 US; ℜ, ≈, ⊗; after the Moorea Beach, ☎ 223-8703, ♯ 538-7545)* is a most charming hotel, located close to the beach and adorned with magnificent tropical gardens. The quality accommodation consists of vast, elegant, airy, well-furnished rooms with balconies, all in an enchanting setting. One of the hotel's major assets is its huge terrace, furnished with rattan chairs, where guests can spend hours contemplating the blue ocean stretching out into the distance. To top it all off, the restaurant serves fine French cuisine. The Villa Serena is one of the most pleasant hotels on the peninsula.

The largest hotel complex around Las Galeras, the **Casa Blanca** *($100 US; ℜ, ≈, ≡; on the outskirts of Las Galeras, ☎ 682-8913 or 535-3450)* occupies a large property on the outskirts of town. Guests have direct access to the beach, and can enjoy all sorts of activities and sports, including tennis, horseback riding and scuba diving.

RESTAURANTS

The Samaná peninsula boasts a great number of places offering excellent food. Whether in Las Terrenas, Santa Barbara de Samaná or Las Galeras, local recipes are quite often prepared with something of a European flavour.

Las Terrenas

The **Bario Latino** *($-$$; Las Terrenas)* is a small, palm-roofed restaurant with the atmosphere of a French bistro, located in the vicinity of the beach, close to Las Terrenas' main road. Light meals are served here throughout the day. This restaurant is especially renowned for its good and inexpensive pizzas.

The **Paco Cabana** *($$; Las Terrenas)* offers a rather full menu, as suitable for a light lunch as it is for a longer, more relaxed dinner. It is most notable for its wide variety of fish dishes.

Another place whose menu is suitable for any time of day is the **Casa Azul** *($$; Las Terrenas)*, a small outdoor spot near the beach. It opens early in the morning and serves good breakfasts.

The **Araya** hotel's restaurant *($$-$$$; Punta Bonita)* is certainly worth a stop for dinner. Under a roof of palms, and in a rather convivial atmosphere, this establishment offers a menu including a wide variety of very well-prepared seafood, fish and meat dishes. Service is attentive. Be sure to ask the proprietress for a glass of her delicious lime-flavoured liqueur after your meal.

A visit to the **Tropic Banana's** restaurant *($$-$$$; Las Terrenas)* starts during cocktail hour, as guests slowly sip their drinks in the pleasant and refreshing atmosphere of the hotel's little bar. When the proprietor is in a good mood, lucky patrons are offered tasty hors d'oeuvres to pique their appetites. The guests can then make their way to the dining room, which opens out on the garden and the swimming pool. It is in this relaxed ambiance that guests savour dishes, each more delicious than the other, like the oven-roasted filet of sea bream in mushroom sauce or the seafood stew, brimming with large, tasty morsels.

The **Salsa** *($$-$$$; Las Terrenas)* is a romantic little palm-roofed restaurant located right on the beach, an ideal place for sipping a cocktail while admiring the sunset. It is in this enchanting setting that visitors can sample one of the most refined cuisines in Las Terrenas. The menu is varied, with seafood, fish and meat dishes all prepared with equal panache. Every one of the dishes will leave you wanting more, be it the succulent Noilly sea bream, or the beef fillet with green pepper. Guests should make sure to leave a little room for dessert though, as these are also quite delectable.

Samaná

Many restaurants are clustered along Avenida le Malecón, facing the bay, on the east side of the city, where most nightlife takes place. Most have electric generators to compensate for the frequent power outages in Samaná.

The **Black and White** *($-$$; on the Malencón, near the port)* is a small open-air restaurant serving simple meals at all hours of the day.

The **Café de Paris** *($-$$; on Avenida le Malecón, near the port)* offers simple, inexpensive cuisine. Sandwiches, crepes, pizza and ice cream are the big favourites here. This pleasant spot becomes a lively bar as the evening progresses.

The **Cotubanamá** restaurant *($$; Cotubanamá hotel, ☎ 538-2557)* is a quiet establishment where service is attentive. Its principal drawing point is that it serves Dominican specialties, which are always delicious. In fact, for those who have yet to try this cuisine, this is a must. French specialties are also served. The atmosphere is peaceful, the service, attentive. There is also a pleasant little bar.

The **Don Juan** *($$; in the Tropical Lodge hotel)* restaurant serves mainly French cuisine and seafood in a warm setting. The small bar is a relaxing place for an aperitif.

Known as a great spot for many years now, the charming **Le France** restaurant *($$; on Avenida le Malecón, near the port)* serves French cuisine, as its name suggests, as well as a few local delights, including succulent *mérou au coco*. Don't hesitate to ask the jolly, friendly host to help you pick your meal.

Cayo Levantado

Fish, seafood and chicken is sold at food stalls on the north side of Cayo Levantado. If you are looking for a more elaborate menu, there is also a restaurant in the Cayo Levantado Hotel.

Las Galeras

Ideally located near the beach, the bar-restaurant **Jardin Tropical** *($$; in the centre of Las Galeras)* serves mainly fish and seafood, prepared according to local recipes.

The **Villa Serena** *($$-$$$; Villa Serena hotel)* specializes in French gourmet cuisine and every day the menu includes succulent specialties. The restaurant looks out on a beautiful flowering garden, a realm of tranquillity perfect for intimate meals.

 SHOPPING

Las Terrenas

Las Terrenas has a certain number of shops, most of which are located near the beach. Among these are **Haitian Indian Art** and **Ginger Bread**, which specialize in arts and crafts, the beachware store, **Playa Melisa**, and **Indigo**, which sells a vast range of local cigars.

Samaná

The city of Samaná is a good place to buy souvenirs. Most shops are clustered along the Melancón; **Indiana** offers a wide choice of jewellery and local handicrafts.

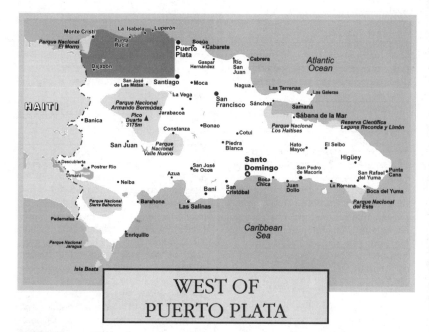

WEST OF PUERTO PLATA

T he western part of the Atlantic coast is above all remembered for having been at the heart of an event that would irrevocably change the course of history. In 1493, Christopher Columbus, while on his second voyage to the Americas chose to found La Isabela, the first settlement in the New World, on this coast.

Despite its precocious beginnings, however, this portion of the coast, extending over 150 kilometres from Puerto Plata to the Haitian border, remains one of the most undeveloped regions in the coun-try. There are no big urban cen-tres in the area; the small population is concentrated mostly in villages where fishing and farming are the main economic activities.

So far there has not been any major tourist development along this stretch of the coast, though a few good hotels have been built here. The beautiful sandy beaches are for the most part untouched and virtually deserted. A day trip along this part of the coast is easy from Puerto Plata.

 FINDING YOUR WAY AROUND

The highway to Monte Cristi is in good condition, which is not always the case with the secondary roads. To reach La Isabela, Luperón or Punta Rucia, the gravel roads are in particularly bad shape, but still passable by car.

Luperón

The town of Luperón lies approximately 45 kilometres from Puerto Plata. Day trips are possible from Puerto Plata if you don't want to stay overnight. To get there, take the highway to the village of Imbert. From there, a narrow winding road on the right (facing the gas station) leads to Luperón. Avoid driving on this road after nightfall.

La Isabela

To get to La Isabela from Puerto Plata, first drive to Luperón, and from there take the dirt road for just under 15 kilometres. The road is in pitiful condition, but safe for both cars and motorcycles. Helpful road signs are virtually nonexistent, but the site is clearly visible from the road. If in doubt, do not hesitate to ask people in the area for directions.

Punta Rucia

Punta Rucia is accessible via the dirt road that follows the ocean from Luperón. However, it is quicker to take the highway toward Monte Cristi, and turn right at Villa Elisa. It takes at least an hour and a half to drive the 90 kilometres between Puerto Plata and Punta Rucia.

 EXPLORING

Luperón

Nestled alongside a pretty deepwater bay. This peaceful village of about 18,000, where fishing is the main economic activity, is named after General Luperón, a hero of the *Restoración*. While the city is pleasant enough, and the sheltered port is picturesque, most visitors are attracted by the neighbouring **beach ★**. The area is best suited to those seeking peace and quiet outside the larger tourist centres. There is only one big hotel, the Luperón Beach Resort, located right near the beach and offering the opportunity to enjoy all sorts of water sports.

La Isabela

When, on his second voyage to America, Columbus discovered that Fuerte Navidad had been destroyed, he chose this location near the Río Bajabonico to build the first city in the New World (1493). Named La Isabela after Isabela de Castillo, it was divided into two sections, one military, the other civilian. Although La Isabela even became the seat, or *Ajuntamiento*, of the colonial administration at one point, it was abandoned in 1496 after epidemics and famine claimed the lives of 1,500 men and much of the cattle. The centre of the colony thus moved to the southern coast of the island to an area baptised Santo Domingo, which is today the capital of the country. Today few vestiges of that earlier era remain, and the town is generally of interest only to diehard archaeology enthusiasts and romantic historians.

Punta Rucia

Punta Rucia, a tiny fishing village bordered by a pretty white-sand **beach ★**, is located near the town of Estero Hondo. In 1959, a group opposing the Trujillo regime met here to draw up plans before battling the dictator's troops. Today this serene and picturesque village's military past seems faraway. Fishing is the main activity here, as indicated by the numerous little boats moored along the shore. From Punta Rucia, visitors can set out

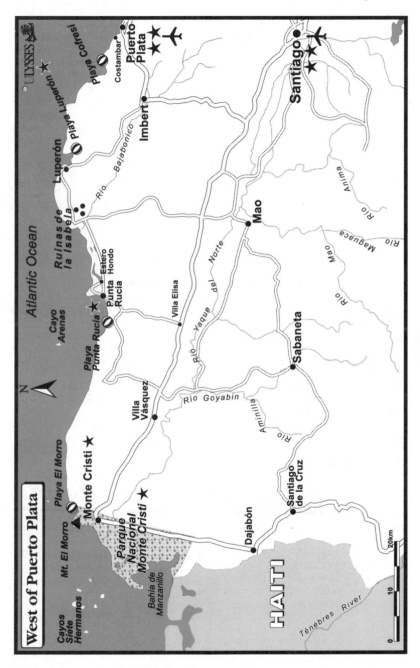

West of Puerto Plata

on excursions to **Cayo Arenas**, a tiny island of white sand lost out in the Atlantic about 10 kilometres offshore. Swimming and snorkelling are excellent here and absolute tranquillity is guaranteed! Only those with an appreciation for deserted beaches and tranquillity should stay in Punta Rucia.

Villa Vasquez

To reach Monte Cristi from Santiago, you have to pass through the prosperous-looking little town of Villa Vasquez. Although it has little to offer in terms of sights or activities, the town does have a few decent restaurants, making it a pleasant and convenient place to stop.

Monte Cristi ★

Founded in the 16th century, Monte Cristi, like many towns in the region, was abandoned in 1606 when the population was forced by royal decree to move to the region around Santo Domingo. The city became active once again a century later, and enjoyed a certain prosperity at the turn of the 20th century when precious timbers and agricultural products from the centre of the country were shipped out from its port.

Today the city is a major salt producer. Not many foreign travellers venture all the way to Monte Cristi, and a rare few are familiar with its long unspoiled **beaches**, frequented by numerous species of birds, its beautiful sunsets and the extraordinary sight of Mount El Morro silhouetted against the sky. Monte Cristi itself is not a particularly attractive city, but it does have a certain charm. There are a number of interesting buildings here, including Victorian-style residences built during the last century, in Monte Cristi's heyday, as well as an **old clock** *(Parque Central)* purchased in France in 1895. The best time to visit Monte Cristi is in February, during **Carnival**. The big celebrations take place each Sunday throughout the month.

Máximo Gomez's house *(free admission; open every day; Avenida Mella)*, where the hero of the Dominican Restoration and Cuban independence lived, has been converted into a museum, offering an interesting perspective on daily life during the last century. It was in Monte Cristi that Máximo Gomez and José Martí signed a mutual aid agreement for the liberation of the Dominican Republic and Cuba.

East of Monte Cristi, the road passes by an impressive **saltern**, runs along the ocean, then cuts inland to **Parque Nacional El Morro ★**. Mount El Morro rises several hundred metres into the sky and its strange silhouette is visible from all around. Its summit offers a panoramic view of the surroundings. Several species of birds can be seen near the rocky beach at the foot of the mountain's eastern side.

Los Cayos Siete Hermanos ★, a group of seven little islands off Monte Cristi, make up a unique tropical bird sanctuary. The islands also harbour a few beautiful, unspoiled beaches, which are occasionally frequented by sea turtles. The easiest way to get there is to make arrangements with one of the fishermen along the coast.

Some Dominican Heroes

When travelling though the Dominican Republic, you will soon notice that the names of streets and parks are much the same from town to town. Very often, they are named for historical figures who played a central part in the fight for Dominican or Cuban independence.

Juan Pablo Duarte (Santo Domingo 1813 – Caracas 1876) was the leader of a rebel group that drove Haitian invaders out of the Dominican Republic in 1844. Soon after the country regained its independence, a civil war broke out; Duarte was ousted from power and went into exile in Venezuela.

José Martí (Cuba 1853 – Cuba 1895) is considered the father of Cuban independence. His zeal to see the country throw off the yoke of colonialism landed him in exile. Martí nevertheless remained an influential figure throughout Latin America. He was also a respected author.

Máximo Gómez (Baní 1836 – Havana 1905) fought Haitian and Spanish attempts to take over the Dominican Republic. When Spain annexed the country again, he fled to Cuba, where he became the leader of the revolutionary forces. In 1895, he fought Spain once again, this time in a successful bid to liberate Cuba.

Dajabon

Dajabon is a border town, and trade with Haiti is the main local activity. Passes to visit Haiti for a few hours can be obtained here.

 PARKS

Parque Nacional El Morro ★ occupies a vast territory on the outskirts of the little town of Monte Cristi, at the western extremity of the country. The park contains several wild beaches near Mount El Morro, which are great places to observe species of tropical birds. Offshore from Monte Cristi, the archipelago known as **Los Cayos Siete Hermanos** ★ is another protected area, featuring an interesting bird sanctuary.

The shores of these seven clustered islands are occasionally visited by sea turtles. You'll have to arrange transportation to these islands with the local fishermen. If you are equipped to go scuba diving, the Monte Cristi region offers some interesting dives, especially around Los Cayos Siete Hermanos.

Sea turtle

BEACHES

Playa Luperón ★, located near the Caribbean Village Luperón, is a good place for swimming and other water sports. This long ribbon of white sand is lined with coconut palms.

Playa Punta Rucia ★ is a pretty stretch of sand lined from one end to the other with coconut palms. Little fishing vessels are pulled up on the sand. The spot is nothing if not picturesque. Swimming is possible near the Discovery Hotel, and at various other spots along the coast.

Wild beaches dot the coast around Monte Cristi. There are several at the base of **Mount El Morro**. Swimming is also possible at the deserted beaches of the **Los Cayos Siete Hermanos** archipelago, offshore from Monte Cristi.

 ACCOMMODATIONS

Luperón

The **Caribbean Village Luperón** *($140 US all-inclusive; ≡, ≈, ℜ, tv; ☎ 571-8303, ↹ 571-8180)* is located in a charming, tranquil setting, right on Luperón's beautiful beach. The level of comfort is what one would expect from a luxury hotel. Guests can enjoy all sorts of activities and take part in excursions to the region's major tourist centres. Ideal for people looking for an isolated spot.

Monte Cristi

The most idyllic place to stay in Monte Cristi is, of course, at the water's edge, and there are often a few *cabañas* for rent. You might check out **Las Caravelas** *($15 US; ⊗; after Monte Cristi, on the beaches)*, which has a few basic rooms for rent.

Another option is the **Chic** hotel *($15 US; ⊗, 44 Calle Benito Monsion, ☎ 579-2316)*, whose rooms may be furnished with mismatched pieces, but nevertheless are comfortable. The hotel is located in downtown Monte Cristi.

 RESTAURANTS

Villa Vasquez

Mi Casa *($; on the main street as you come into town)* serves traditional Dominican dishes, including the popular chicken, beans and rice combo. It is an attractive, airy restaurant with a large palm-thatched roof, whose beautiful decor is somewhat surprising in a small village like Villa Vasquez.

GLOSSARY

GREETINGS

Goodbye	*adiós, hasta luego*
Good afternoon and good evening	*buenas tardes*
Hi (casual)	*hola*
Good morning	*buenos días*
Good night	*buenas noches*
Thank-you	*gracias*
Please	*por favor*
You are welcome	*de nada*
Excuse me	*perdone/a*
My name is...	*mi nombre es...*
What is your name?	*¿cómo se llama usted?*
yes	*no*
no	*sí*
Do you speak English?	*¿habla usted inglés?*
Slower, please	*más despacio, por favor*
I am sorry, I don't speak Spanish	*Lo siento, no hablo español*
How are you?	*¿qué tal?*
I am fine	*estoy bien*
I am American (male/female)	*Soy estadounidense*
I am Australian	*Soy autraliano/a*
I am Belgian	*Soy belga*
I am British (male/female)	*Soy británico/a*
I am Canadian	*Soy canadiense*
I am German (male/female)	*Soy alemán/a*
I am Italian (male/female)	*Soy italiano/a*
I am Swiss	*Soy suizo*
I am a tourist	*Soy turista*
single (m/f)	*soltero/a*
divorced (m/f)	*divorciado/a*
married (m/f)	*casado/a*
friend (m/f)	*amigo/a*
child (m/f)	*niño/a*
husband, wife	*esposo/a*
mother	*madre*
father	*padre*
brother, sister	*hermano/a*
widower widow	*viudo/a*
I am hungry	*tengo hambre*
I am ill	*estoy enfermo/a*
I am thirsty	*tengo sed*

DIRECTIONS

beside	*al lado de*
to the right	*a la derecha*
to the left	*a la izquierda*
here	*aquí*
there	*allí*
into, inside	*dentro*
outside	*fuera*
behind	*detrás*
in front of	*delante*
between	*entre*
far from	*lejos de*
Where is ... ?	*¿dónde está ... ?*
To get to ...?	*¿para ir a...?*
near	*cerca de*
straight ahead	*todo recto*

MONEY

money	*dinero / plata*
credit card	*tarjeta de crédito*
exchange	*cambio*
traveller's cheque	*cheque de viaje*
I don't have any money	*no tengo dinero*
The bill, please	*la cuenta, por favor*
receipt	*recibo*

SHOPPING

store	*tienda*
market	*mercado*
open	*abierto/a*
closed	*cerrado/a*
How much is this?	*¿cuánto es?*
to buy	*comprar*
to sell	*vender*
the customer	*el / la cliente*
salesman	*vendedor*
saleswoman	*vendedora*
I need...	*necesito...*
I would like...	*yo quisiera...*
batteries	*pilas*
blouse	*blusa*
cameras	*cámaras*
cosmetics and perfumes	*cosméticos y perfumes*
cotton	*algodón*
dress jacket	*saco*
eyeglasses	*lentes, gafas*
fabric	*tela*
film	*película*

gifts	*regalos*
gold	*oro*
handbag	*bolsa*
hat	*sombrero*
jewellery	*joyería*
leather	*cuero, piel*
local crafts	*artesanía*
magazines	*revistas*
newpapers	*periódicos*
pants	*pantalones*
records, cassettes	*discos, casetas*
sandals	*sandalias*
shirt	*camisa*
shoes	*zapatos*
silver	*plata*
skirt	*falda*
sun screen products	*productos solares*
T-shirt	*camiseta*
watch	*reloj*
wool	*lana*

MISCELLANEOUS

a little	*poco*
a lot	*mucho*
good (m/f)	*bueno/a*
bad (m/f)	*malo/a*
beautiful (m/f)	*hermoso/a*
pretty (m/f)	*bonito/a*
ugly	*feo*
big	*grande*
tall (m/f)	*alto/a*
small (m/f)	*pequeño/a*
short (length) (m/f)	*corto/a*
short (person) (m/f)	*bajo/a*
cold (m/f)	*frío/a*
hot	*caliente*
dark (m/f)	*oscuro/a*
light (colour)	*claro*
do not touch	*no tocar*
expensive (m/f)	*caro/a*
cheap (m/f)	*barato/a*
fat (m/f)	*gordo/a*
slim, skinny (m/f)	*delgado/a*
heavy (m/f)	*pesado/a*
light (weight) (m/f)	*ligero/a*
less	*menos*
more	*más*
narrow (m/f)	*estrecho/a*
wide (m/f)	*ancho/a*

new (m/f)	*nuevo/a*
old (m/f)	*viejo/a*
nothing	*nada*
something (m/f)	*algo/a*
quickly	*rápidamente*
slowly (m/f)	*despacio/a*
What is this?	*¿qué es esto?*
when?	*¿cuando?*
where?	*¿dónde?*

TIME

in the afternoon, early evening	*por la tarde*
at night	*por la noche*
in the daytime	*por el día*
in the morning	*por la mañana*
minute	*minuto*
month	*mes*
ever	*jamás*
never	*nunca*
now	*ahora*
today	*hoy*
yesterday	*ayer*
tomorrow	*mañana*
What time is it?	*¿qué hora es?*
hour	*hora*
week	*semana*
year	*año*

Sunday	*domingo*
Monday	*lunes*
Tuesday	*martes*
Wednesday	*miércoles*
Thursday	*jueves*
Friday	*viernes*
Saturday	*sábado*
January	*enero*
February	*febrero*
March	*marzo*
April	*abril*
May	*mayo*
June	*junio*
July	*julio*
August	*agosto*
September	*septiembre*
October	*octubre*
November	*noviembre*
December	*diciembre*

WEATHER

It is cold	*hace frío*
It is warm	*hace calor*
It is very hot	hace mucho calor
sun	*sol*
It is sunny	hace sol
It is cloudy	está nublado
rain	*lluvia*
It is raining	está lloviendo
wind	viento
It is windy	hay viento
snow	nieve
damp	húmedo
dry	seco
storm	tormenta
hurricane	huracán

COMMUNICATION

air mail	*correos aéreo*
collect call	*llamada por cobrar*
dial the number	*marcar el número*
area code, country code	*código*
envelope	*sobre*
long distance	*larga distancia*
post office	*correo*
rate	*tarifa*
stamps	*estampillas*
telegram	*telegrama*
telephone book	*un guia telefónica*
wait for the tone	*esperar la señal*

ACTIVITIES

beach	*playa*
museum or gallery	*museo*
scuba diving	*buceo*
to swim	*bañarse*
to walk around	*pasear*
hiking	*caminata*
trail	*pista, sendero*
cycling	*ciclismo*
fishing	*pesca*

TRANSPORTATION

arrival	*llegada*
departure	*salida*
on time	*a tiempo*
cancelled (m/f)	*anulado/a*
one way ticket	*ida*
return	*regreso*

round trip	*ida y vuelta*
schedule	*horario*
baggage	*equipajes*
north	*norte*
south	*sur*
east	*este*
west	*oeste*
avenue	*avenida*
street	*calle*
highway	*carretera*
expressway	*autopista*
airplane	*avión*
airport	*aeropuerto*
bicycle	*bicicleta*
boat	*barco*
bus	*bus*
bus stop	*parada*
bus terminal	*terminal*
train	*tren*
train crossing	*crucero ferrocarril*
station	*estación*
neighbourhood	*barrio*
collective taxi	*colectivo*
corner	*esquina*
express	*rápido*
safe	*seguro/a*
be careful	*cuidado*
car	*coche, carro*
To rent a car	*alquilar un auto*
gas	*gasolina*
gas station	*gasolinera*
no parking	*no estacionar*
no passing	*no adelantar*
parking	*parqueo*
pedestrian	*peaton*
road closed, no through traffic	*no hay paso*
slow down	*reduzca velocidad*
speed limit	*velocidad permitida*
stop	*alto*
stop! (an order)	*pare*
traffic light	*semáforo*

ACCOMMODATION

cabin, bungalow	*cabaña*
accommodation	*alojamiento*
double, for two people	*doble*
single, for one person	*sencillo*
high season	*temporada alta*
low season	*temporada baja*

bed	*cama*
floor (first, second...)	*piso*
main floor	*planta baja*
manager	*gerente, jefe*
double bed	*cama matrimonial*
cot	*camita*
bathroom	*baños*
with private bathroom	*con baño privado*
hot water	*agua caliente*
breakfast	*desayuno*
elevator	*ascensor*
air conditioning	*aire acondicionado*
fan	*ventilador, abanico*
pool	*piscina, alberca*
room	*habitación*

NUMBERS

1	*uno*	30	*treinta*
2	*dos*	31	*treinta y uno*
3	*tres*	32	*treinta y dos*
4	*cuatro*	40	*cuarenta*
5	*cinco*	50	*cincuenta*
6	*seis*	60	*sesenta*
7	*siete*	70	*setenta*
8	*ocho*	80	*ochenta*
9	*nueve*	90	*noventa*
10	*diez*	100	*cien*
11	*once*	101	*ciento uno*
12	*doce*	102	*ciento dos*
13	*trece*	200	*doscientos*
14	*catorce*	300	*trescientos*
15	*quince*	400	*quatrocientoa*
16	*dieciséis*	500	*quinientos*
17	*diecisiete*	600	*seiscientos*
18	*dieciocho*	700	*sietecientos*
19	*diecinueve*	800	*ochocientos*
20	*veinte*	900	*novecientos*
21	*veintiuno*	1,000	*mil*
22	*veintidós*	1,100	*mil cien*
23	*veintitrés*	1,200	*mil doscientos*
24	*veinticuatro*	2000	*dos mil*
25	*veinticinco*	3000	*tres mil*
26	*veintiséis*	10,000	*diez mil*
27	*veintisiete*	100,000	*cien mil*
28	*veintiocho*	1,000,000	*un millón*
29	*veintinueve*		

INDEX

Other Ulysses Guides

Acapulco (Mexico)
Ulysses Due South guide offers a fresh look at Acapulco, the most famous Mexican resort: Acapulco Bay, its beaches, restaurants and captivating nightlife are all in there, but so are the neighbouring mountains, as well as an enlightened look at the people and history of this spot.
Marc Rigole, Claude-Victor Langlois
150 pages, 5 maps
$14.95 CAN $9.95 US   £6.99
2-89464-062-5

The Islands Of The Bahamas
Vacationers will find extensive coverage of the big favourites of New Providence (Nassau) and Grand Bahama (Freeport) with their spectacular beaches, glittering casinos and great scuba diving, but they will also find the most extensive coverage of the Out Islands. Here island-hoppers enjoy world-class fishing, scuba diving and boating, friendly people and pristine deserted beaches.
Jennifer McMorran
288 pages, 25 maps
8 pages of colour photos
$24.95 CAN $17.95 US   £12.99
2-89464-123-0
June 1998

Cancún & Cozumel (Mexico)
The entirely man-made resort of Cancún on the Yucatán Peninsula attracts visitors from the world-over. They come to enjoy a unique travelling experience with fabulous archaeological sites, the last remnants of the Mayan civilization, and the island of Cozumel, a scuba-diver's paradise, both close by.
Caroline Vien, Alain Théroux
200 pages, 20 maps
$17.95 CAN $12.95 US   £8.99
2-89464-040-4

Costa Rica
This fresh look at Costa Rica provides travellers with the most extensive choice of practical addresses, no matter what their budget while also placing special emphasis on eco-tourism, independent travel and the culture, history and natural wonders of this Central American gem.
Francis Giguère, Yves Séguin
368 pages, 35 maps
8 pages of colour photos
$27.95 CAN $19.95 US   £13.99
2-89464-144-3
September 1998

Cuba, 2nd edition
Already a second edition for this unique guide to Cuba. The island's spirit is revealed, from colonial Havana, to the world-heritage site of Trinidad and to Santiago with it Afro-Cuban culture. The guide also covers the famous beaches and provides travellers with countless shortcuts and tips for independent travel in Cuba.
Carlos Soldevila
336 pages, 40 maps
8 pages of colour photos
$24.95 CAN $17.95 US   £12.99
2-89464-143-5
current edition 2-89464-047-1
September 1998

Ecuador and the Galápagos Islands
All the major sites of this South American country are explored including extensive coverage of the capital city, Quito, but also the extraordinary Galapagos Islands. Hundreds of addresses for all budgets as well as countless useful hints for discovering this fascinating and ancient land of the Incas.
Alain Legault
300 pages, 25 maps
8 pages of colour photos
$24.95 CAN $17.95 US   £12.99
2-89464-059-5

El Salvador
This guide provides everything the traveller needs to discover this fascinating Central American country: explanation of cultural and political contexts, advice on how to travel in the area, descriptions of the various attractions, detailed lists of accommodation, restaurants, entertainment.
Eric Hamovitch
152 pages, 7 maps
$22.95 CAN $14.95 US   £11.50
2-921444-89-5

Guadeloupe, 3rd edition
This is the only guide to provide such extensive cultural and practical coverage of this destination. The charm of this dramatically beautiful Caribbean island is revealed along winding picturesque roads through typical villages and towns. Magnificent colour plates help to identify Guadeloupe's birds and plants.
Pascale Couture
224 pages, 15 maps
8 pages of colour photos
$24.95 CAN $17.95 US   £12.99
2-89464-135-4
current edition 2-89464-004-8
August 1998

Guatemala-Belize
Historic peace talks have once again allowed tourism to develop in Guatemala, providing a spectacular glimpse at a country whose native traditions are so strong and omnipresent. Travellers can also discover Belize, a tiny country that has become a veritable paradise for divers.
Carlos Soldevila
336 pages, 30 maps
$24.95 CAN $17.95 US   £12.99
2-89464-175-3
August 1998

Honduras, 2nd edition
The prospects for tourism in Honduras are among the brightest – promising travellers a first-rate vacation, whether they are in search of spectacular deserted beaches, fascinating archaeological sites or supreme diving locations. This guide offers numerous suggestions for outdoor adventure plus practical tips and information on everything from A to Z.
Eric Hamovitch
224 pages, 20 maps
$24.95 CAN $17.95 US   £12.99
2-89464-132-X
August 1998

Jamaica
Jamaica offers everything from a seaside vacation in a luxurious seaside mega-resort to an edenic Caribbean getaway in a remote jungle village and Ulysses shows you how to make that choice with suggestions for every budget range. An insightful portrait of this birthplace of Bob Marley provides the backdrop.
Pierre Longnus
288 pages, 20 maps
$24.95 CAN $17.95 US   £12.99
2-89464-142-7
September 1998

Martinique, 3rd edition
A perfect marriage of cultural and practical information provides the best coverage of Martinique. Numerous tours lead across the island of flowers, from Fort-de-France to Saint-Pierre, with stops in Grande Anse and Montagne Pelée. Everything you need to know about hiking and water sports. Magnificent colour plates help to identify birds and plants.
Claude Morneau
256 pages, 18 maps
8 pages of colour photos
$24.95 CAN $17.95 US   £12.99
2-89464-136-2
current edition 2-89464-003-X
August 1998

Nicaragua

Once a headline-maker the world over, Nicaragua is more often featured in the "Travel" section these days. Besides the capital city of Managua and the popular resort of Montelimar, this guide traverses the whole country, discovering the touching cities of León and Granada, among other places, along the way.

Carol Wood

224 pages, 15 maps

$24.95 CAN $16.95 US   £11.50

2-89464-034-X

Panamá, 2nd edition

Famous for its impressive canal, Panamá offers magnificent beaches on two different oceans, nestled in a diverse ethnic and cultural environment. This guide will help the traveller discover an infinite variety of landscapes, with unequalled flora and fauna.

Marc Rigole, Claude-Victor Langlois

208 pages, 16 maps

8 pages of colour photos

$24.95 CAN $16.95 US   £11.50

2-89464-005-6

Portugal, 2nd edition

A new edition of the most practical guide covering every region in Portugal. *Pousadas*, *quintas*, medieval chateaux, museums, festivals, Algarve beaches... it's all in there! The riches of Porto are also revealed as is Lisbon, host-city of the 1998 World Exposition.

Marc Rigole, Claude-Victor Langlois

384 pages, 32 maps

8 pages of colour photos

$24.95 CAN $17.95 US   £12.99

2-89464-080-3

current edition 2-89464-012-9

February 1998

Provence-Côte d'Azur, 2nd edition

Once again Ulysses offers both these magnificent French regions in one book. Monaco, Nice, Marseille and Avignon are just some of the legendary sites covered. Spend some time by the seaside, in the casinos or explore hillside villages on the Vaucluse plateau and in the Luberon.

Hans Jörg Mettler, Benoit Éthier, Howard Rombough

368 pages, 38 maps

8 pages of colour photos

$29.95 CAN $21.95 US   £14.99

2-89464-112-5

current edition 2-921444-37-2

April 1998

Puerto Vallarta (Mexico)
What began as a tiny fishing village nestled between sea and mountains has blossomed into one of the Mexican Riviera's most splendid resorts. This guide reveals the splendour of Puerto Vallarta, from its luxuriant flora to its quaint tile-roofed houses and countless excellent restaurants.
Richard Bizier, Roch Nadeau
160 pages, 5 maps
$14.95 CAN $9.95 US   £6.50
2-89464-039-0

Cartagena, 2nd edition
Here is the new edition on this colonial jewel. Declared a World Heritage Site by UNESCO, Cartagena boasts historic charm, cultural riches, luxurious hotels, beautiful beaches and the possibility of exciting excursions, all the ingredients for an extraordinary vacation.
Marc Rigole
128 pages, 10 maps
$12.95 CAN $9.95 US   £6.50
2-89464-018-8
current edition 2-921444-21-6
August 1998

Saint Martin - Saint Barts, 2nd edition
Jewels of the French and Dutch Caribbean, Saint Martin and Saint Barts offer a kaleidoscope of attractions – beautiful beaches, charming villages, first-class tourist facilities – and they have been combined for this guide. Whether it's international Saint Martin or tiny Saint Barts, or both, this handy pocket guide has all the great restaurants, luxurious hotels, outdoor activities, plus a glossary, maps and a historical overview.
Pascale Couture
192 pages, 10 maps
$16.95 CAN $12.95 US   £8.99
2-89464-071-4
current editions Saint Martin 2-89464-001-3
*   Saint Barts 2-89464-002-1*
September 1997

Enjoy more...

ULYSSES
TRAVEL PUBLICATIONS

Travel better...
enjoy more

Travel Notes

Travel Notes _____

Travel Notes _____

Travel Notes _____

■ ULYSSES TRAVEL GUIDES

☐ Affordable Bed & Breakfasts in
   Québec .... $12.95 CAN
                      $9.95 US
☐ Beaches of Maine .... $12.95 CAN
                      $9.95 US
☐ Canada's Maritime Provinces .. $24.95 CAN
                     $14.95 US
☐ Chicago .... $19.95 CAN
                     $14.95 US
☐ Cuba .... $24.95 CAN
                     $16.95 US
☐ Dominican Republic .... $24.95 CAN
                     $17.95 US
☐ Ecuador Galapagos Islands .... $24.95 CAN
                     $17.95 US
☐ El Salvador .... $22.95 CAN
                     $14.95 US
☐ Guadeloupe .... $24.95 CAN
                     $16.95 US
☐ Honduras .... $24.95 CAN
                     $16.95 US
☐ Martinique .... $24.95 CAN
                     $16.95 US
☐ Montréal .... $19.95 CAN
                     $14.95 US
☐ Nicaragua .... $24.95 CAN
                     $16.95 US
☐ Ontario .... $24.95 CAN
                     $14.95 US
☐ Panamá .... $24.95 CAN
                     $16.95 US
☐ Portugal .... $24.95 CAN
                     $16.95 US
☐ Provence - Côte d'Azur ...... $24.95 CAN
                     $14.95 US

☐ Québec .... $24.95 CAN
                     $14.95 US
☐ Toronto .... $18.95 CAN
                     $13.95 US
☐ Vancouver .... $14.95 CAN
                     $10.95 US
☐ Western Canada .... $24.95 CAN
                     $16.95 US

■ ULYSSES GREEN ESCAPES

☐ Cycling in France .... $22.95 CAN
                     $16.95 US
☐ Hiking in the Northeastern
   United States .... $19.95 CAN
                     $13.95 US
☐ Hiking in Québec .... $19.95 CAN
                     $13.95 US

■ ULYSSES DUE SOUTH

☐ Acapulco .... $14.95 CAN
                     $9.95 US
☐ Cartagena (Colombia) .... $9.95 CAN
                     $5.95 US
☐ Cancun Cozumel .... $17.95 CAN
                     $12.95 US
☐ Puerto Vallarta .... $14.95 CAN
                     $9.95 US
☐ St. Martin and St. Barts ...... $16.95 CAN
                     $12.95 US

■ ULYSSES TRAVEL JOURNAL

☐ Ulysses Travel Journal .... $9.95 CAN
                     $7.95 US

QUANTITY	TITLES	PRICE	TOTAL
	Sub-total		
	Postage & Handling	$8.00*	
	Sub-total		
	G.S.T.in Canada 7%		
	TOTAL		

NAME:_____

ADDRESS:_____

_____

_____

Payment: ☐ Money Order ☐ Visa ☐ MasterCard

Card Number:_____Exp.:_____

Signature:_____

ULYSSES TRAVEL PUBLICATIONS
4176 St-Denis, Montréal, Québec, H2W 2M5
(514) 843-9447 fax (514) 843-9448
*$15 for overseas orders

U.S. ORDERS: **GLOBE PEQUOTE PRESS**
P.O. Box 833, 6 Business Park Road,
Old Saybrook, CT 06475-0833
1-800-243-0495 fax 1-800-820-2329
www.globe-pequot.com